Tableau Cookbook – Recipes for Data Visualization

Create beautiful data visualizations and interactive dashboards with Tableau

Shweta Sankhe-Savale

BIRMINGHAM - MUMBAI

Tableau Cookbook – Recipes for Data Visualization

First published: December 2016

Production reference: 1161216

Published by Packt Publishing Ltd.
Livery Place
35 Livery Street
Birmingham B3 2PB, UK.

ISBN 978-1-78439-551-3

www.packtpub.com

Credits

Author

Shweta Sankhe-Savale

Reviewer

Sally Zhang

Commissioning Editor

Veena Pagare

Acquisition Editor

Chaitanya Nair

Content Development Editor

Sumeet Sawant

Technical Editor

Akash Patel

Copy Editor

Safis Editing

Project Coordinator

Shweta H Birwatkar

Proofreader

Safis Editing

Indexer

Aishwarya Gangawane

Graphics

Disha Haria

Production Coordinator

Nilesh Mohite

Cover Work

Nilesh Mohite

About the Author

Shweta Sankhe-Savale is the Co-founder and Head of Client Engagements at Syvylyze Analytics (pronounced as "civilize"), a boutique business analytics firm specializing in visual analytics. Shweta is a Tableau Desktop Qualified Associate and a Tableau Accredited Trainer. Being one of the leading experts on Tableau in India, Shweta has translated her experience and expertise into successfully rendering analytics and data visualization services for numerous clients across a wide range of industry verticals. She has taken up numerous training as well as consulting assignments for customers across various sectors like BFSI, FMCG, Retail, E-commerce, Consulting & Professional Services, Manufacturing, Healthcare & Pharma, ITeS etc. She even had the privilege of working with some of the renowned Government and UN agencies as well.

Combining her ability to breakdown complex concepts, with her expertise on Tableau's visual analytics platforms, Shweta has successfully trained over a 1300+ participants from 85+ companies.

LinkedIn: https://in.linkedin.com/in/shwetasavale

About the Reviewer

Sally Zhang is an aspiring data scientist and software engineer. She graduated with a BS in Statistics and Computer Science in May 2014 and an MS in Computer Science in Dec 2015 from University of Illinois Urbana-Champaign. Sally is currently working at Apple, Inc. as a Machine Learning Software Engineer. Before this, she worked at Neustar, Bazaarvoice, and Groupon, where she worked on data analytics, data engineering and infrastructures with tools and languages such as Tableau, Hadoop, Splunk, Python/Bash/R, Java, and SQL.

www.PacktPub.com

eBooks, discount offers, and more

Did you know that Packt offers eBook versions of every book published, with PDF and ePub files available? You can upgrade to the eBook version at www.PacktPub.com and as a print book customer, you are entitled to a discount on the eBook copy. Get in touch with us at customercare@packtpub.com for more details.

At www.PacktPub.com, you can also read a collection of free technical articles, sign up for a range of free newsletters and receive exclusive discounts and offers on Packt books and eBooks.

https://www.packtpub.com/mapt

Get the most in-demand software skills with Mapt. Mapt gives you full access to all Packt books and video courses, as well as industry-leading tools to help you plan your personal development and advance your career.

Why subscribe?

- ▶ Fully searchable across every book published by Packt
- ▶ Copy and paste, print, and bookmark content
- ▶ On demand and accessible via a web browser

Customer Feedback

Thank you for purchasing this Packt book. We take our commitment to improving our content and products to meet your needs seriously—that's why your feedback is so valuable. Whatever your feelings about your purchase, please consider leaving a review on this book's Amazon page. Not only will this help us, more importantly it will also help others in the community to make an informed decision about the resources that they invest in to learn.

You can also review for us on a regular basis by joining our reviewers' club. **If you're interested in joining, or would like to learn more about the benefits we offer, please contact us**: customerreviews@packtpub.com

Table of Contents

Preface

Tableau is a suite of business analytics and data visualization tools that allows people to explore and analyze data quickly and easily with simple drag-and-drop operations.

Tableau software Inc. (http://www.tableau.com/**)** was founded in 2003 by Chris Stolte, Christian Chabot, and Pat Hanrahan. What began as a research project in Stanford University between 1999 and 2002 soon changed the way people see and interact with their data. Through the development of a database visualization language called VizQL (Visual Query Language), which is a combination of a structured query language for databases and a descriptive language for rendering graphics, Tableau was able to give great power to the end users and allowed them to *visualize* and interact with their data with simple drag-and-drop operations.

Giving people the ability to analyze their data and interact with it at the *speed of thought*, Tableau software empowered end users to ask questions on the fly by using their self-service analysis products suite.

The Tableau product suite – differences between the products

Before we actually get started on any visualization, it would be useful to understand the overall range and purpose of the various products offered by Tableau.

The overall suite of products can be broadly bifurcated into two categories; the ones built for creation of dashboards and visualizations and those built for collaboration, sharing, and management of these dashboards and visualizations.

Tableau Desktop

Tableau Desktop is the primary tool most of us will spend most of our time on. It is where we actually create the visualizations, analytics, and dashboards. It is the tool in which all our development will be done.

Tableau Desktop comes in two editions; the Desktop Professional edition which most of us will typically use, and the Desktop Personal edition, which is typically used by people with limited data connectivity needs. To explain this just a bit further, the Desktop Professional edition is a full feature version that can connect to a wide range of data sources, including flat files as well as large database formats (which we will cover in more detail a bit later). Correspondingly the Desktop Personal edition is a limited version in the sense that it can connect only to flat file formats as a data source (Excel, Access, Statistical files, and so on) and does not give the option to connect to any database formats. However, in terms of all other features, the Desktop Professional and the Desktop Personal editions are essentially identical.

Tableau Public

Tableau Public is a free edition that is very similar to Desktop Personal in most ways. It has virtually the full range of features available in the Desktop editions and connects only to flat file formats and not database formats, but with one key distinction. The Tableau Public edition is meant for anyone wanting to post their dashboards and visualizations on the Web, typically for bloggers, journalists, researchers, and the like dealing with public or open data. Hence, the Tableau Public edition does not allow you to save your work offline to your laptop, but publishes your visualizations directly to the Web, on your Tableau Public account on the Tableau public cloud server. The Tableau Public edition is a great tool for anyone wanting to build great visualizations for public consumption, but is not recommended for anyone working with confidential data.

Tableau Server

Tableau Server is an on-premise hosted browser and mobile-based collaboration platform used to publish dashboards created in Tableau Desktop and share them throughout your organization. It allows you to share, to some extent edit, and publish dashboards within your organization while managing access rights and making your visualizations accessible securely over the Web. It also allows you to maintain live data connectivity to backend data sources, which in turn allows users to view up-to-date dashboards online from anywhere. The Tableau Server also allows you to view your dashboards on a mobile tablet through an app available on iOS as well as Android.

Tableau Online

Tableau Online is a cloud hosted version or SaaS version of Tableau Server. It brings Server's capabilities on the cloud without the infrastructure cost.

Tableau Reader

Tableau Reader is a free desktop application that you can use to open, view, and interact with dashboards and visualizations built in Tableau Desktop. Since the dashboards built in Tableau Desktop can package the data within the workbook itself when you save it, Tableau Reader allows you to filter, drill down, view the details of the data, and interact with the dashboards to the full extent of what the author has intended. That said, it being a reader, you cannot make any changes or edit the dashboard in any way beyond what has already been built in by the author.

With this brief introduction to Tableau's suite of products, you will notice that the entire process of creating a dashboard or visualization is done within Tableau Desktop, and thereby this is the product we will be focusing on for the purposes of this book.

In this book, we will go through a bunch of recipes and create a Tableau workbook. The idea is that we follow the recipes and create them from scratch; however, a final copy of the Tableau workbook has been uploaded on the following link.

```
https://1drv.ms/u/s!Av5QCoyLTBpnhlRBwZcWGGJKpasC.
```

What this book covers

Chapter 1, Keep Calm and Say Hello to Tableau, covers the fundamentals of Tableau. We learn how to connect to data, get acquainted with the Tableau workspace and terminologies, and finally see how to save the workbook as a Tableau workbook.

Chapter 2, Ready to Build Some Charts? Show Me!, focuses on the data visualization part. We learn to create some basic charts such as text table, highlight table, heat map, bar chart, stacked bar, pie chart, line chart, area chart, tree map, packed bubble chart, and word cloud.

Chapter 3, Hungry for More Charts? Dig In!, focuses on the advanced chart types in Tableau. We learn how to create charts to compare multiple measures by creating a blended axes chart, dual axes chart, combination chart, scatter plot, and so on. We will also understand how we can create a Gantt chart, build maps and use background images.

Chapter 4, Slice and Dice – Grouping, Sorting, and Filtering Data, teaches you how to do various analyses on the data such as grouping members into higher levels, sorting, filtering unnecessary information, and creating custom hierarchies.

Chapter 5, Adding Flavor – Create Calculated Fields, looks at various calculations in Tableau. The idea is that not every single field will come from the database, and hence one needs to create some calculations in the tool. We will look at creating custom calculations, level-of-detail calculations, and the use of table calculations and parameters.

Chapter 6, Serve It on a Dashboard!, is about building one holistic view for end users and giving them a consolidated snapshot of the business. We will look at building dashboards, the use of actions to link multiple sheets on the dashboard, the use of images on the dashboard, formatting dashboards, and using cross-data-source filters.

Chapter 7, The Right MIX – Blending Multiple Data Sources, walks us through the options of connecting to data from multiple data sources. We will look at concepts such as data blending, multiple table joins, cross-database joins, unions, custom SQL, and working with Tableau extracts.

Chapter 8, Garnish with Reference Lines, Trends, Forecasting, and Clustering, focuses on some specific analytics in terms of computing and understanding trends in the data. We do a forecast by using the in-built forecasting model and lastly understand the use of reference lines as benchmark. We will look at topics like trend lines, forecast, reference lines, bullet charts and clustering.

Chapter 9, Bon Appétit! Tell a Story and Share It with Others, covers the storytelling feature in Tableau. We also look at the various ways in which one can save and share their work with others.

Chapter 10, Formatting in Tableau for Desserts, focuses on the various formatting options in Tableau.

What you need for this book

You'll need any one of the following for the book:

Tableau Desktop Professional version 10.1 or higher

Tableau Desktop Personal version 10.1 or higher

Tableau Public version 10.1 or higher

Please note that it is ideal if you use Tableau Desktop Professional. However, in case you are using Tableau Desktop Personal or Tableau Public, then some of the functionalities mentioned in the book may change.

Who this book is for

This book is for anyone who wishes to use Tableau. It will be of use to both beginners who want to learn Tableau from scratch and to more seasoned users who simply want a quick reference guide. This book is a ready reckoner guide for you. The book will be such that both new and existing Tableau users who don't know or can't recall how to perform different Tableau tasks can use it and be benefited from it.

Sections

In this book, you will find several headings that appear frequently (Getting ready, How to do it..., How it works..., There's more..., and See also).

To give clear instructions on how to complete a recipe, we use these sections as follows:

Getting ready

This section tells you what to expect in the recipe, and describes how to set up any software or any preliminary settings required for the recipe.

How to do it...

This section contains the steps required to follow the recipe.

How it works...

This section usually consists of a detailed explanation of what happened in the previous section.

There's more...

This section consists of additional information about the recipe in order to make the reader more knowledgeable about the recipe.

See also

This section provides helpful links to other useful information for the recipe.

Conventions

In this book, you will find a number of text styles that distinguish between different kinds of information. Here are some examples of these styles and an explanation of their meaning.

Code words in text, database table names, folder names, filenames, file extensions, pathnames, dummy URLs, user input, and Twitter handles are shown as follows: "We can include other contexts through the use of the include directive."

A block of code is set as follows:

```
[default]
exten => s,1,Dial(Zap/1|30)
exten => s,2,Voicemail(u100)
exten => s,102,Voicemail(b100)
exten => i,1,Voicemail(s0)
```

When we wish to draw your attention to a particular part of a code block, the relevant lines or items are set in bold:

```
[default]
exten => s,1,Dial(Zap/1|30)
exten => s,2,Voicemail(u100)
exten => s,102,Voicemail(b100)
exten => i,1,Voicemail(s0)
```

Any command-line input or output is written as follows:

```
# cp /user/src/asterisk-addons/configs/cdr_mysql.conf.sample
    /etc/asterisk/cdr_mysql.conf
```

New terms and **important words** are shown in bold. Words that you see on the screen, for example, in menus or dialog boxes, appear in the text like this: "Clicking the **Next** button moves you to the next screen."

 Warnings or important notes appear in a box like this.

 Tips and tricks appear like this.

Reader feedback

Feedback from our readers is always welcome. Let us know what you think about this book—what you liked or disliked. Reader feedback is important for us as it helps us develop titles that you will really get the most out of.

To send us general feedback, simply e-mail feedback@packtpub.com, and mention the book's title in the subject of your message.

If there is a topic that you have expertise in and you are interested in either writing or contributing to a book, see our author guide at www.packtpub.com/authors.

Customer support

Now that you are the proud owner of a Packt book, we have a number of things to help you to get the most from your purchase.

Downloading the example code

You can download the example code files for all Packt books you have purchased from your account at http://www.packtpub.com. If you purchased this book elsewhere, you can visit http://www.packtpub.com/support and register to have the files e-mailed directly to you.

1. You can download the code files by following these steps:
2. Log in or register to our website using your e-mail address and password.
3. Hover the mouse pointer on the **SUPPORT** tab at the top.
4. Click on **Code Downloads & Errata**.
5. Enter the name of the book in the **Search** box.
6. Select the book for which you're looking to download the code files.
7. Choose from the drop-down menu where you purchased this book from.
8. Click on **Code Download**.

Once the file is downloaded, please make sure that you unzip or extract the folder using the latest version of:

- WinRAR / 7-Zip for Windows
- Zipeg / iZip / UnRarX for Mac
- 7-Zip / PeaZip for Linux

The code bundle for the book is also hosted on GitHub at https://github.com/PacktPublishing/Tableau-Cookbook-Recipes-for-Data-Visualization. We also have other code bundles from our rich catalog of books and videos available at https://github.com/PacktPublishing/. Check them out!

If you are using Tableau Public, you'll need to locate the workbooks that have been published to Tableau Public. These may be found at the following link: http://goo.gl/wJzfDO.

Downloading the color images of this book

We also provide you with a PDF file that has color images of the screenshots/diagrams used in this book. The color images will help you better understand the changes in the output. You can download this file from https://www.packtpub.com/sites/default/files/downloads/TableauCookbookRecipesforDataVisualization_ColorImages.pdf.

Errata

Although we have taken every care to ensure the accuracy of our content, mistakes do happen. If you find a mistake in one of our books—maybe a mistake in the text or the code—we would be grateful if you could report this to us. By doing so, you can save other readers from frustration and help us improve subsequent versions of this book. If you find any errata, please report them by visiting http://www.packtpub.com/submit-errata, selecting your book, clicking on the **Errata Submission Form** link, and entering the details of your errata. Once your errata are verified, your submission will be accepted and the errata will be uploaded to our website or added to any list of existing errata under the Errata section of that title.

To view the previously submitted errata, go to https://www.packtpub.com/books/content/support and enter the name of the book in the search field. The required information will appear under the **Errata** section.

Piracy

Piracy of copyrighted material on the Internet is an ongoing problem across all media. At Packt, we take the protection of our copyright and licenses very seriously. If you come across any illegal copies of our works in any form on the Internet, please provide us with the location address or website name immediately so that we can pursue a remedy.

Please contact us at copyright@packtpub.com with a link to the suspected pirated material.

We appreciate your help in protecting our authors and our ability to bring you valuable content.

Questions

If you have a problem with any aspect of this book, you can contact us at questions@packtpub.com, and we will do our best to address the problem.

1
Keep Calm and Say Hello to Tableau

In this chapter, we will cover the following recipes:

- ▶ Starting with Tableau Desktop
- ▶ Introduction to My Tableau Repository and connecting to the sample data source
- ▶ Building our first visualization and understanding the Tableau workspace
- ▶ Saving a Tableau workbook

Introduction

Earlier, in the preface, we saw the various products that are available under Tableau's product suite. The focus of this book will be on Tableau Desktop, the UI authoring tool of Tableau that will help us analyze and visualize our data. So, let's get started by familiarizing ourselves with Tableau Desktop.

Starting with Tableau Desktop

To get started in terms of creating our visualizations, we will be using **Tableau Desktop Professional Edition Version 10.1**. This is the latest version of Tableau products and offers compatibility with both Windows OS as well as Mac OS. However, for the sake of a wider audience, we will be using the Windows-OS-compatible version in this book. That said, those using version 10.1 on a Mac OS should not see much of a difference since the User Interface and functionality is essentially the same.

Getting ready

Before we get started, we need to make sure that **Tableau Desktop Professional Edition Version 10.1** is downloaded and installed on our machines.

 Note that if we use **Tableau Public**, then some of the protocols for saving our work will change since Tableau Public doesn't allow us to save our work locally. Also, if we use **Tableau Desktop Personal Edition**, then apart from certain limitations, such as being able to connect to databases, the rest of the functionality will mostly remain the same.

If you are an existing licensed user of Tableau Desktop, then make sure that you are using the latest version. If the version is anything below 10.1, then it is recommended that you upgrade it to the latest version, as there are significant changes in terms of the User Interface as well as features. Nonetheless, even if we decide to continue with the earlier versions, the majority of the fundamental concepts and features outlined in this book would remain the same, although their implementation may differ.

If you do not have a license, the 14-day full-feature trial of **Tableau Desktop Professional Version 10.1** can be installed and downloaded from Tableau's website (http://www.tableau.com/).

Tableau, being a plug and play software, simply needs to be downloaded and installed just like any .exe or .dmg installable.

How to do it...

1. Download and install Tableau Desktop Professional 10.1.

2. Upon installation, you can activate the trial version by registering your details; alternatively, if you have a license key, then you can activate the license by entering the same. We are now ready to get started.

3. When we click on the **Tableau 10.1** icon on the desktop, we will see the starting or landing page of Tableau. Check out the following screenshot:

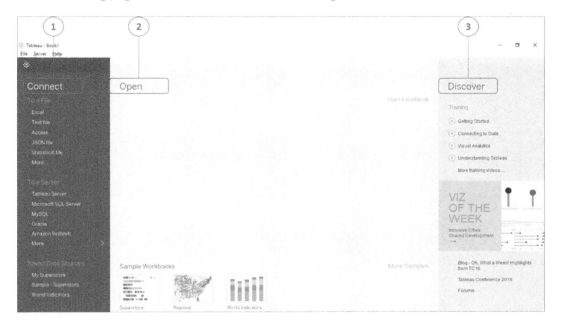

How it works...

The **Start Page** of Tableau is divided into three parts, namely **Connect**, **Open**, and **Discover**; refer to the numbers **1**, **2**, and **3** respectively in the preceding screenshot.

The top-left corner, which says **Connect** (number 1), consists of three sections called **To a File**, **To a Server**, and **Saved Data Sources**. In each of these sections, we will see the list of data sources that Tableau can connect to.

The **To a File** section consists of flat file data sources such as Excel files, Access files, Text files, JSON files, and statistical files, including **SAS**, **SPSS**, and **R**. Clicking on the **More...** option under this section allows us to even connect to Tableau's data extract files, which we will understand in detail in the later chapters.

The **To a Server** section consists of data sources such as Microsoft SQL Server, MySQL, Oracle, and so on. To see a more detailed list of data sources that Tableau can connect to, we need to click on the **More...** option and expand the section by clicking on the arrow. Refer to the following image that illustrates this:

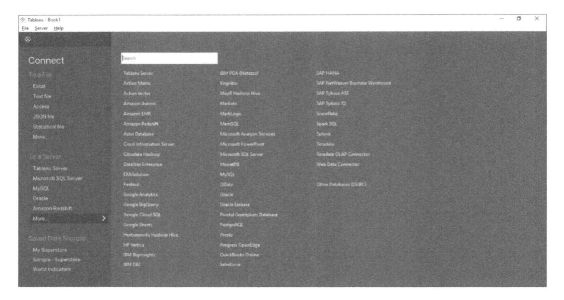

Just below the **To a Server** section, we will see the **Saved Data Sources** section. This section essentially points to those data sources that have been previously worked on and then saved for later purposes. Currently, we will not use this option and we will start by connecting to the raw data and not use any of the existing saved data sources.

Adjacent to the **Connect** header is an empty section that is covered under the header **Open** (number 2). This is the section where we will see the thumbnails of all our recently opened workbooks. This section is blank to begin with; however, as we create and save new workbooks, this section will display the thumbnails of the nine most recently opened workbooks.

This section also gives us access to some sample workbooks that are provided by Tableau for our reference. We can open these workbooks in Tableau Desktop to see how certain functionalities are used or how a particular visualization is created in Tableau.

A **workbook** in Tableau is similar to that of Excel. Just as an Excel workbook consists of multiple sheets, the workbook in Tableau contains multiple worksheets, and/or dashboards, and/or stories. The worksheet in Tableau consists of one view/visualization/report, whereas a dashboard is a combination of multiple worksheets which when viewed will provide the viewer with a holistic view.

The next section is the **Discover** section (number 3). This section basically provides links to resources that are available on the Tableau website. Apart from the training videos, this section also shows the blogs, forums, latest news about Tableau, as well as the views that are selected as the **Viz of the week** on Tableau Public.

 Viz is short for visualization/visual. In the Tableau community, this word is used very regularly to describe the visualizations done in Tableau.

Introduction to My Tableau Repository and connecting to the sample data source

Tableau is a very versatile tool and is being used across various industries, businesses, and organizations. These include government and non-profit organizations, the BFSI sector, consulting, construction, education, healthcare, manufacturing, retail, FMCG, software and technology, telecommunications, and many more. The good thing about Tableau is that it is industry- and business-vertical-agnostic, and hence, as long as we have data, we can analyze and visualize it.

Tableau can connect to a wide variety of data sources, and many of the data sources are implemented as native connections in Tableau. This ensures that the connections are as robust as possible.

 To view the comprehensive list of data sources that Tableau connects to, we can visit the technical specification page on the Tableau website by clicking on http://www.tableau.com/products/techspecs.

Getting ready

Tableau provides some sample datasets with the Desktop edition. In this book, we will frequently use the sample datasets that have been provided by Tableau. We can find these datasets in the Datasources folder within the My Tableau Repository folder, which gets created in the Documents folder when Tableau Desktop is installed on the machine. We can look for these data sources in the repository or quickly download them from https://1drv.ms/f/s!Av5QCoyLTBpnhj06IKTNX0S9hK48. Once you do this, you save them in a new folder called Tableau Cookbook data that you'll find by navigating to Documents\My Tableau Repository\Datasources.

There are three files that have been uploaded, and these are the ones that we will primarily use throughout the book. They are as follows:

▸ Microsoft Excel data called `Sample - Superstore.xls`

▸ Microsoft Access data called `Sample - Coffee Chain.mdb`

▸ Microsoft Excel data called `Sample - CoffeeChain (Use instead of MS Access).xlsx`

In the following section, we will see how to connect to the sample data source. We will be connecting to the Excel data called `Sample - Superstore.xls`.

This Excel file contains transactional data for a retail store. There are three worksheets in this Excel workbook. The first sheet, called the `Orders` sheet, contains the transaction details, The `Returns` sheet contains the status of returned orders. And the `People` sheet contains the region names and the names of the managers associated with those regions. Refer to the following image to get a glimpse of how the Excel data is structured:

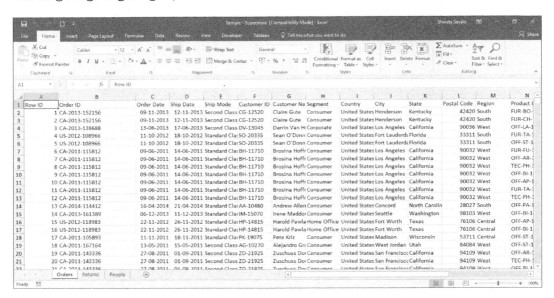

Now that we have looked at the Excel data, let's see how to connect to this data in the following recipe. To begin with, we will work on the `Orders` sheet of the `Sample - Superstore.xls` data. This worksheet contains the order details in terms of the products purchased, the name of the customer, sales, profits, discounts offered, day of purchase, and the order shipment date, among many other transactional details.

How to do it...

1. Open Tableau Desktop by double-clicking on the Tableau 10.1 icon on the desktop. You can also right-click on the icon and select **Open**. When you do this, you will see the **Start** page of Tableau, as shown in following image:

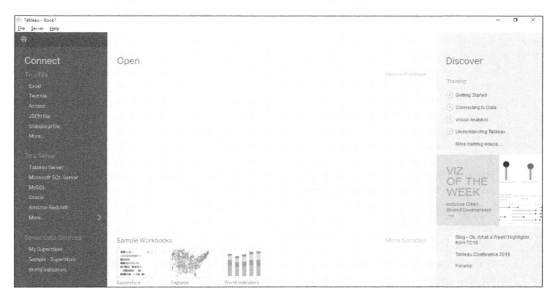

2. Select the **Excel** option from under the **Connect** header on the left-hand side of the screen.

3. Once you do this, browse the Excel file called `Sample - Superstore.xls`, which is saved in `Tableau Cookbook data` under `Documents | My Tableau Repository | Datasources`.

4. Once we are able to establish a connection to the referred Excel file, we will get a view as shown in the following image:

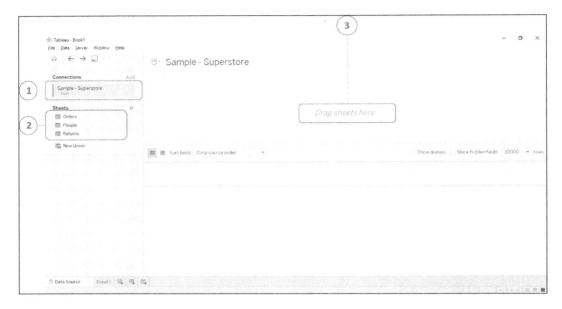

5. The number 1 in the preceding image refers to the data that we have connected to, and 2 refers to the list of worksheets/tables/views in our data.

6. Let's double-click on the **Orders** sheet or drag and drop the **Orders** sheet from the left-hand side section of the screen into a blank space that says **Drag sheets here**. Refer to the number 3 in the preceding image.

7. Once we select the **Orders** sheet, we will get to see the preview of our data, highlighted using the number 1 in the following image. We will see the column headers, their data type (#, Abc, and so on), and the individual rows of data:

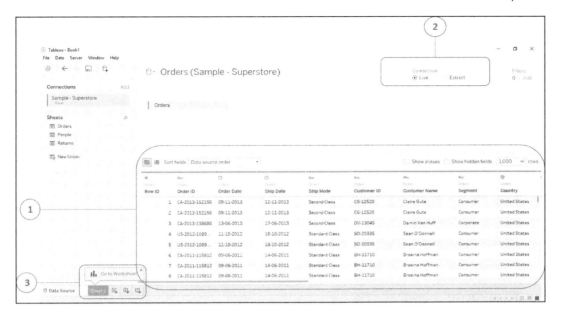

8. While connecting to a data source, we can also read data from multiple tables/ sheets from that data source. However, this is something that we will explore a little later. Moving on, we will need to specify what type of connection we wish to maintain with the data source. Do we wish to connect to our data directly and maintain a **Live** connectivity with it or do we wish to import the data into Tableau's data engine by creating an **Extract**? Refer to the number 2 in the preceding image. We will understand these options in detail in the next section. However, to begin with, we will select the **Live** option.

9. Next, to get to our Tableau workspace, where we can start building our visualizations, click on the **Go to Worksheet** option and then **Sheet 1**, which we will find at the bottom left-hand side corner. Refer to the number 3 in the preceding image.

10. This is how we can connect to the data in Tableau. If we have a database to connect to, then we can select the relevant data source from the list and fill in the necessary information in terms of the server name, username, password, and so on. Refer to the following image to see what options we get when we connect to the Microsoft SQL Server:

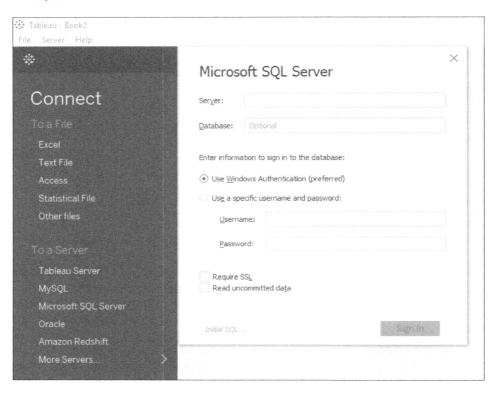

How it works...

Before we connect to any data, we need to make sure that our data is clean and in the right format. The Excel file that we connected to was stored in a tabular format where the first row of the sheet contained all the column headers and every other row is basically a single transaction in the data. This is the ideal data structure for making the best use of Tableau. Typically, when we connect to databases, we get a columnar/tabular type of data. However, flat files, such as Excel, can have data even in cross-tab formats. Although Tableau can read cross-tab data, we may end up facing some limitations in terms of creating certain chart types, thereby aggregating and slicing and dicing our data in Tableau.

Having said that, there may be situations where we have to deal with such cross-tab or preformatted Excel files. These files will essentially need cleaning up before being pulled into Tableau. Refer to `http://kb.tableausoftware.com/articles/knowledgebase/preparing-excel-files-analysis` to understand more about how we can clean up these files and make them Tableau-ready. Refer to the following article to quickly understand how we can quickly pivot the data in Excel. `http://kb.tableau.com/articles/knowledgebase/addin-reshaping-data-excel`.

If it is a cross-tab file, then we will have to pivot it into normalized columns either at the data level or at the Tableau level on the fly. We can do so by selecting multiple columns that we wish to pivot and then selecting the **Pivot** option from the drop-down menu that appears when we hover over any of the columns. Refer to the following image:

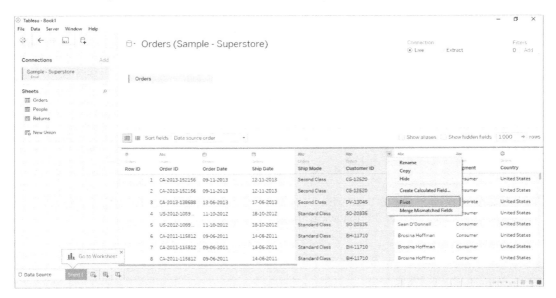

Further, if the format of the data in our Excel file is not suitable for analysis in Tableau, then we can turn on the **Data Interpreter** option, which becomes available when Tableau detects any unique formatting or any extra information in our Excel file. For example, the Excel data may include some empty rows and columns or extra headers and footers. Refer to the following image:

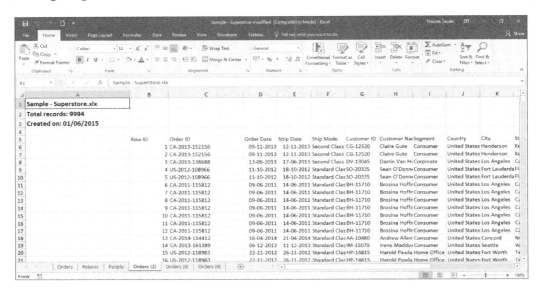

Data Interpreter can remove that extra bit of information to help prepare our Tableau data source for analysis. Refer to the following image:

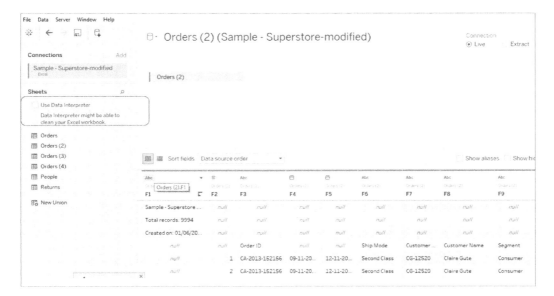

When we enable **Data Interpreter**, the preceding view will change to what is shown in the following image:

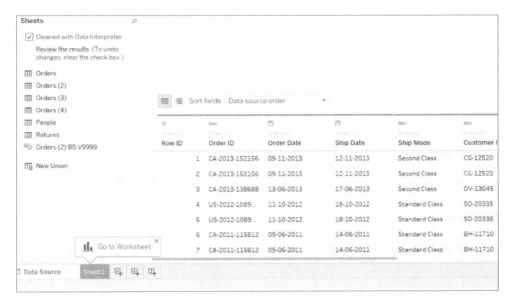

This is how **Data Interpreter** works in Tableau.

Now, many a times, there may also be situations where our data fields are compounded or clubbed in a single column. Refer to the following image:

	A	B	C	D	E
1	Customer Na	Segment	Geography	Postal Code	Region
2	Claire Gute	Consumer	United States/Henderson/Kentucky	42420	South
3	Claire Gute	Consumer	United States/Henderson/Kentucky	42420	South
4	Darrin Van H	Corporate	United States/Los Angeles/California	90036	West
5	Sean O'Donn	Consumer	United States/Fort Lauderdale/Florida	33311	South
6	Sean O'Donn	Consumer	United States/Fort Lauderdale/Florida	33311	South
7	Brosina Hoffr	Consumer	United States/Los Angeles/California	90032	West
8	Brosina Hoffr	Consumer	United States/Los Angeles/California	90032	West
9	Brosina Hoffr	Consumer	United States/Los Angeles/California	90032	West
10	Brosina Hoffr	Consumer	United States/Los Angeles/California	90032	West
11	Brosina Hoffr	Consumer	United States/Los Angeles/California	90032	West
12	Brosina Hoffr	Consumer	United States/Los Angeles/California	90032	West
13	Brosina Hoffr	Consumer	United States/Los Angeles/California	90032	West
14	Andrew Aller	Consumer	United States/Concord/North Carolina	28027	South
15	Irene Maddo	Consumer	United States/Seattle/Washington	98103	West
16	Harold Pawla	Home Office	United States/Fort Worth/Texas	76106	Central
17	Harold Pawla	Home Office	United States/Fort Worth/Texas	76106	Central
18	Pete Kriz	Consumer	United States/Madison/Wisconsin	53711	Central
19	Alejandro Gr	Consumer	United States/West Jordan/Utah	84084	West
20	Zuschuss Dor	Consumer	United States/San Francisco/California	94109	West
21	Zuschuss Dor	Consumer	United States/San Francisco/California	94109	West
22	Zuschuss Dor	Consumer	United States/San Francisco/California	94109	West
23	Ken Black	Corporate	United States/Fremont/Nebraska	68025	Central
24	Ken Black	Corporate	United States/Fremont/Nebraska	68025	Central

In the preceding image, the highlighted column is basically a concatenated field that has the **Country**, **City**, and **State** fields. For our analysis, we may want to break these and analyze each geographic level separately. To do so, we simply need to use the **Split** or **Custom Split** option in Tableau. Refer to the following image:

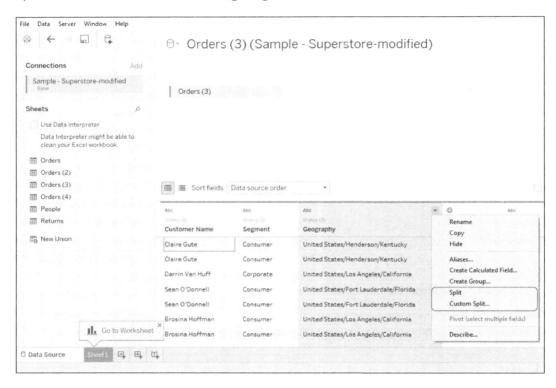

Once we do this, our view would be as shown in the following image:

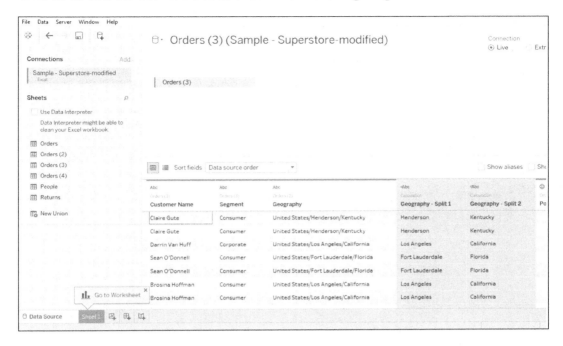

Further, when preparing some data for analysis, at times a list of fields may be easy to consume as against the current preview of our data. The **Metadata** grid in Tableau allows us to do the same along with many other quick functions such as renaming fields, hiding columns, changing data types, changing aliases, creating calculations, splitting fields, merging fields, and pivoting the data. Refer to the following image:

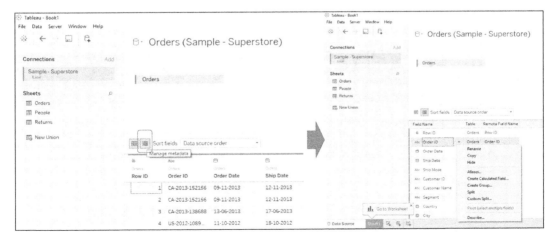

After having established the initial connectivity by pointing to the right data source, we need to specify how we wish to maintain that connectivity. We can choose between the **Live** option and the **Extract** option.

The **Live** option helps us connect to our data directly and maintains a live connection with the data source. Using this option allows Tableau to leverage the capabilities of our data source, and in this case, the speed of our data source will determine the performance of our analysis.

The **Extract** option, on the other hand, helps us import the entire data source into Tableau's fast data engine as an extract. This option basically creates a .tde file, which stands for Tableau Data Extract. In case you wish to extract only a subset of your data, then you can select the **Edit** option, as highlighted in following image. The **Add** link in the right-hand side corner helps us add filters while fetching the data into Tableau:

One point to remember about **Extract** is that it is a snapshot of our data stored in a Tableau proprietary format, and as opposed to a **Live** connection, the changes in the original data won't be reflected in the dashboard unless and until the **Extract** is updated.

Note that we will have to decide between **Live** and **Extract** on a case-to-case basis. Refer to http://www.tableausoftware.com/learn/whitepapers/memory-or-live-data for more clarity.

Building our first visualization and understanding the Tableau workspace

Tableau is a very user-friendly tool that helps us visualize our data with a simple drag and drop technique. In the previous recipe, we saw how to connect to the data, and in this section, we will create our very first visualization and get acquainted with the Tableau workspace.

Getting ready

We will continue from where we left in the previous recipe where we are still connected live to the `Orders` sheets of `Sample - Superstore.xls`. Let's quickly build our first view and then understand the workspace of Tableau.

How to do it...

1. If you haven't already connected to the data, then make sure that you are connected live to the `Orders` sheets of `Sample - Superstore.xls` by following the steps mentioned in the previous recipe.

2. Click on the **Go to Worksheet** option and then the **Sheet 1** tab. Refer to the following image:

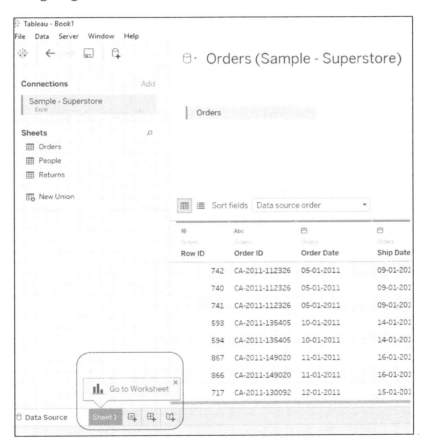

3. Once we do this, we will get a view as shown in the following image:

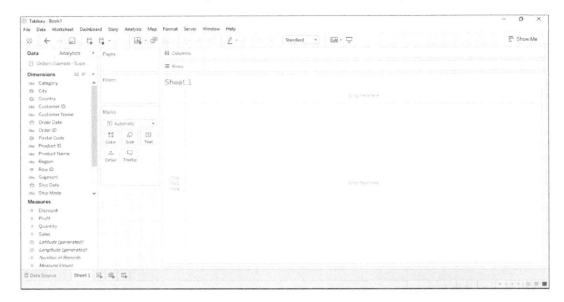

4. Then, let us drag **Region** field from the left-hand side pane and drop it into the **Rows** shelf. Refer to the following image:

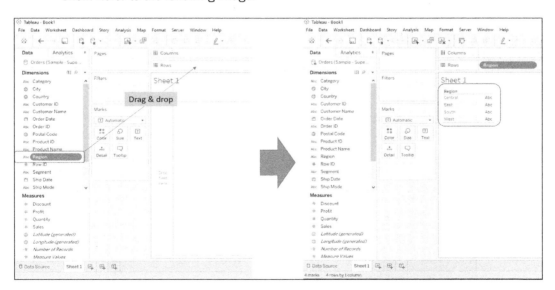

5. Once you do this, drag **Sales** and drop it into the **Columns** shelf, and our view will be updated as shown in the following image:

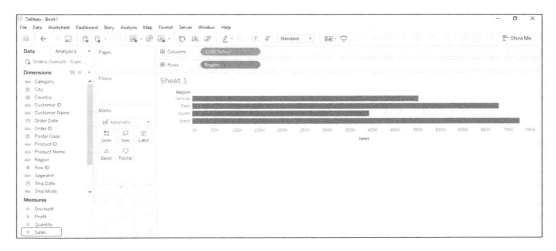

6. What we see in the preceding image is a bar chart that shows region-wise **Sales**.

How it works...

After having established the connection to the data and having read the data in Tableau by clicking on the **Go to Worksheet** option and then the **Sheet 1** tab, we get the view where we will create our visualizations. Refer to the following image:

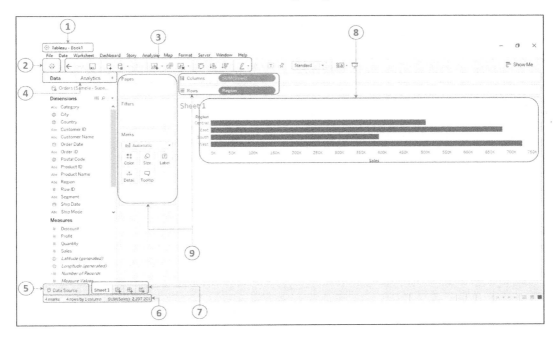

The preceding image gives us a quick glimpse into the Tableau workspace. Let's understand this workspace in more detail:

▶ **Workbook name**: Refer to the number 1 in the preceding image. This is the name of the workbook. By default, it is Tableau - Book 1 or so. However, we can change the name once we save the workbook.

▶ **Go to the start page:** Refer to the number 2 in the preceding image. This helps us navigate back to the start page of Tableau.

▶ **Toolbar**: Refer to the number 3 in the preceding image. This is Tableau's toolbar that consists of various commands that help us enable/disable various features and functionalities.

▶ **Side bar**: The number 4 in the preceding image refers to the sidebar that provides two panes: the **Data** pane and the **Analytics** pane.

The **Data** pane, as the name suggests, shows the data to begin with, which is populated from the data source that we have connected to. The top section of the **Data** pane displays the data source that we have connected to. In the case of multiple data sources, we will see a list of data sources.

Further, just below the data source section are the fields available in that data source. Refer to the following image:

The **Data** pane is primarily divided into two sections: **Dimensions** and **Measures**.

Dimensions are all the **descriptive fields** in our data. These are fields that hold **categorical/ discrete qualitative data**. In short, any field that contains text or date values will be identified as **Dimensions**, for example, customer name, purchase date, customer state, and so on.

On the other hand, **Measures** are all the fields that contain **numeric values**. These are fields that hold quantitative data, for example, sales, profit, budget, and so on. Typically, **Measures** are the fields that will be aggregated while analyzing. For example, we may want to see the sum of sales across regions, the average sales for a particular category, and so on.

Basically, **Dimensions** and **Measures** are Tableau's way of classifying our data fields. At a little later point in time, you will understand how Tableau is capable of doing this classification, and in case we wish to change it, then how to go about it.

Further, the **Data** pane may additionally accommodate sections for **Sets** and **Parameters**, functionalities that we will explore later.

The **Analytics** pane, on the other hand, provides quick and easy access to features such as reference lines, box plots, trend lines, forecasts, and so on. We will explore these options at a later stage. To begin with, the **Analytics** pane may be disabled/grayed out. However, once we start creating our visualizations, then depending on the visualization, some of the options from this pane will be enabled/disabled for us. Refer to the following image:

- ▸ **Go to the data source page**: Refer to the number 5. This helps us navigate back to the data source page of Tableau.

- ▸ **Status bar**: Refer to the number 6. The **status bar** shows us the number of rows and marks that we are dealing with. It also displays occasional warning icons.

- ▶ **Worksheet tabs**: Refer to the number 7. The worksheet tab helps us view our worksheets, dashboards, or story. These can either be shown as tabs or filmstrips.

- ▶ **Worksheet view**: Refer to the number 8. The worksheet view is the place where we build a view/visualization.

- ▶ **Cards and shelves**: Refer to the number 9. These are containers for shelves, such as the **Column** shelf, the **Row** shelf, the **Filter** shelf, and the **Page** shelf. This is where we define what the columns, rows, and filters of our worksheet are. The **Marks** card consists of a drop-down list that helps us specify the mark type (for example, bar, line, pie, circles, and many more) and also contains shelves for **Color, Size, Text, Detail,** and **Tooltip**. This is where we can define the appearance of our worksheet in terms of the visualization type, color scheme, labels, and many more. Depending on what kind of chart we create, we would see the **Label** shelf, the **Shape** shelf, the **Path** shelf, and the **Angle** shelf as well. However, the availability of these shelves is dependent on the visualization that we create. Refer to the following image to see the options from the **Marks** dropdown:

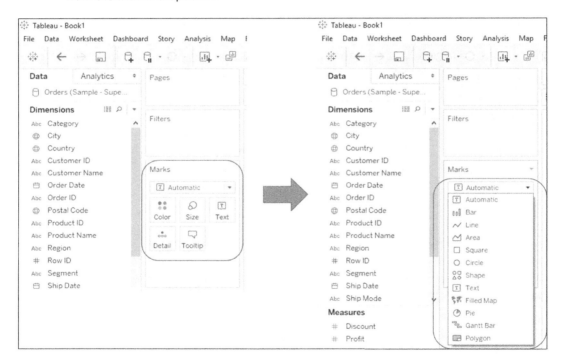

We shall explore these various shelves in more detail as we progress with our understanding of Tableau.

In the earlier section, we read about **Dimensions** and **Measures**. As a quick recap, **Dimensions** are basically fields that contain categorical/descriptive/qualitative data, such as text and dates, whereas, **Measures** are fields that contain numeric/quantitative data that can be aggregated.

Dimensions and **Measures** are the fundamental building blocks of our analysis, and it is very important that they are identified correctly. As mentioned earlier, Tableau is capable of classifying our data fields as either a **Dimension** or a **Measure**, and it does so based on the data type of the fields.

So, what data types are supported by Tableau and how does Tableau identify them? When we connect to a database, the data types are already defined in the database and that is what Tableau would read. However, when we connect to typical flat file formats, such as Excel, Access, or CSVs, Tableau will read the data types of the first 10,000 rows of an Excel data source or the first 1,024 rows of a text file data source. Once it does this, it will accordingly decide the data type of that field. So, in an Excel file, if most of the first 10,000 rows are numeric values, the entire column is mapped as Integer.

> Before version 8.2 came out, Tableau used Microsoft Jet Engine to connect to Excel, Access, and CSVs. We call this a **legacy connection**. However, with the latest versions, there are new connectors that are being used for connectivity to Excel and CSVs. With the legacy connection, the datatype mapping was done by reading the first 16 rows of the data for Excel, Access, and CSVs.

Each field under the **Dimensions** and **Measures** section will have a prefixed icon before it. These are the data types supported by Tableau and are identified in the **Data** pane by one of the following icons:

Abc	Text / String / Character values
#	Numeric / Integer values
📅	Date values
📅⊙	Date and Time values
T|F	Boolean (True/False) values
⊕	Geographic values that are to be used with Maps

Is it possible to change the datatype of the fields in Tableau? Yes! Ideally, it is recommended that we handle all the data-related changes at the data source level. However, if we feel that Tableau has incorrectly identified the data type of a certain field, then we can right-click on the field in the **Data** pane, select **Change Data Type**, and then select the appropriate data type. Refer to the following image:

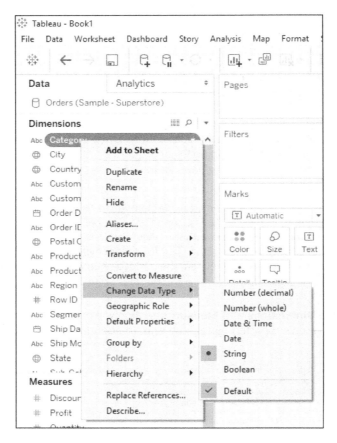

Once Tableau identifies the data type, it simply classifies all **String** and **Date / Date & Time** data types as **Dimensions** and all **Integer** data types as **Measures**.

Why is Row ID a Dimension even though its datatype is Integer? Even though **Row ID** is a numeric field in this case, taking a sum or average of **Row ID** won't be useful. It is actually a descriptive field that gives us information about the transaction. Since the header/field name contains the word **ID**, Tableau assumes that it is an identifier and hence places it in the **Dimensions** shelf.

Is it possible to convert a Dimension to a Measure and vice versa? Yes! It is easily possible to convert **Dimension** to **Measure** and vice versa. To do so, we can simply right-click on the **Dimension** field and select the option of **Convert to Measure**. If we right-click on the **Measure** field, then we get an option of **Convert to Dimension**. Refer to the following image:

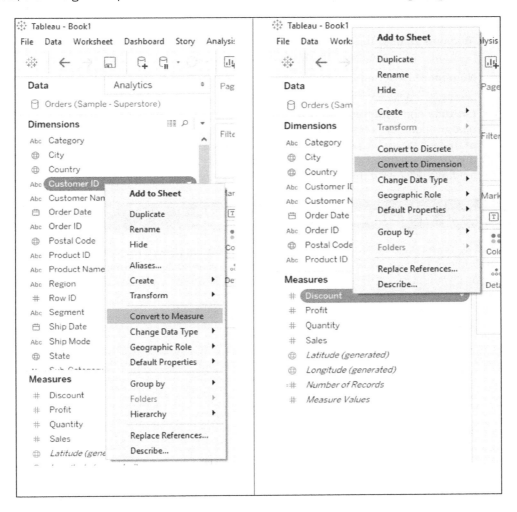

We can also drag **Dimension** fields and then drop them into the **Measures** pane and vice versa to convert them from **Dimensions** to **Measures**. The same method can be used to convert **Measures** to **Dimensions** as well.

When we connect to the data, apart from reading the data fields and classifying them as **Dimensions** or **Measures**, Tableau also autogenerates certain new fields in both the **Dimensions** and **Measures** pane. They are as follows:

- ► **Measure Names**: This contains the names of all our measures in a single dimension and is shown at the bottom of the **Dimensions** pane.

- ► **Measure Values**: This contains the values of all our measures into a single field and is shown at the bottom of the **Measures** pane.

- ► **Number of Records**: This shows the number of records that we are dealing with after we have connected to our data.

- ► **Latitude** and **Longitude**: Tableau has the ability to create geographic maps and plot any point on a Map; we would essentially require the latitudes and longitudes of these geographic points. Tableau understands certain geographic roles and will automatically generate these two measures if it identifies any field as a geographic field. We will revisit this in more detail when we discuss Maps in the later chapters.

Saving a Tableau workbook

Now that we have connected to data, built our first visualization, and have learned the fundamentals of Tableau, we will go ahead and save our workbook so that we can continue working on it without losing what we have already done. To do so, let's follow the following recipe.

Getting ready

In the coming chapters, we will learn how to create various charts in Tableau. However, before we go there, let's understand how we can save the file that we are currently working on:

How to do it...

1. After following the steps mentioned in the previous recipe, we will first right-click on the **Sheet** tab, which currently says **Sheet 1**, and select the **Rename Sheet** option as shown in the following image:

2. We will rename the sheet to My first Tableau view.

3. Then, we will click on the **File** menu in the toolbar and select the **Save** option as shown in the following image:

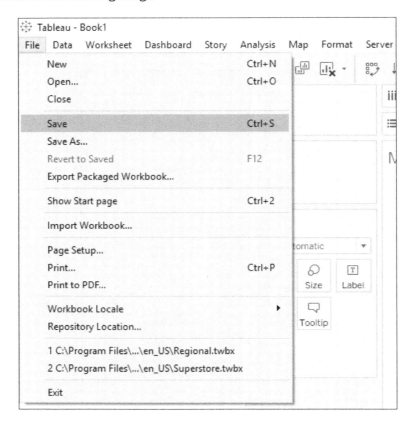

4. We will now have to decide where the workbook needs to be saved. Let's save it in Documents | My Tableau Repository | Workbooks.

5. We will name our workbook My first Tableau Workbook.

6.   We will select the `.twb` extension that stands for **Tableau Workbook**, and once we have done this, our workbook name will be changed to `My first Tableau Workbook`. Refer to the following image:

 A `.twb` file is a Tableau proprietary file format to save your work and it stands for Tableau Workbook. We will look into the various other ways of saving and sharing our work in detail in the upcoming chapters.

2
Ready to Build Some Charts? Show Me!

In this chapter, we will cover the following recipes:

- ▶ Building views manually
- ▶ Building views automatically
- ▶ Understanding Show Me!
- ▶ Creating a Text table
- ▶ Creating a Highlight table
- ▶ Creating a Heat map
- ▶ Creating a Bar chart
- ▶ Creating a Stacked Bar chart
- ▶ Creating a Pie chart
- ▶ Creating a Line chart
- ▶ Creating an Area chart
- ▶ Creating a Treemap
- ▶ Creating a Packed Bubble chart
- ▶ Creating a Word cloud

Introduction

In the previous chapter, we saw how to connect to data, got ourselves acquainted with Tableau's User Interface, and created a simple visualization. Moving forward, in this chapter we will focus on how we can visualize our data and get introduced to the various chart types in Tableau.

Tableau is a new-generation data visualization tool with a user-friendly interface, and empowers users with the ability to quickly analyze their data and instantly create rich, powerful, and interactive visualizations. We can create visualizations in Tableau by adopting the **Manual** approach or the **Automatic** approach. Let's understand both these approaches in the following sections.

Building views manually

The Manual approach in Tableau is a simple drag and drop functionality that users can adopt to build visualizations. This approach gives the users power and flexibility to decide how they want to create their views. In the following recipe, we will build some basic views using the Manual approach.

Getting ready

We can manually build a view in Tableau by dragging and dropping the **Dimensions** and **Measures** pane into the **Rows** or **Columns** shelf. We will see this approach in the following recipe, and to do this, we will continue working in the workbook named **My first Tableau Workbook**, which we created and saved in *Chapter 1, Keep Calm and Say Hello to Tableau.*

How to do it...

1. If the workbook isn't already open, then open it by double-clicking on `My first Tableau Workbook.twb` by navigating to `Documents | My Tableau Repository | Workbooks`. Once we do this, we will see the view shown in the following screenshot:

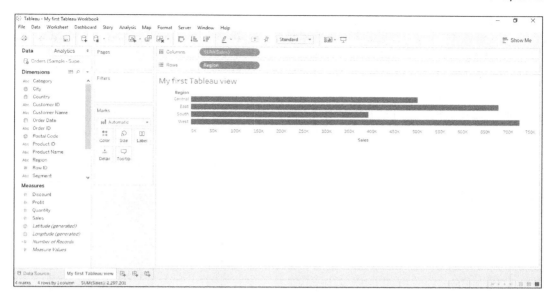

2. Now, to create our next visualization, create a new worksheet by right-clicking on the tab that says **My first Tableau view** and selecting the **New Worksheet** option; alternatively, you can do this by clicking on the first tab right next to the **My first Tableau view** tab. You can also create a new worksheet by selecting the **New Worksheet** icon on the toolbar or by typing *Ctrl + M* on the keyboard. Refer to the following image:

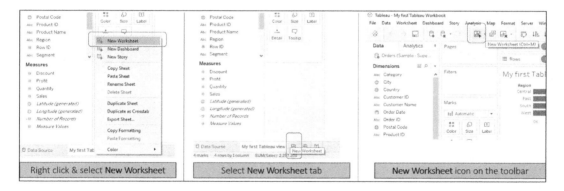

3. Once we do this, we will get a blank new worksheet named **Sheet 2**. In **Sheet 2**, first let us drag the **Ship Mode** field from the **Dimensions** pane and drop it into the **Columns** shelf. We will then drag the **Sales** field from the **Measures** pane and drop it into the **Rows** shelf. Refer to the following image:

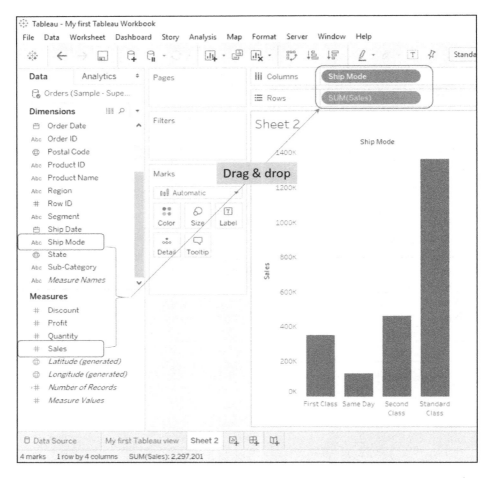

4. This is how we can use the **drag and drop** approach to manually build views in Tableau. However, as the last finishing touch for this recipe, right-click on **Sheet tab**, which says **Sheet 2**, and rename it to **Manual approach**. Refer to the following image:

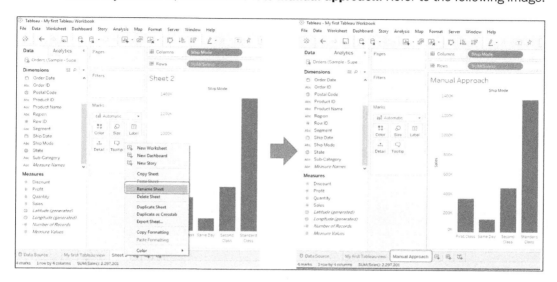

 When we drop the **Sales** field into the **Rows** shelf, the field becomes **Sum(Sales)**. This is because Tableau aggregates the sales value to show it at the **Ship Mode** level. For relational databases, the default aggregation is **Sum**. However, this aggregation can be changed to suit our requirements.

How it works...

When we use the **Manual approach**, there is no hard-and-fast rule for dragging and dropping fields into a particular shelf. We can place our **Dimensions** and **Measures** fields in either the **Rows** shelf or the **Columns** shelf; alternatively, we can also use the **Color**, **Size**, **Text**, or **Detail** shelf.

Further, instead of directly dropping fields into the **Rows** or **Columns** shelf, we can also drop them into the section that says **Drop field here**. Refer to the following image:

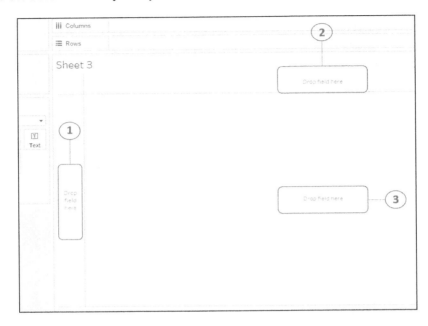

Dropping the field into the vertical section (refer to annotation 1) is the same as placing the field in the **Rows** shelf. When we do this, the field automatically gets placed in the **Rows** shelf. Similarly, dropping the field into the horizontal section (refer to annotation 2) is equivalent to dropping it into the **Columns** shelf. And, if we drop **Dimension** into the middle section (refer to annotation 3), then by default, Tableau will place it in the **Rows** shelf. However, if we place **Measure** in the middle section, then Tableau will place the field in the **Text** shelf in the **Marks** card. This is the default behavior of Tableau.

What are those Blue and Green pills?

In an earlier recipe, where we created a bar chart to show **Sales** by **Ship Mode**, we also saw that **Ship Mode** in the **Columns** shelf is shown as a **Blue pill** and **Sum(Sales)** in the **Rows** shelf is shown as a **Green pill**. This is because **Ship Mode** is a discrete field, whereas **Sales** is a continuous field.

Discrete fields are always shown as a Blue pill and will always result in headers being drawn whenever they are placed on the **Rows** or **Columns** shelves.

However, **Continuous fields** are always shown as a Green pill and will always result in axes when we add them to the view.

Building views automatically

In the previous recipe, we saw how we could use the manual **Drag and Drop** approach to build our visualizations. There are, however, two ways in which we can automatically create views in Tableau, and they are as follows:

- Add to Sheet: Double-Click
- Show Me!

In the following recipe, we will understand the **Add to Sheet: Double-Click** approach, which is simply the act of double-clicking on the **Dimensions** and **Measures** fields that we want to analyze.

Getting ready

We will continue working in our existing workbook, **My first Tableau Workbook**, and recreate the same example that we used in the previous recipe by using the **Ship Mode** and **Sales** fields. Let's see how this is done.

How to do it...

1. To use the **Double-click** approach, first create a new worksheet by pressing *Ctrl + M* on your keyboard.
2. Then, let us rename the sheet from **Sheet 3** to **Automatic approach-double-click**.

3. Next, double-click on **Sales** in the **Measures** pane, followed by double-clicking on the **Ship Mode** field from the **Dimensions** pane. Once we do this, we will see a vertical bar chart, as shown in the following image:

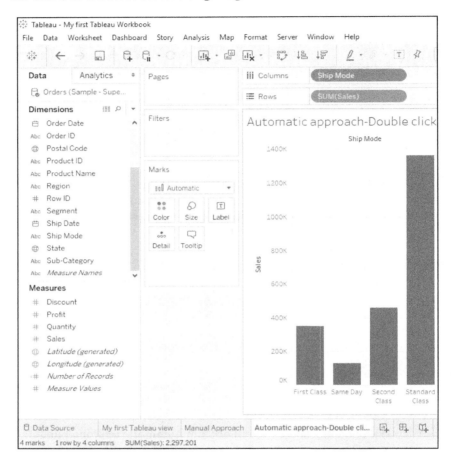

How it works...

The manual drag and drop approach lets us decide which field will be placed where. However, the double-click method follows more of a default behavior, where Tableau automatically starts placing fields in the **Rows** or **Columns** shelf.

If we double-click on a **Dimension** pane first followed by a **Measure**, then Tableau will create a text table; however, if we double-click on the **Measure** first and follow it up with **Dimension**, then Tableau will create a chart. This is a very intuitive and powerful feature of Tableau.

The other way to automatically build views is by using the **Show Me!** button, which is explained in the next recipe.

Understanding Show Me!

Representing data in a visual format is essential from the point of view of faster and better decision making. The only problem is that not all analysts are familiar with the graphical design principles that could help them build visualizations that can be further used for decision making.

However important an insight, if visualized unclearly, it can mar the effectiveness of the decision-making process. A visual analysis tool that can automatically show the data using the best practices of data visualization is the answer to this.

Tableau is a great data visualization tool that is intuitive and incorporates the best practices of data visualization. Among the many fascinating features of Tableau, **Show Me!** is one of the most powerful features and helps us visually display our data while abiding by the principles of data visualization. Depending on the selected **Dimensions** and **Measures**, the **Show Me!** panel gives us all the possible visualization choices. It also has an in-built best practice recommendation, which essentially helps us show data in an apt visualization feature. Let's understand how to use **Show Me!** for building charts, discussed in the following recipe.

Getting ready

To understand how to automatically create a chart using **Show Me!**, we will start by creating a new worksheet in our existing Tableau workbook. Perform the following steps.

How to do it...

1. First create a new worksheet by pressing *Ctrl + M* on a keyboard and renaming the sheet from **Sheet 4** to **Automatic approach-Show Me!**.

2. Then, select **Order Date** from the **Dimensions** pane via a single left-click. Next, press *Ctrl* on your keyboard and select **Sales** from the **Measures** pane. While selecting **Sales**, that is the second field, continue pressing *Ctrl* on the keyboard. In short, to select multiple fields from the **Dimensions** or **Measures** pane, we need to press *Ctrl + Select*. Refer to the following image:

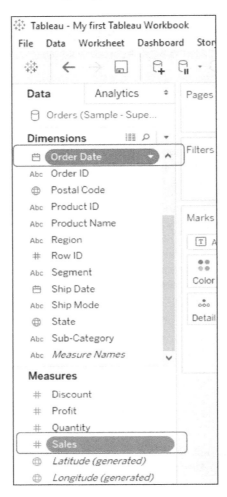

3. Keeping the current selection as is, click on the **Show Me!** button on the extreme right-hand side of your Tableau workspace. Refer to the following image:

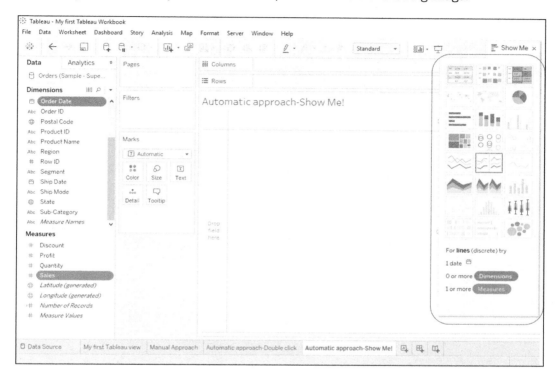

4. Select the **Line chart** option, which is highlighted with a brown color border, and our view will be updated to show a chart as shown in the following image:

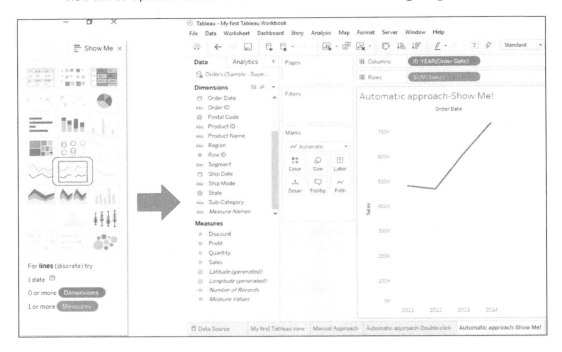

How it works...

When we select fields and click on the **Show Me!** button, Tableau automatically evaluates the selected fields and gives us the option of various views that can be created using those fields. Since Tableau makes an educated guess at how the data should be displayed, we will see that some charts are enabled and others disabled.

Further, when we hover over any chart in the **Show Me!** panel, we will see all the necessary options that are required to enable that chart. This section is available at the bottom of the **Show Me!** panel. Refer to the highlighted section in the following image:

Once we select the fields that we want to use, we will also see a specific chart highlighted with a brown color border. This is the built-in best practice recommendation given by Tableau.

Tableau will follow a series of logic to suggest the most suitable chart to represent the selected **Dimensions** and **Measures**, and this ability of Tableau is best explained in an article, *Show Me: Automatic Presentation for Visual Analysis*, written by Jock D. Mackinlay, Pat Hanrahan, and Chris Stolte.

 Refer to `http://www.tableau.com/whitepapers/ show-me-automatic-presentation-visual- analysis` for more information on the paper.

Creating a Text table

It is said that a *picture is worth a thousand words*, and hence, instead of just looking at numbers in a grid format and trying to make sense out of them, it is always better to analyze the data visually. Having said that, there may be occasions when we are required to represent some data as numbers. This is where we can use Text tables in Tableau.

Text tables are also known as **Crosstabs** views and are typically used to show important numbers at a glance. They are very similar to Excel's pivot table.

Getting ready

Let's create a Text table view that shows the sales for different product categories across different regions. Let's see how we can build this.

How to do it...

1. Create a new worksheet by pressing *Ctrl + M* on your keyboard. This will create a new sheet called **Sheet 5**. Let us rename it as **Text table**.

2. Then let us drag the **Region** field from the **Dimensions** pane and drop it into the **Columns** shelf.

3. Next, let us drag the **Category** field from the **Dimensions** pane and drop it into the **Rows** shelf.

4. After we have done this, we will drag the **Sales** field from the **Measures** pane and either drop it into the **Text shelf** in the **Marks** card, or into **Abc** in the view. Refer to the following image:

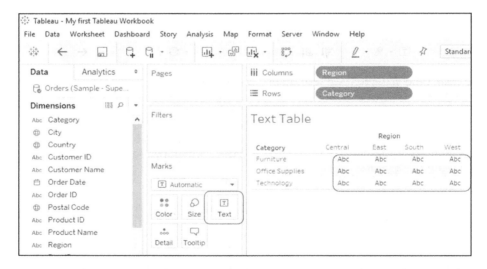

5. After we drop **Sales** into the **Text** shelf, we will get to see the view shown in the following image:

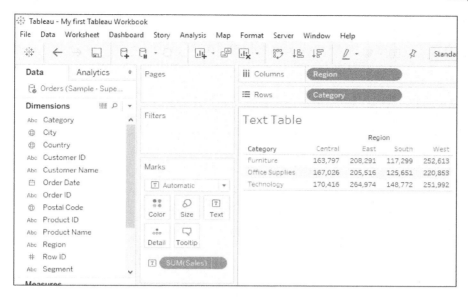

6. This is how we create a Text table in Tableau. Now, these are just numbers that show the **Sales** of each product **Category** across each **Region**. However, we still don't know the total sales of product categories or the total sales of the different **Regions**. To achieve this, we will click on **Analysis** in the **Menu** bar or toolbar. Select **Total** and then select **Show Row Grand Totals** and **Show Column Grand Totals**. See the following image:

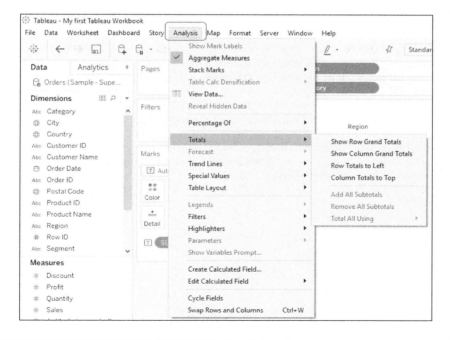

Since Tableau doesn't allow us to simultaneously select Show **Row Grand Totals** and Show **Column Grand Totals**, we will have to take the total for rows and columns separately.

7. Once we have selected both the respective grand totals of both the rows and columns, we will get the output as shown in the following image:

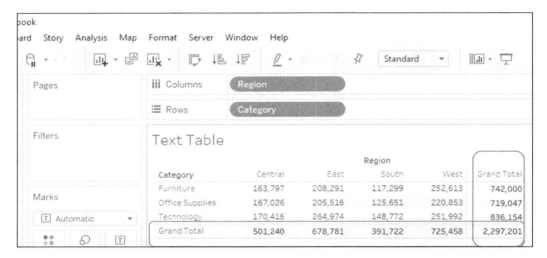

How it works...

The mark used for creating a Text table in Tableau is Text. When we put **Category** in the **Rows** shelf and **Region** in the **Columns** shelf, we create a crosstab output and the number in a cell is basically the **Sales** value for a particular **Category** in a particular **Region**.

For example, the first value from the left is 163797 and is shared between **Furniture** and **Central**. This is the **Sales** value of **Furniture** in the **Central** region.

Since this is a Text table, we will see that the Sales field is placed in the Text shelf in the Marks card and the icon in front of the **Sum(Sales)** pill is to let the user know which shelf is used to represent the field. Refer to the following image:

Creating a Highlight table

A **Highlight** table is actually a Text table with conditional formatting where the color of the cell will denote the value of **Measure**. When we create a Highlight table, we make use of colors to show values from the highest to the lowest. This is great for comparing a field's value within a row or column or even within an entire table.

Getting ready

To get started with the recipe for creating a Highlight table, we will continue working in our existing Tableau workbook. Since this is an extension of the Text table, we will first recreate the Text table in a separate sheet and continue working on it. As shown in the previous recipe, our Highlight table will show the sales for different product categories across different regions. Let's check out the steps.

How to do it...

1. Since we are going to take up the same example as discussed in our previous recipe, let's duplicate the **Text table** sheet and rename it as **Highlight table**. We can either right-click on the **Text table** tab and select the **Duplicate Sheet** option, or click on the **Duplicate Sheet** option from the toolbar. Refer to the following image:

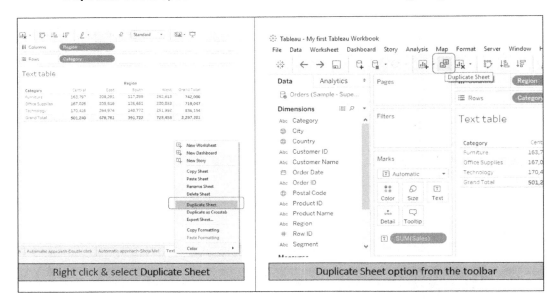

Right click & select Duplicate Sheet	Duplicate Sheet option from the toolbar

2. Once we are done with this, the next step is to drag **Sales** again from the **Measures** pane and drop it into the **Color** shelf in the **Marks** card:

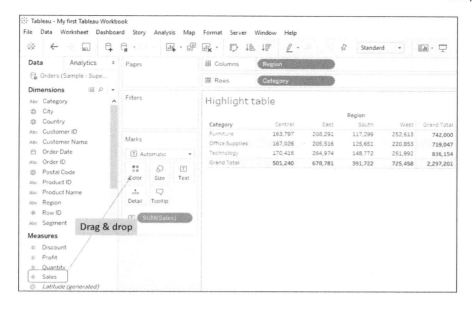

3.   When we do this, we will get the view as shown in the following image:

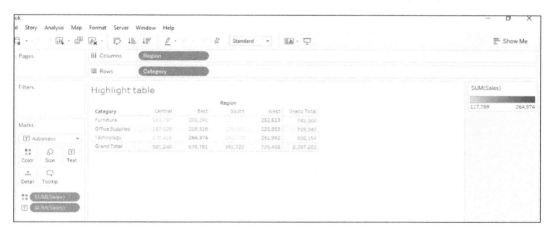

4. As the last step, change the mark type from **Automatic** to **Square** via the Marks drop-down in the **Marks** shelf. Refer to the following image:

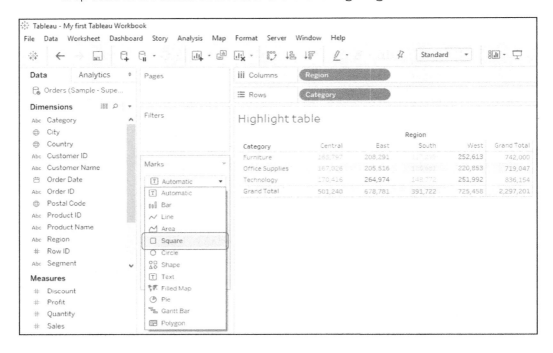

5. Once we do this, we will get the view as shown in the following image. This is the Highlight table:

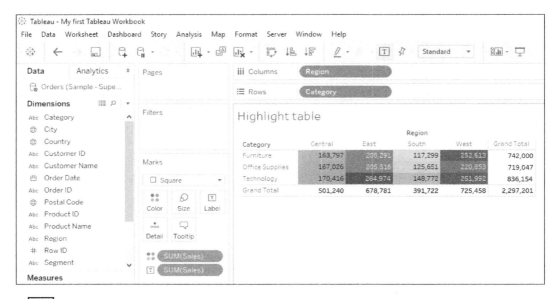

How it works...

When we look at a chart with just numbers, it may sometimes be difficult to quickly compare them.

However, when we use a Highlight table, we use color to depict the values. The darker the color of the cell, the higher the value; the lighter the color of the cell, the lower the value.

Thus, in the preceding chart, the **Technology** category in **East Region** has the **Highest Sales**.

Since we only have positive sales values, Tableau has automatically taken the diverging blue color, which can be changed by clicking on the dropdown of **Color Legend** drop-down and selecting the **Edit Colors...** option. Refer to the following image:

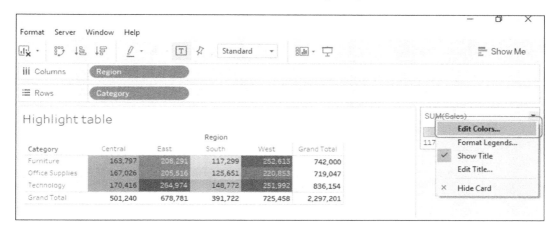

Further, in the Highlight table that we have created, notice that the **Totals** are not taken into consideration while assigning the colors. This is the default functionality of Tableau. However, when we click on the **Edit Colors...** option, we will get an option to include the totals as well. Refer to the following image:

Creating a Heat map

In the earlier sections, we read about the Text table, which just shows numbers. Then we read about the Highlight table where we used a color in addition to the text to find out which values were high and which values were low. A **Heat map** is a step advanced than the Highlight table. With a Heat map, we can compare both the size and color values. In a Heat map, we can also compare two different **Measures** for a combination of **Dimensions**.

Getting ready

To create a Heat map, we will compare **Sales** and **Profit** for product categories across **Regions**. Let's understand how to build a Heat map.

How to do it...

1. Create a new sheet by pressing *Ctrl + M* on your keyboard and rename it to `Heat map`.

2. Next, let us drag **Category** into the **Rows** shelf and **Region** into the **Columns** shelf.

3. Then we will change the mark type to **Squares** from the marks dropdown in the **Marks** shelf. Refer to the following image:

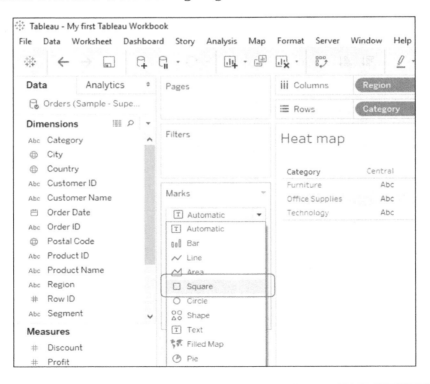

4. Next we will **Sales** from the **Measures** pane and drop it into the **Size** shelf in the **Marks** card. Refer to the following image:

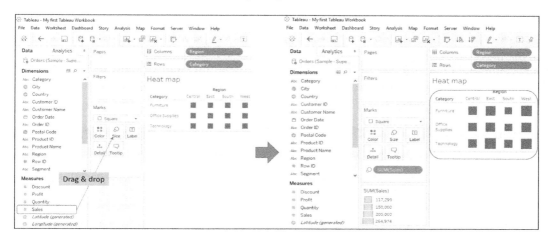

5. Next, we will drag **Profit** from the **Measures** pane and drop it into the **Color** shelf in the **Marks** card. With this, we will get the output shown in the following image:

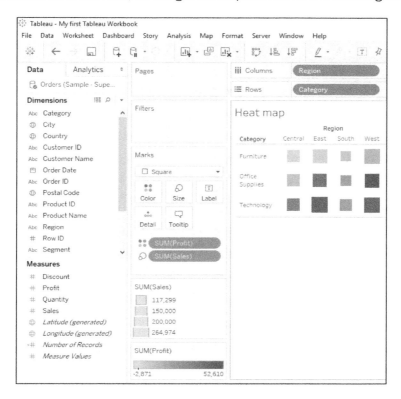

How it works...

Size in the preceding image shows **Sales** and **Color** indicates profit. Thus, the bigger the square, more the sales, and the darker the blue square, the greater the profit.

In the preceding image, we can see that **Furniture** in the **Central** region is light orange in color, indicating that it is a non-profitable venture. Further, **Technology** in the **East** region has the biggest square, which indicates that it has the highest number of sales among other categories across regions.

Creating a Bar chart

Bar chart is one of the most commonly used chart type that will help us quickly compare information across various categories. In a bar chart, the height (in the case of a vertical bar chart) or the length (in the case of a horizontal bar chart) of the bar is what determines the value. They are very effective when we want to split our quantifiable data into different categories and find quick trends in the data, for example, the number of sales across different customer segments, the profit across various product categories, and so on. The bar chart in Tableau uses the Bar mark type.

Getting ready

In the following recipe, we will continue working in our existing workbook to create a bar chart that shows the sales across different regions. We will use the **Sales** field from the **Measures** pane and the **Region** field from the **Dimensions** pane. Let's see how this is done.

How to do it...

1. We will create a new worksheet by pressing *Ctrl + M* on your keyboard and rename it to Bar chart.

2. Next, we will drag **Region** from the **Dimensions** pane and drop it into the **Columns** shelf.

3. Then, we will drag **Sales** from the **Measures** pane and drop it into the **Rows** shelf. Once we do this, we will see the view as shown in the following image:

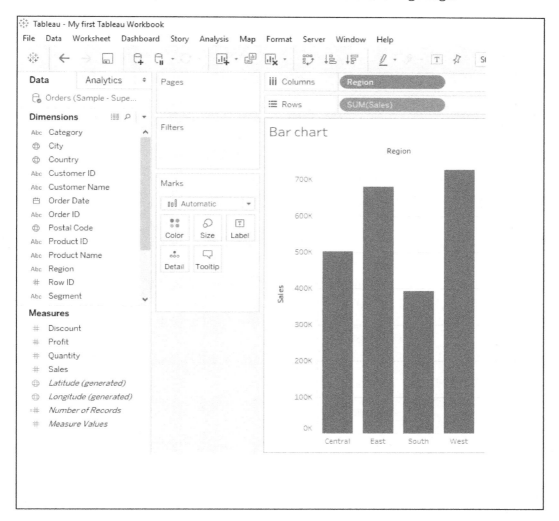

4. This is how we can create a Bar chart in Tableau. Further, to see the **Sales** value on top of the bars, we will again drag **Sales** from the **Measures** pane and drop it into the **Label** shelf in the **Marks** card. Refer to the following image:

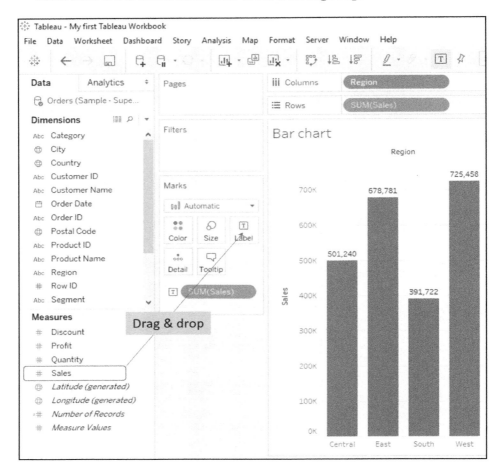

How it works...

In the first chapter, we read about the **Rows** and **Columns** shelves. Since we place **Region** in the **Columns** shelf, we get a column for each region; **Sales** in the **Rows** shelf creates the y axis.

This is because a continuous field, such as **Sales**, will result in an axis being drawn when placed in the **Rows** or **Columns** shelf. However, a **Discrete field**, such as **Region**, will result in the headers being drawn when placed in the **Rows** or **Columns** shelf.

We could have also created the same bar chart using the **Show Me!** button, and to do this, we simply have to select **Region** in the **Dimensions** pane and do a *Ctrl + Select* on **Sales** in the **Measures** pane first. Then, click on the **Show Me!** button to select the **Bar chart** option, which is already highlighted with a **Brown border**. Refer to the following image:

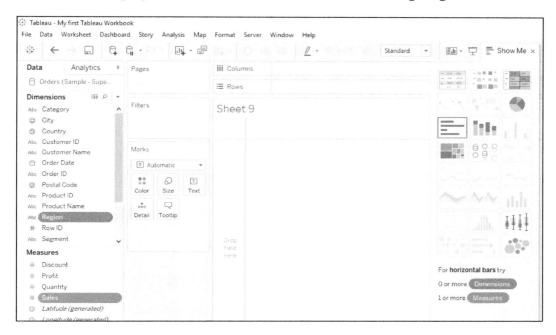

Once we select the Bar chart option from **Show Me!**, we will get a horizontal bar chart that can be made vertical by swapping the **Rows** and **Columns** shelves by clicking on the **Swap** button in the toolbar. Refer to the following image:

 The default bar chart created using **Show Me!** is a **Horizontal bar chart** that can later be converted into a **Vertical** chart by using the **Swap** option, as seen in the preceding screenshot.

Creating a Stacked Bar chart

A **Stacked Bar** chart is an extension of the bar chart where we use colors to represent additional information. These are typically used when we are trying to show a comparison within a particular category as well as across categories.

So, for example, in the previous recipe where we created a bar chart showing **Sales across Region**, we would additionally want to look at the performance of various product categories within a particular region and compare their performance across regions. To understand this, we will create a Stacked Bar chart.

How to do it...

1. Let us duplicate the **Bar chart** sheet by right-clicking on the sheet tab of **Bar chart** and then selecting the **Duplicate Sheet** option. Refer to the following image:

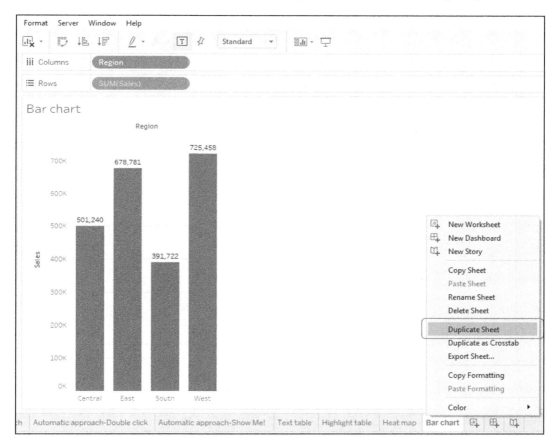

2. We will then rename the new sheet to **Stacked bar chart**.

3. Next, we will drag **Category** from the **Dimensions** pane and drop it into the **Color** shelf in the **Marks** card. Refer to the following image:

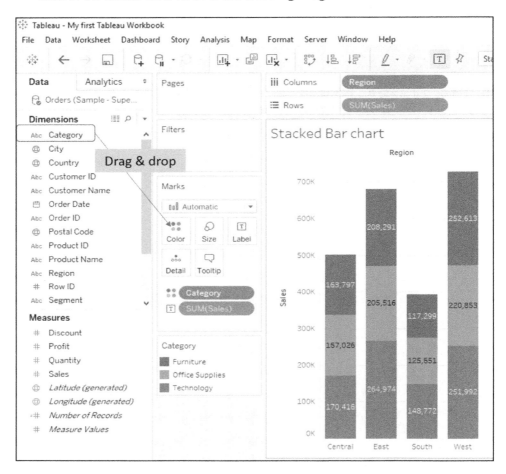

How it works...

In the earlier bar chart, the **Sales across Region** bar chart, we showed the total number of sales across different regions. The taller or longer the bar, the greater the sales. However, when we drop **Category** into the **Color** shelf, we break the total sales for that region into three parts. These parts are shown with different colors, and the color legend helps us identify the exact product category. Thus, we get to see how each category is performing when compared to other categories in terms of sales within a particular region, and we can also compare the **Sales** of these product **Categories** across **Regions**.

For example, in the preceding chart, if we look at just the bar for the **East** region, we get to see that the red block that represents **Technology** is taller as compared to the blue and orange blocks that represent **Furniture** and **Office Supplies**, respectively. This indicates that **Technology** has more sales as against **Furniture** and **Office Supplies** in the **East** region.

Further, if we now look at the entire view instead of just focusing on one region, we can see how the performance of **Technology** has been across all the regions. Thus, we have the ability to compare product **Categories** within a **Region** and also across different **Regions**.

Creating a Pie chart

Just like bar charts, pie charts too are very widely used. They are typically used to show relative proportions or percentage distributions, and the size of the slice indicates the contribution to the total value.

The pie chart in Tableau uses the **Pie mark type**.

Getting ready

In the following recipe, we will create a Pie chart to show the sales across different customer segments. We can create a Pie chart by selecting the necessary fields from the **Dimensions** and **Measures** fields and then selecting the Pie chart option from **Show Me!**. However, in the following recipe, we will build it manually using the Marks card. Let's see how this can be done.

How to do it...

1. Create a new sheet and rename it to `Pie chart`.

2. Then select **Pie mark** from the **Marks** dropdown in the **Marks** card. Refer to the following image:

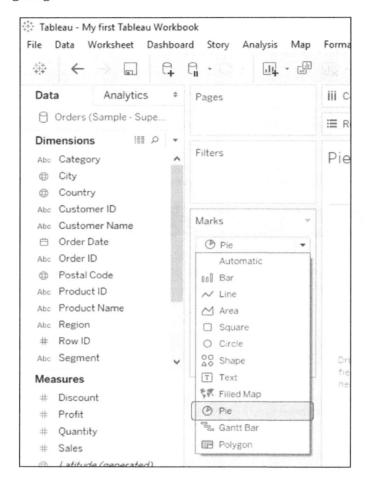

3. Next, let us drag **Sales** from the **Measure** pane and drop it into the **Size** shelf. Follow this up by dragging the **Sales** field again from the **Measure** pane and this time dropping it into the **Angle** shelf in the Marks card.

4. Since we want to show the distribution of the customer segment, we will drop **Customer Segment** into the **Color** shelf. Refer to the following image:

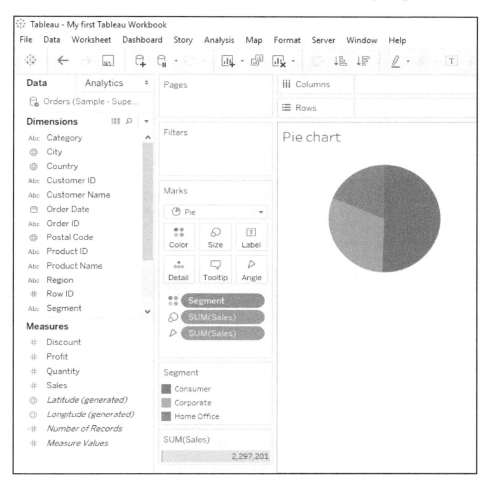

How it works...

When we select Pie as a mark from the **Marks** dropdown, an additional shelf called **Angle** is available and determines the angular measure of the pie slices/wedges.

In the preceding image, when we place **Sales** in the angle shelf, the complete 360 degrees circle, representing the total sales, is divided into three slices/wedges, and shows the value for each customer segment.

When we look at the chart, we get to see how much of sales is being contributed by which customer segment, and these segments can be identified by referring to the **Color** legend.

Thus, in the preceding chart, most sales are contributed by the **Consumer** segment.

Even though pie charts are widely used, many data visualization experts do not encourage their use. Some of the many reasons are mentioned as follows:

- The human eye is not very good at estimating area but are better at comparing heights. For example, if there are two categories with approximately the same values and we decide to create a Pie chart, then it would be very difficult to say which category has more value as both slices will more or less be of the same size. But if we represent the same information in a bar chart, then it would be easier to compare the height or the length of the bars and determine which category has more value.

- In a pie chart, we can only compare slices that are right next to each other.

- If we have a greater number of categories to plot, then creating a pie chart will only make it difficult to quickly and meaningfully interpret the slices of the pie as there would be too much color and this can be distracting; also, the slices would be small. Imagine creating a pie chart to show 20 categories. Experts suggest that if we have more than six proportions to communicate, then one should consider a bar chart instead of a pie chart.

Creating a Line chart

Another frequently used chart type is the **Line chart**, which is primarily used to show trends over a period of time. This chart type helps us focus on the peaks and dips in the values over a period of time.

The line chart in Tableau uses the **Line mark type**.

Getting ready

To understand this chart type better, let's create a **Line chart** to show profit for all the months over the last 4 years.

How to do it...

1. Let us create a new sheet and rename it to **Line chart**.
2. Next, we will drag **Order Date** from the **Dimensions** pane and drop into the **Columns** shelf.

3. Drag **Profit** from the **Measures** pane and drop it into the **Rows** shelf. Refer to the following image:

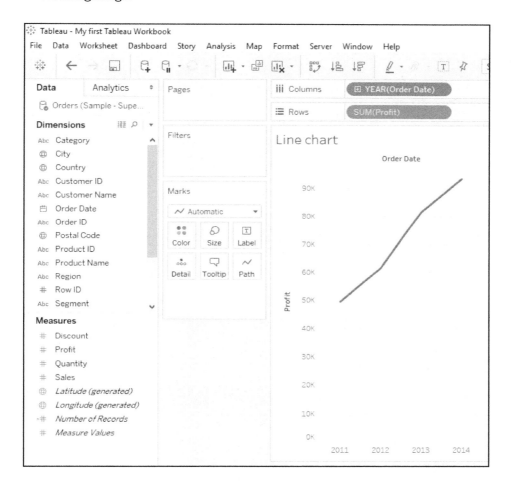

4. Next, we will click on the dropdown for the Blue pill in the **Rows** shelf, which says **Year(Order Date)**, and select the **Month** option from the second list—not the first list, which is identical—showing **Year**, **Quarter**, **Month**, and so on. Refer to the following image:

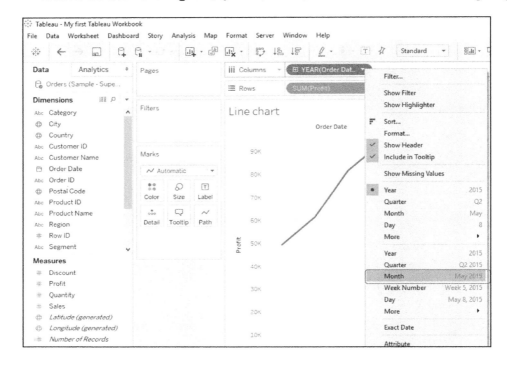

5. Once we do this, we will get the view as shown in the following image:

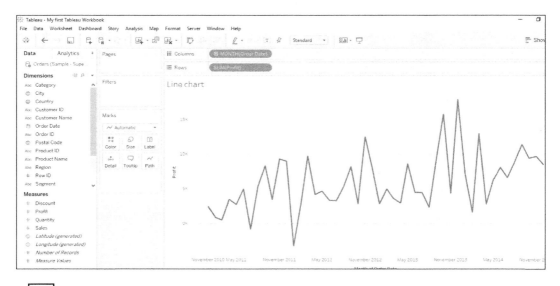

How it works...

In the recipe for Bar chart, we had **Region** in the **Columns** shelf and **Sales** in the **Rows** shelf. This is a similar situation where we have **Dimension** in the **Columns** shelf and **Measure** on the **Rows** shelf.

However, in the preceding recipe, the **Dimension** that is placed in the **Columns** shelf is not an ordinary dimension. It is a date field, and in addition to this when we get a measure in the **Rows** shelf, Tableau will create a line chart.

Further, when we get **Order Date** in the view, Tableau intelligently aggregates the dates at the highest level possible. For example, if the date field includes multiple years, the default level is year. However, if the date field contains data for just one year but includes multiple months, then the default level is month. In the preceding scenario, the highest level is **Year**.

We can drill down to the desired level of date by clicking on the plus button on the **Date** field. Refer to the following image:

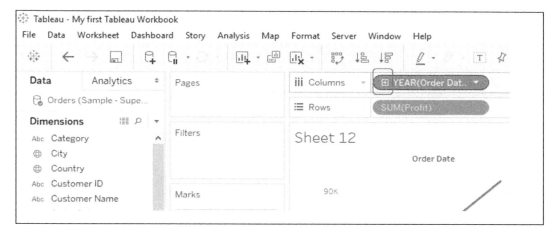

Further, a date can be discrete as well as continuous. In the preceding recipe, when clicked on the dropdown of **Year(Order Date)**, we saw that there were two sections that showed the year, quarter, month, and so on. We selected the month from the second section, which was for a continuous month and thus got a continuous line chart. See the following image to understand the difference between a discrete line chart versus a continuous line chart.

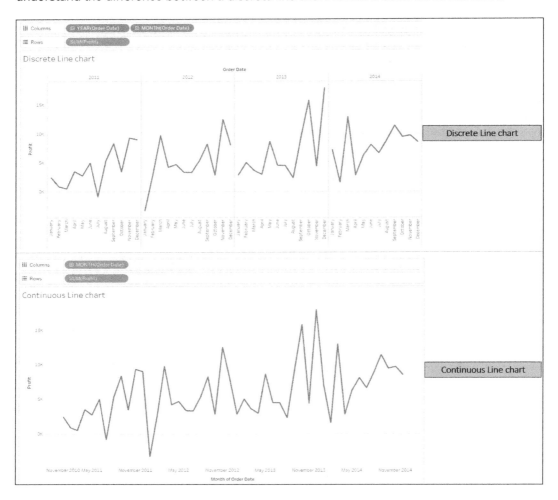

In the first chart in the preceding image, we have the years on the top and the months at the bottom. This view creates a small table for each year and hence the line is broken after each year. However, in the second chart, the month is combined with the year to show one data point (notice the x axis). These data points when connected via a line create a continuous line chart.

Creating an Area chart

In a very simplistic way, an **Area chart** is a stacked line chart. It is an essentially a line chart where the space between each line and the next line is filled with a color. These charts are typically used to *show the relative proportions of totals or percentage relationships*. This type of chart is not the best way to show specific values along the line, but it can clearly show the total values so you can get an idea of how a dimension contributes to an overall trend.

Getting ready

The **Area chart** is an extension of the Line Chart and hence we will work on the line chart that we created earlier. In the Line chart recipe, we showed the profit for every month over the last four years. For the Area Chart, we will show the sales for every month over the last four years. Let's see how this is done.

How to do it...

1. While on the **Line chart** sheet, let us right-click on the sheet name and select the **Duplicate sheet** option. We will get a new sheet; rename it to **Area chart**.

2. We will then remove the **Profit** field in the **Rows** shelf by dragging it from the **Rows** shelf and dropping it outside the view in the gray area or by simply clicking on the dropdown and selecting the **Remove** option. Refer to the following image:

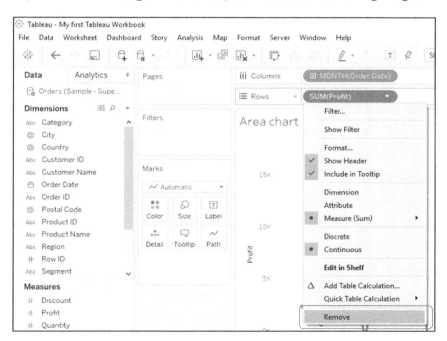

3. Next, let us drag **Sales** from the **Measures** pane and drop it into the **Rows** shelf. After we do this, we will then drag **Segment** from the **Dimensions** pane and drop it into the **Color** shelf. We will then get the view as shown in the following image:

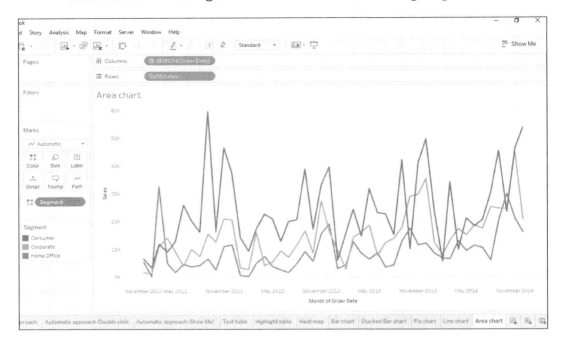

4. Then, we will change the mark from **Line** to **Area** by selecting the **Area** mark in the **Marks** dropdown in the marks card. Refer to the following image to see the desired output:

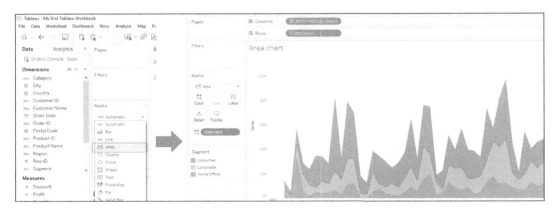

How it works...

When we get **Segment** in the **Color** shelf and change **Marks** to **Area**, we stack up the line chart. When we do this, we will notice a change in **Value** of **Axis** for the line chart and the area chart.

This is because, in the **Line chart**, we show the sales per segment; however, in the **Area chart**, the **Sales** value is stacked up to show the total sales for all the segments together. The area shows the trend of sales for each segment.

Creating a Treemap

Treemaps are useful for representing hierarchical (tree-structured) data as a part-to-whole relationship. It shows data as a set of nested rectangles, and each branch of the tree is given a rectangle, which represents the amount of data it comprises. These can then be further divided into smaller rectangles that represent subbranches, based on its proportion to the whole.

We can show information via the color and size of the rectangles and find out patterns that would be difficult to spot in other ways. They make efficient use of the space and hence can display a lot of items in a single visualization simultaneously.

Getting ready

We will create a **Treemap** to show the sales and profit across various product subcategories. Let's see how to create a Treemap.

How to do it...

1. We will first create a new sheet and rename it as `Treemap`.
2. Next, we will drag **Sales** from the **Measures** pane and drop it into the **Size** shelf.
3. We will then drag **Profit** from Measures pane and drop it into the **Color** shelf.

4. Our **Mark** type will automatically change to show squares. Refer to the following image:

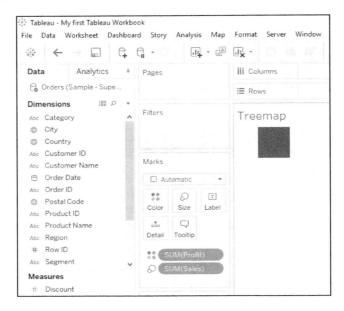

5. Next, we will drop **Sub-Category** into the **Label** shelf in the **Marks** card, and we will get the output as shown in the following image:

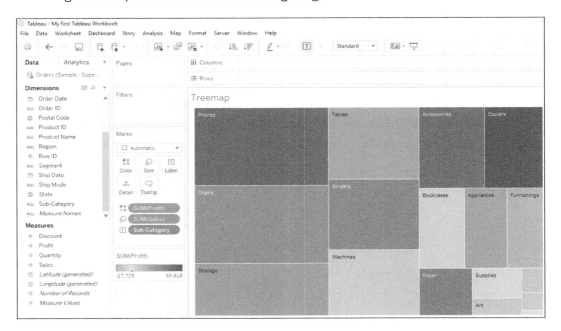

How it works...

In the preceding image, since we have placed **Sales** in the **Size** shelf, we are inferring this: the greater the size, the higher the sales value; the smaller the size, the smaller the sales value.

Since the Treemap is sorted in descending order of **Size**, we will see the biggest block in the top left-hand side corner and the smaller block in the bottom right-hand side corner.

Further, we placed **Profit** in the **Color** shelf. There are some subcategories where the profit is negative and hence Tableau selects the orange/blue diverging color.

Thus, when the color blue is the darkest, it indicates the **Most profit**. However, the orange color indicates that a particular subcategory is in a loss scenario.

So, in the preceding chart, **Phones** has the maximum number of sales. Further, **Copiers** has the highest profit. **Tables**, on the other hand, is non-profitable.

Creating a Packed Bubble chart

A **Packed bubble** chart is a cluster of circles where we use dimensions to define individual bubbles, and the size and/or color of the individual circles represent measures. Bubble charts have many benefits and one of them is to let us spot categories easily and compare them to the rest of the data by looking at the size of the bubble. This simple data visualization technique can provide insight in a visually attractive format.

The Packed Bubble chart in Tableau uses the **Circle mark type**.

Getting ready

To create a packed bubble chart, we will continue with the same example that we saw in the **Treemap** recipe. In the following section, we will see how we can convert the Treemap we created earlier into a **Packed Bubble** chart.

How to do it...

1. Let us duplicate the `Tree Map` sheet name and rename it to `Packed Bubble chart`.

2. Next, change the marks from **Square** to **Circle** from the **Marks** dropdown in the **Marks** card. The output will be as shown in the following image:

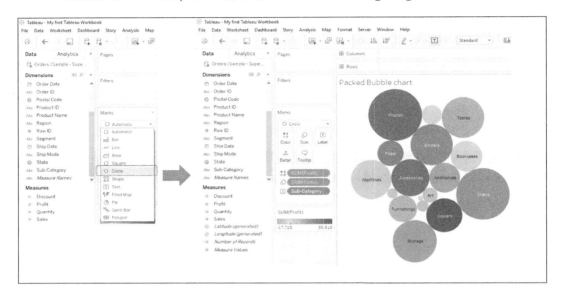

How it works...

In the Packed Bubble chart, there is no specific sort of order for **Bubbles**. The size and/or color are what defines the chart; the bigger or darker the circle, the greater the value.

So, in the preceding example, we have **Sales** in the **Size** shelf, **Profit** in the **Color** shelf, and **Sub-Category** in the **Label** shelf.

Thus, when we look at it, we understand that **Phones** has the most sales. Further, **Copiers** has the highest profit. **Tables**, on the other hand, is non-profitable even though the size indicates that the sales are fairly good.

Creating a word cloud

A **word cloud** is also called a **Tag cloud**. It is a visual representation for text data and is usually used to depict the frequently searched keywords/tags on websites. It could also be used to visualize free form text. Tags are usually single words, and the importance of each tag is shown with the font size or color. Word clouds are typically used for website analytics and text mining. Let's see how we can build a word cloud.

Getting ready

To create a word cloud, we will continue with the same example that we used in the Treemap and in the Packed Bubble chart. Let's convert the Packed Bubble chart that we created in the previous recipe into a word cloud.

How to do it...

1. Let us duplicate the Packed Bubble chart sheet and rename the new sheet to `Word cloud`.

2. Next, we will change the marks from **Circle** to **Text** from the marks dropdown in the marks card. The output will be as shown in the following image:

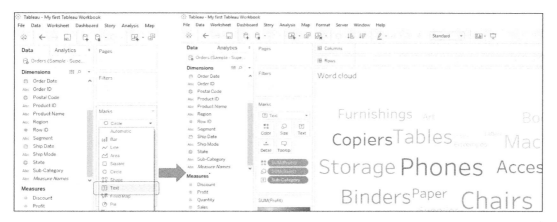

How it works...

Just like the Packed Bubble chart, the size of the word indicates the sales and the color indicates profit. However, the only difference is that instead of showing circles, we show the text itself.

3
Hungry for More
Charts? Dig In!

In this chapter, we will cover the following recipes:

- ▶ Creating an individual axes chart
- ▶ Creating a blended axes chart
- ▶ Creating a side by side bar chart
- ▶ Creating a dual axes chart
- ▶ Creating a combination chart
- ▶ Creating a scatter plot
- ▶ Creating a box and whisker plot
- ▶ Creating a Gantt chart
- ▶ Creating maps
- ▶ Using background images

Introduction

In the previous chapter, we saw how to create basic visualizations in Tableau. In this chapter, we will focus on some of the advanced chart types in Tableau.

Creating an Individual axes chart

Just showing a single measure may not always give us a complete picture. For example, a bar chart showing region-wide sales only gives us information about how much sales each region has done. Although this is useful information for us, there isn't much insight in it to take any decisions. This would be even more useful to us if we could compare the sales of each region with targets of those regions. This way we could find out which regions are not meeting their targets and which regions are hitting or over-achieving the target.

There can be plenty of instances where we would want to compare multiple measures; and creating an individual axes chart is one of the many ways to do so.

Getting ready

For our next recipe, we will continue working in our existing workbook `My first Tableau Workbook` which is stored in the `Workbooks` folder in our `My Tableau Repository`. We will also continue working on the same **Orders** data of the `Sample - Superstore.xls` file.

How to do it...

1. If the workbook isn't already open, then we need to open it by double-clicking on `My first Tableau Workbook.twb` from `Documents | My Tableau Repository | Workbooks`.

2. After opening it, we will create a new sheet by pressing *Ctrl + M* and rename it as `Individual axes chart`.

3. Next, we will continue hold down the right-click on the **Order Date** in the **Dimensions** pane in order to drag and drop it into the **Columns** shelf. This action will give us a dialog box, as shown in the following screenshot:

4. Select the **MY(Order Date)** option. Once we do that, drag **Sales** from the **Measures** pane and drop it into the **Rows** shelf. This action gives us the following view:

5. In the next step, we will drag **Profit** from the **Measures** pane and drop it into the **Rows** shelf, just after the green pill for **SUM(Sales)**. This view is called as an **Individual axes chart**. Refer to the following image:

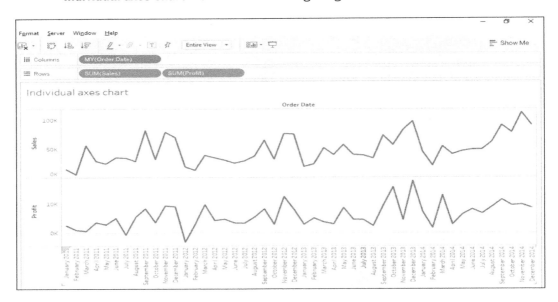

How it works...

The **Individual axes** chart is a very commonly used chart type and is one of the many charts that we can use for comparing multiple measures. In the preceding screenshot, we can see that we have a common *X-axis* of **Date** which is shown as **Month Year** and there are two independent *Y-axes*, one of which is **Sales** and the other is **Profit**. One can compare the **Sales** and **Profit** trend over the months by using this chart. This chart is typically used when independent axes are required for each measure without being in the same pane. Here, we analyze the data by placing each measure in a separate independent axis.

Even though the Individual axes chart is a fairly common and simple chart type, at times it may seem difficult to read and interpret this chart as the measures are completely separate and not in the same pane. In the above chart, one has to look at the top graph to find out the **Sales** value and then look at the bottom chart to find out the **Profit** value. Also, since the axes are independent, the interpretation could often be misleading. For example, in the preceding screenshot, there is a spike in both the **Sales** and **Profit** for December 2013. When we look at the chart, the spike looks more or less the same for **Sales** as well as **Profit**. However, that doesn't mean that the **Profit** in December 2013 is equal to the **Sales** in December 2013. Even though the spike looks the same, the **Sales** for December 2013 are approximately $100K, whereas the **Profit** in the same period is approximately $20K.

Thus, when working with an Individual axes chart, we cannot simply make inferences by just looking at the chart. Focusing on the axes is also very important.

Creating a Blended axes chart

In the preceding individual axes chart, we saw that, because the measures were not in the same pane, it was difficult to draw inferences by just looking at the chart and without taking the axes' values into consideration.

It would be great if, in the preceding example, we could get both the **Profit** and **Sales** in the same pane and have a unified axis for both, so that it is quicker and easier to interpret the chart. This is where we use a **Blended axes chart**.

As the name suggests, the axis is blended to have a common unified scale to refer to.

Getting ready

We will continue working in the same workbook, and we will also work with the same example that we discussed in the previous recipe, where we compared **Profit** and **Sales** across various months for all the years. Let us see how to create a **Blended axes chart**.

How to do it...

1. Let us create a new sheet by pressing *Ctrl + M* and rename it as **Blended axes chart**.
2. Next, we will right-click and drag the **Order Date** field from the **Dimensions** pane and drop it into the **Columns** shelf. This step is exactly the same as step 3 in the previous recipe. Select the **MY(Order Date)** option.

3. We will then drag **Profit** from the **Measures** pane and drop it into the **Rows** shelf. Refer to the following screenshot:

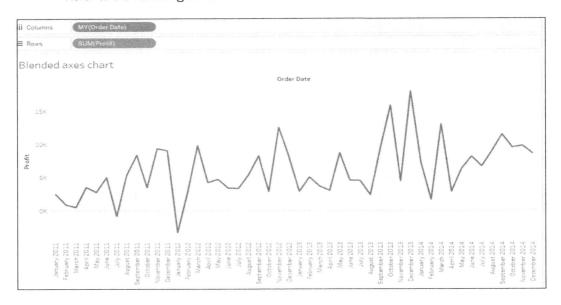

4. We will then **Sales** from the **Measures** pane and drop it on the **Profit** axis. Refer to the following screenshot:

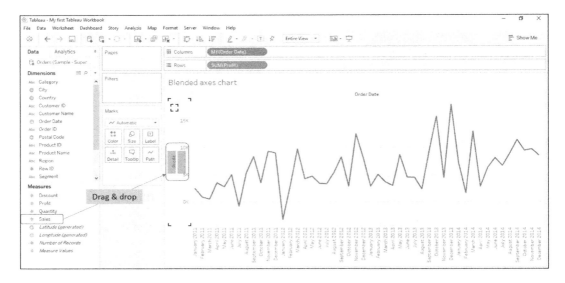

5. Once we drop the **Sales** field on the **Profit** axis, we will get the Blended axes chart, as shown in the following screenshot:

When we put the **Sales** field on the axis which already has **Profit**, we are actually **Blending** the **Sales** and **Profit** values to create a common axis. This common axis is now called **Value**. Further more, notice that the scale of the axis, which was initially showing **Profit** values, has now changed to accommodate the **Sales** values as well. The field **Measure Value** is placed in the **Rows** shelf instead of just **Profit**, and the field **Measure Names** is placed in the **Color** shelf.

As discussed in *Chapter 1, Keep Calm and Say Hello to Tableau, Measure Names* contain the names of all our measures in a single dimension, and **Measure Values** contain the values of all our measures in a single field; since the **Measure Names** field is in the **Color** shelf, we get to see two colored lines: the orange line represents the **Sales**, and the blue line represents the **Profit**.

In the preceding screenshot, we can quickly compare the **Sales** and **Profit** across various months and years. Further, the spike for December 2013 that we discussed in the Individual axes chart, is now much easier to read and compare.

We use **Blended axes** chart when two or more measures need to share an axis. In Blended axes charts, each measure is represented as a different color. The chart is most appropriate to use when comparing measures that have similar scale and units of measurement.

Creating a Side by Side Bar chart

A **Side by Side Bar** chart is an extension of the Blended axes chart. It helps us compare values side by side. Let us follow the steps in the following recipe to quickly create a Side by Side Bar chart

Getting ready

Since this is an extension of the **Blended axes**, we will first duplicate the Blended axes sheet and then modify it. Let us follow the following steps and create a Side by Side Bar chart.

How to do it...

1. Firstly, we will duplicate the **Blended axes** sheet and rename it to `Side by Side Bar chart`.

2. Next, we will drag **Measure Names** from the **Dimensions** pane and drop it into the **Columns** shelf, just after the **MY(Order Date)** field. Refer to the following screenshot:

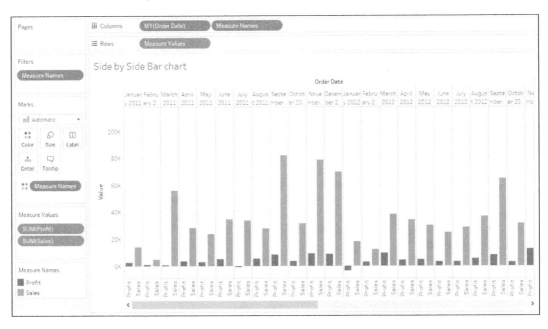

3. This is a **Side by Side Bar chart**. However, you'll notice a horizontal scroll bar below the view. This is because; there are a lot of values that are placed horizontally. To remove the scroll, click on the dropdown in the toolbar which currently says **Standard**, and change it to **Entire View**. Refer to the following image:

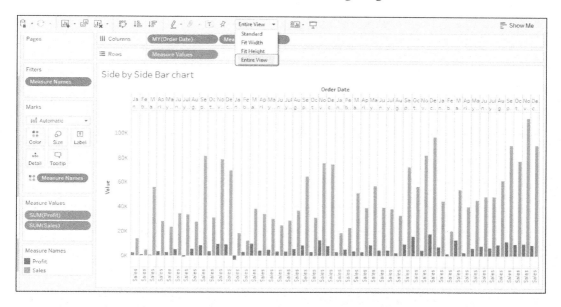

How it works...

When we get the **Measure Names** field and drop it in the **Columns** shelf, we are creating a column for each measure. This way we can compare them in side by side columns. Just like the Blended axes chart, this chart type is useful when we are comparing measures that have the same scale and unit of measurement.

The Side by Side Bar chart could also be created by simply selecting the **side-by-side bars** option from **Show Me!**.

Further, if we change the Mark type in the Marks dropdown of the Marks shelf from Bar to Shapes, the preceding Side by Side Bar chart can be converted into Side by Side Circles. Selecting the side-by-side circles option from **Show Me!**, would also give us the Side by Side Circles which are shown in the following image:

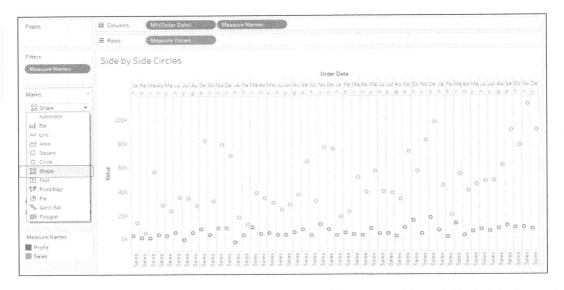

Creating a Dual axes chart

If we are to compare measures that have the same scale and unit of measurement, then we can use the Blended axes chart. However, what if the measures don't have the same scale and unit of measurements and we still wish to compare them? For example, we may want to compare the revenue earned and the discounts offered. Revenue will be an absolute number whereas discount is going to be a percentage. The scales and the units of these measures are completely different.

In this case, we will use a **Dual axes** chart, where we have a secondary *Y* axis, which will contain the other measure that is to be compared. Let us see how we can create a Dual axes chart.

Getting ready

We will continue with the same example we have used for both Individual axes and Blended axes charts, where we are comparing Sales and Profit across different months for all the years. Let us quickly create a Dual axes chart by following the steps mentioned in the following recipe.

How to do it...

1. We will create a new sheet by pressing *Ctrl + M* and rename it **Dual axes chart**.

2. Next, we will right-click and drag the **Order Date** field from the **Dimensions** pane and drop it into the **Columns** shelf. This step is exactly the same as step 3 in the recipe where we created the **Individual axes chart**. Let us select the **MY(Order Date)** option.

3. Then, we will drag **Sales** from the **Measures** pane and drop it into the **Rows** shelf.

4. Next, we will drag **Profit** from the **Measures** pane and drop it on the axis opposite to that of the **Sales** axis. When we get **Profit** on the opposite side of the **Sales** axis, we will get to see a black dotted line at the right-most part. Refer to the following image:

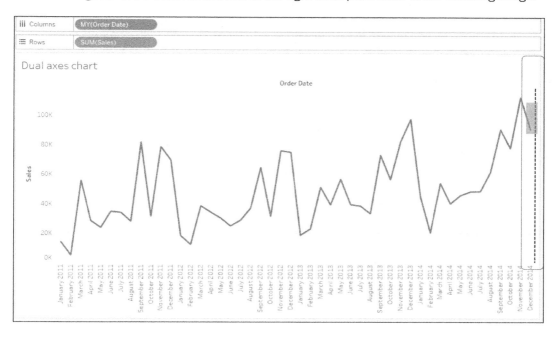

5. Once we have dropped the **Profit** field, we will get the following view:

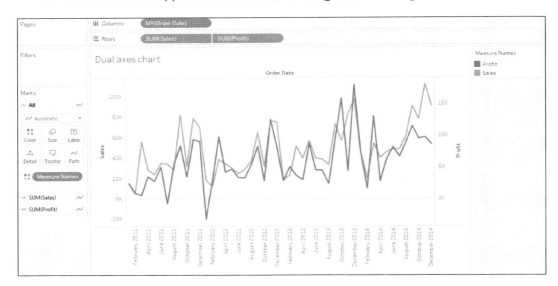

6. This is how we can create a Dual axes chart. In a Dual axes chart, we can keep the axes independent of each other, or we can synchronize them by right-clicking on the secondary axis and selecting the option of **Synchronize Axis**. Refer to the following image:

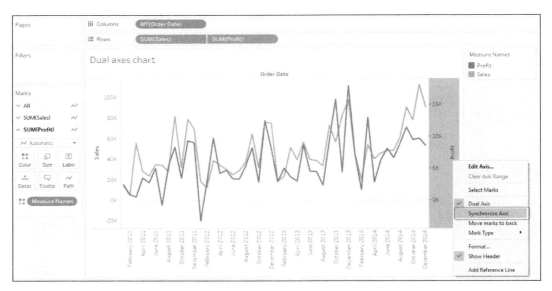

7. Once we have synchronized the axes, we will get the following view:

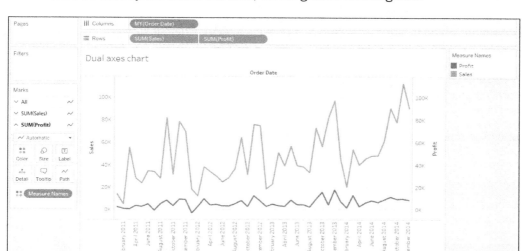

How it works...

As mentioned earlier, we will use a **Dual axes chart** while comparing measures that have **different scales** and **units of measurement**.

A simpler way to create a Dual axes chart would have been to first create an Individual axes chart and then click on the dropdown of the Green pill of the secondary measure and select the **Dual Axis** option. Refer to the following image:

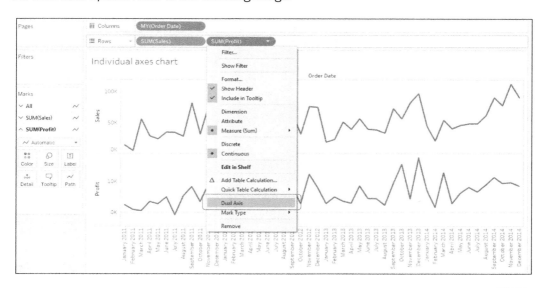

Creating a Combination chart

A **Combination chart** is an extension of a Dual axes chart, where instead of having the measures shown using a single mark, we can have different marks. So, for example, in the preceding Dual axes chart, we have both **Sales** and **Profit** shown as Lines. We may want to show **Sales** as a bar and **Profit** as a line. If we do that, then the chart that will be created will be called as a Combination chart. In simple words, a Combination chart is nothing but a Dual axes chart with multiple marks.

Let us see how to create a Combination chart.

Getting ready

For creating a Combination chart, we will first duplicate the Dual axes chart and then convert it into a Combination chart. The steps are as follows.

How to do it...

1. Firstly, we will duplicate the **Dual axes chart** sheet and rename it to **Combination chart**.

2. Once we do that, we will look at the **Marks** card. Refer to the following image:

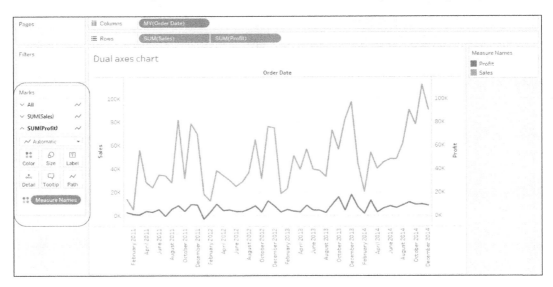

3. In the **Marks** card section, notice that there are three sub-sections called **All**, **SUM(Sales)** and **SUM(Profit)**. If we click on any one of these sections, then that section will expand and we'll see that the Mark type is a **Line**. However, since we want **Sales** as a Bar, click on the **SUM(Sales)** in the **Marks** card and change the **Mark** type from **Line** to **Bar** by clicking on the dropdown of **Marks**. Refer to the following image:

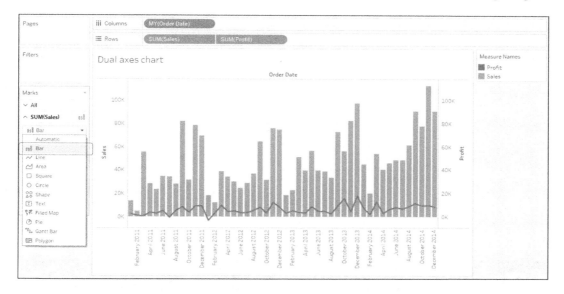

How it works...

In Tableau, each Mark is associated with an Axis. In the Dual axes chart, since we have two separate axes, we can change the **Mark Type** for each axis. However, for the Blended axes chart, since there is a common axis that is being shared across multiple measures, when we change the **Mark Type**, it will be applied to every measure.

When creating the preceding Combination chart, if the line gets hidden behind the bars, then we can right-click on the axis which represents the line and select the option of **Move Marks** to front. Refer to the following image:

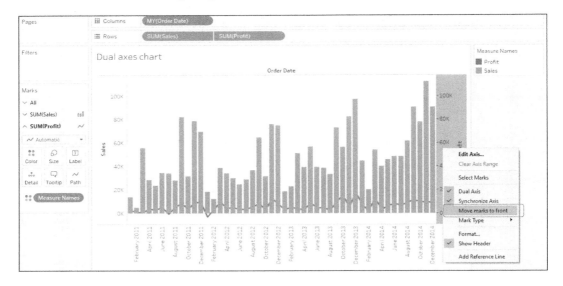

Creating a Scatter plot

Another way of comparing multiple measures is by creating a **Scatter plot**. A scatter plot is an *XY* axis chart with measures on both the *X* axis and the *Y* axis. It helps us find trends, concentrations and outliers by helping us focus on anomalies which are shown by the scattered points.

Getting ready

To create a Scatter plot, we will continue working in the same workbook. However, we will connect to a new data source. We will use the **Access** data, `Sample-Coffee Chain.mdb` which has been uploaded on `https://1drv.ms/f/s!Av5QCoyLTBpnhj06IKTNX0S9hK48`.

For our Mac users, since Tableau doesn't connect to the Access database from Mac, we will have to use the Excel version of this data which is also uploaded on the same link and is called `Sample - CoffeeChain (Use instead of MS Access).xlsx`.

If you haven't already downloaded these files in *Chapter 1, Keep Calm and Say Hello to Tableau,* you can download them now and save the files in a new folder called Tableau Cookbook data under `Documents | My Tableau Repository | Datasources`.

We will use the `Sample-Coffee Chain.mdb` or `Sample - CoffeeChain (Use instead of MS Access).xlsx` data source to create the Scatter plot that compares the marketing expenses and the profits we are making for different products across different markets. Let us follow the recipe below and quickly create a Scatter plot.

How to do it...

1. Let us a new sheet by pressing *Ctrl + M* and renaming the sheet to `Scatter plot`.

2. In the toolbar, click on **Data | New Data Source** or press *Ctrl + D*, or click on the cylinder icon in the toolbar. Refer to the following image:

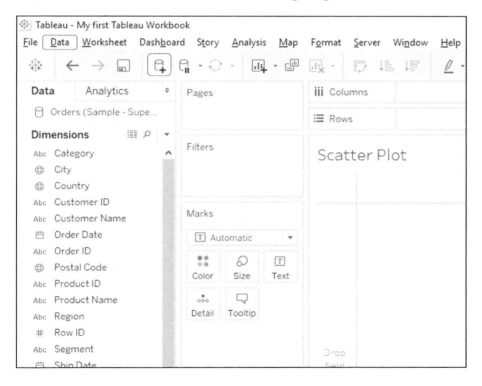

3. Once we use the **Connect to data** option, we'll see the list of data sources that we can connect to. Let us select the **Access** option and connect to the `Sample-Coffee Chain.mdb` data file stored in a folder called `Tableau Cookbook` data under `Documents | My Tableau Repository | Datasources`. If you are a Mac user, select the **Excel** option and connect to the **Sample - CoffeeChain (Use instead of MS Access).xlsx** data file which should be stored in the same folder as mentioned earlier.

4. Select the table named `CoffeeChain Query`. Refer to the following image:

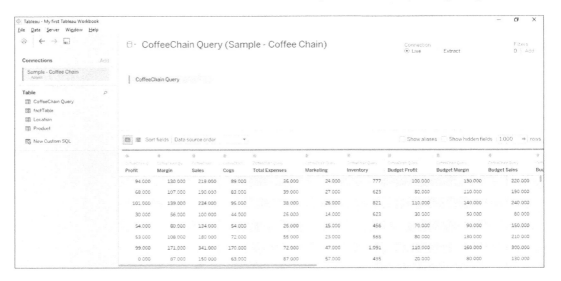

5. Let us go ahead with the **Live** option to connect to this data.

6. Once we are done connecting the data, we'll click on the **New Worksheet** tab to see the **Dimensions** and **Measures** of the new Access database. Refer to the following image:

7. Now let's drag **Marketing** from the **Measures** pane and drop it into the **Columns** shelf.

8. Next we will drag the **Profit** field from **Measures** and drop it into the **Rows** shelf. Refer to the following image:

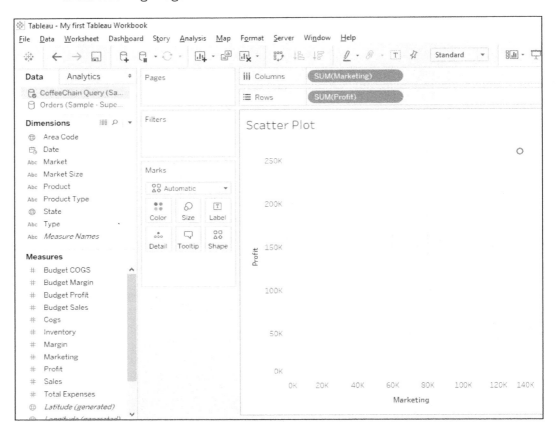

9. We will then drag **Product Type** from the **Dimensions** pane and drop it into the **Shape** shelf in the **Marks** card.

10. Next, let's drag **Product** from the **Dimensions** pane and drop it into the **Color** shelf in the **Marks** card. Refer to the following image:

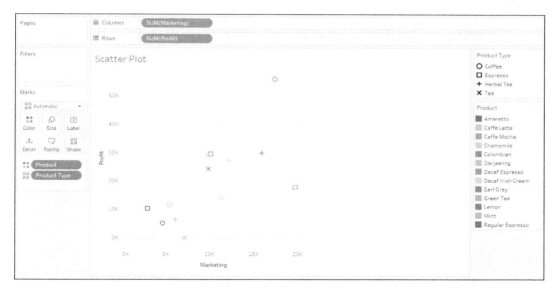

11. The patterns are still not very visible in the above chart. Plus, since we are trying to compare **Profit** and **Marketing**, it makes sense to also add **Market** in the view, as marketing expenses will be different for different products in different markets. So, we will get the **Market** field from the **Dimensions** pane and drop it into the **Label** shelf. Refer to the following image:

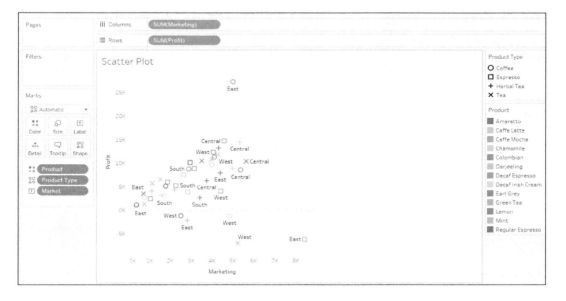

12. With **Market** in the **Label** shelf, the view becomes slightly cluttered. We could put **Market** in the **Detail** shelf so that the additional data points will be visible, but they just won't be explicitly shown via color, size, shape, or label. Thus, the view will be much cleaner, and we can see some patterns in the data. Refer to the following image:

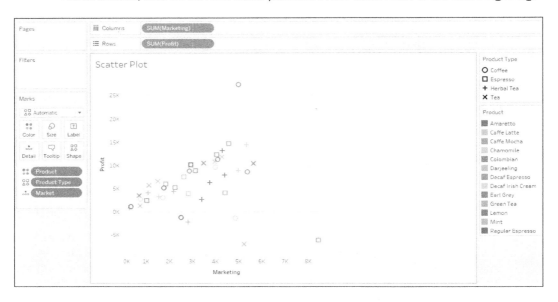

How it works...

The **X axis** represents the money spent as a **Marketing** expense and the *Y* axis represents the **Profit** made. The **Shape** represents the **Product Type**. The **Color** indicates the **Product**. Since the **Market** is placed in the **Level of Detail** shelf, it will be visible to us only when we hover over any data point.

Scatter plots give us a very clear indication of outliers. Typically, the majority of data points will follow a certain pattern and will be placed very close to each other, in such a way that the view looks cluttered and gets difficult to read. However, there will be certain data points that are not following the mainstream pattern, and that is what we can track in a scatter plot. These scattered points are called **Outliers**. These outliers can have a big influence on correlation, and as a good practice, these should be examined to determine whether they are real data values, or some kind of data error.

In the preceding example, we have various scattered points. Refer to the following image:

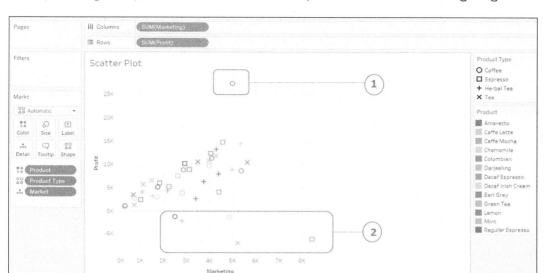

In the preceding image, the green point on the very top, which is a **Colombian** product, belonging to **Coffee** *(refer annotation 1),* is the point where the **Profit** is highest, with a **Marketing** spend of about 5K, whereas the bottom section, *(refer annotation 2)* is showing us all the **Products** that are incurring **Losses**. The worst of the lot is the orange point on the extreme right. This point, **Caffe Mocha**, belongs to **Expresso** type and has the highest **Marketing** spend, yet is incurring heavy **Loss**.

If we hover over these two data points in Tableau, we will get to see that both belong to the East market. So, the point to investigate would be, within a particular region, how is one product highly profitable whereas the other is making heavy losses even after big spending on marketing campaigns. This insight was quick and easy to understand from a Scatter Plot.

Creating a Box and Whisker plot

The **Box plot**, or **Box and Whisker plot** as it is popularly known, is a convenient statistical representation of the variation in a statistical population. It is a great way of showing a number of data points as well as showing the outliers and the central tendencies of data.

This visual representation of the distribution within a dataset was first introduced by American mathematician John W. Tukey in 1969. A box plot is significantly easier to plot than say a histogram and it does not require the user to make assumptions regarding the bin sizes and number of bins; and yet it gives significant insight into the distribution of the dataset.

The box plot primarily consists of four parts:

The median provides the central tendency of our dataset. It is the value that divides our dataset into two parts, values that are either higher or lower than the median. The position of the median within the box indicates the skewness in the data as it shifts either towards the upper or lower quartile.

The upper and lower quartiles, which form the box, represent the degree of dispersion or spread of the data between them. The difference between the upper and lower quartile is called the **Interquartile Range (IQR)** and it indicates the mid-spread within which 50 percentage of the points in our dataset lie.

The upper and lower whiskers in a box plot can either be plotted at the maximum and minimum value in the dataset, or 1.5 times the IQR on the upper and lower side. Plotting the whiskers at the maximum and minimum values includes 100 percentage of all values in the dataset including all the outliers. Whereas plotting the whiskers at 1.5 times the IQR on the upper and lower side represents outliers in the data beyond the whiskers.

The points lying between the lower whisker and the lower quartile are the lower 25 percent of values in the dataset, whereas the points lying between the upper whisker and the upper quartile are the upper 25 percent of values in the dataset.

In a typical normal distribution, each part of the box plot will be equally spaced. However, in most cases, the box plot will quickly show the underlying variations and trends in data and allows for easy comparison between datasets:

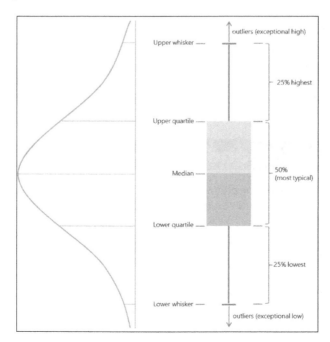

Getting ready

Create a **Box and Whisker plot** in a new sheet in our existing workbook.

For this purpose, we will connect to an Excel file named `Data for Box plot & Gantt chart`, which has been uploaded on `https://1drv.ms/f/ s!Av5QCoyLTBpnhkGyrRrZQWPHWpcY`.

Let us save this Excel file in our `Documents | My Tableau Repository | Datasources | Tableau Cookbook` data folder.

The data contains information about customers in terms of their gender and recorded weight. The data contains 100 records, one record per customer. Using this data, let us look at how we can create a Box and Whisker plot.

How to do it...

Once we have downloaded and saved the data from the link provided in the **Getting started...** section, we will create a new worksheet in our existing workbook and rename it to **Box and Whisker plot**.

1. Since we haven't connected to the new dataset yet, establish a new data connection by pressing *Ctrl + D* on our keyboard.

2. Select the **Excel** option and connect to the **Data for Box plot & Gantt chart** file, which is saved in our `Documents | My Tableau Repository | Datasources | Tableau Cookbook` data folder.

3. Next let us select the table named `Box and Whisker plot data` by double-clicking on it.

4. Let us go ahead with the **Live** option to connect to this data.

5. Next let us multi-select the **Customer** and **Gender** field from the **Dimensions** pane and the **Weight** from the **Measures** pane by doing a *Ctrl + Select*. Refer to the following image:

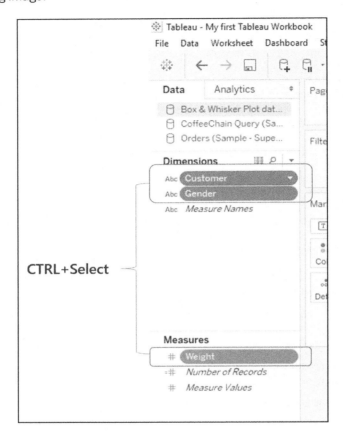

6. Next let us click on the **Show Me!** button and select the **box-and-whisker plot**. Refer to the highlighted section in the following image:

7.   Once we click on the **box-and-whisker plot** option, we will see the following view:

How it works...

In the preceding chart, we get two box and whisker plots: one for each gender. The whiskers are the maximum and minimum extent of the data. Further more, in each category we can see some circles, which are essentially representing a customer. Thus, within each gender category, the graph is showing the distribution of customers by their respective weights. When we hover over any of these circles, we can see details of the customer in terms of name, gender, and recorded weight in the tooltip. Refer to the following image:

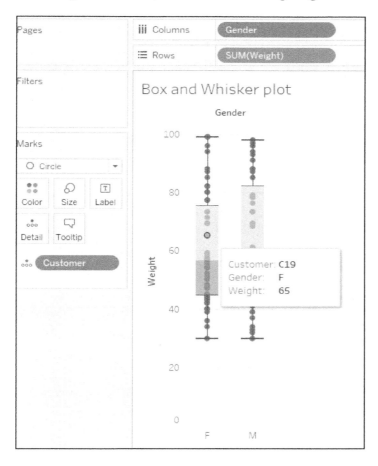

However, when we hover over the box (gray section), we will see the details in terms of median, lower quartiles, upper quartiles, and so on. Refer to the following image:

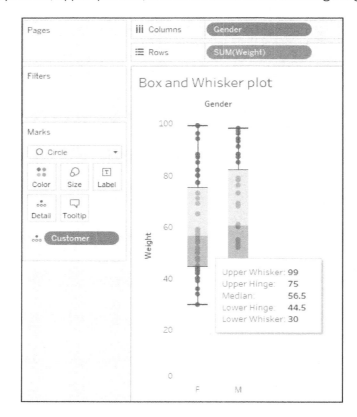

Thus, a summary of the box plot that we created is as follows:

	Female	Male
Minimum weight	30	30
Lower Quartile	44.5	44
Median	56.5	60.5
Upper Quartile	75	82
Maximum weight	99	98

In more simple terms, for the female category, the majority of the population lies between the weight range of 44 to 75, whereas for the male category, the majority of the population lies between the weight range of 44 to 82.

Please note that in our visualization, even though the **Row** shelf displays **SUM(Weight)**, since we have **Customer** in the **Detail** shelf, there's only one entry per customer, so **SUM(Weight)** is actually the same as **MIN(Weight)**, **MAX(Weight)**, or **AVG(Weight)**.

Creating a Gantt chart

A **Gantt chart** is a type of Bar chart which is commonly used in project management, and is one of the most popular and useful ways of showing activities such as tasks or events displayed against time. It was developed by Henry Gantt in the 1910s for tracking project schedules.

Gantt charts show the start and finish dates of various tasks/elements in a project. These elements comprise the work breakdown structure of the project. A Gantt chart can also be used for showing things in use over time, for example, the duration of a machine's use, or how long it took for people to hit a milestone and how that was distributed over time.

Getting ready

In the following recipe, we will create a Gantt chart by connecting to the `Data for Box plot & Gantt` chart Excel file we downloaded earlier. This Excel workbook has a sheet named Gantt Chart data, which contains sample data of various phases in a project-management process.

This is a small dataset, which has a **Start date** for each Task. Let us use this data and follow the steps mentioned in the following recipe to quickly create a Gantt chart, which will show us the duration of each Task.

How to do it...

1. Let us first create a new worksheet and rename it to `Gantt chart`.

2. We will then press *Ctrl + D* on your keyboard and connect to the Excel file named Data for Box plot & Gantt chart file, which is saved in our `Documents | My Tableau Repository | Datasources | Tableau Cookbook` data folder.

3. Next, we will select the **Gantt Chart data** by double-clicking on it.

4. And then go ahead with the **Live** option to connect to this data.

5. Next, we will multi-select the **Start** and **Tasks** field from the **Dimensions** pane and the **Duration** from the **Measures** pane by doing a *Ctrl + Select*.

6. Next, let us click on the **Show Me!** button and select the Gantt view. Refer to the highlighted section in the following image:

7. Once we click on the highlighted chart, we will see the view shown in the following image:

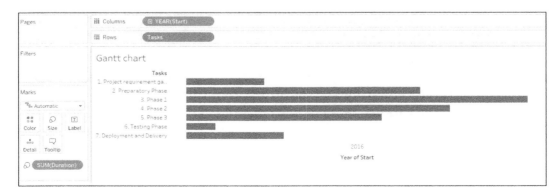

8. Currently, the view is aggregated to show Year of the **Start** field. However, the data consists of various events on various days of a particular year. We will click on the dropdown of the green pill of **Year(Start)** in the **Rows** shelf and select the option **Exact Date**. Refer to the following image:

9. Once we select the **Exact Date** option, we will see the following view:

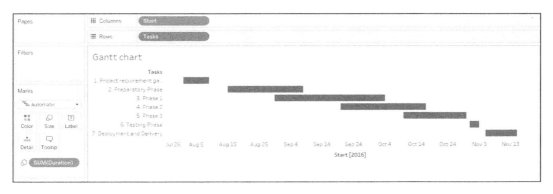

10. For our last step, let us drag the **Tasks** field from the **Dimensions** pane and put it in the **Color** shelf. Refer to the following image:

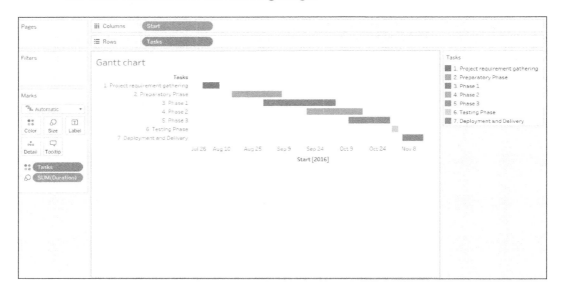

The preceding chart basically tells us the duration and frequency of each **Task** that has occurred in the project management process. We get to know precisely when and for how long each task continued, and whether these were serial tasks, overlapping tasks, and so on.

Creating Maps

Being able to compare data across geographies is critical for any business. Imagine if an organization is doing business in multiple locations; the analysis of interest would be to find out which region is giving high sales, which region is profitable, which region has the maximum customer base, and so on.

Our data may consist of geographic fields such as countries, states, cities, and so on, and when we are analyzing these fields, it makes sense to plot them on a map, primarily because it is easier to compare information across regions to find various geographic trends.

Tableau has many data-map providers and it comes with a set of **Online** and **Offline** maps that one can access to create the maps views. Further more, Tableau understands various geographic roles as well, and once it does that, it will create a small globe icon as a prefix for that field. Refer to the following image:

Tableau will also auto generate two measures: Latitude (generated) and Longitude (generated). We will use these fields to plot the geographical data on the map in Tableau. In the following recipe, we will learn the steps required to create a map.

Getting ready

We will use the **State** field from our **Orders** dataset, `Sample - Superstore.xlsx`. Assuming that Tableau has identified our field as a geographical field and has generated the **Latitude (generated)** and **Longitude (generated)** fields, we will now proceed to create a map in Tableau.

How to do it...

1. Let us create a new sheet by pressing *Ctrl + M* and call it `Symbol map`.

2. Since we have some new datasets added to our workbook, let us make sure we select the **Orders (Sample - Superstore)** data in the data window. Once we do that, we will get to see the **Dimensions** and **Measures** of that dataset. Refer to the following image:

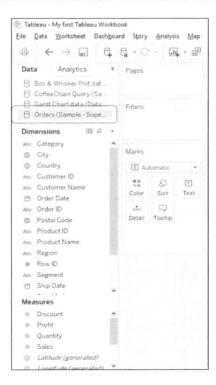

3. Then, we willdrag the **State** field from the **Dimensions** pane and drop it into the **Rows** shelf.

4. Next, let us drag the **Profit** field from the **Measures** pane and drop it into the **Text** shelf. Refer to the following image:

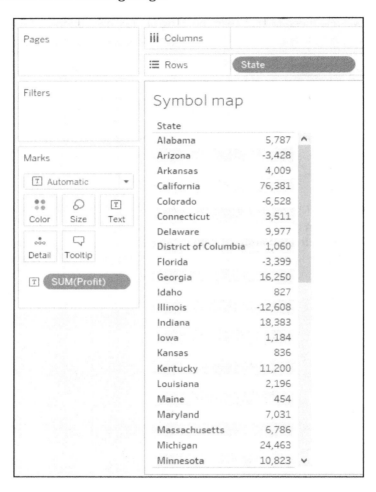

5. Now, click on the **Show Me!** button, and we'll see that the map option has been enabled and highlighted. Refer to the following image:

6. Select the chart which is highlighted in **Show Me!**. Once we do that, we will either get a United States map or a blank world map with no data plotted. In the latter case, there will be an indicator at the bottom of the view saying **49 unknown**. Refer to the following image:

7. If we get the preceding view, click on the indicator and select the option **Edit Locations**. The **Edit Locations** option can also be enabled from the toolbar **Map | Edit Locations...**. Once we do that, we will get a new pop-up window, as shown in the following image:

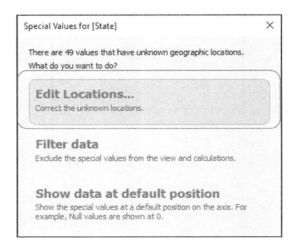

8. Once we do that, we'll get a new window, as shown in the following image:

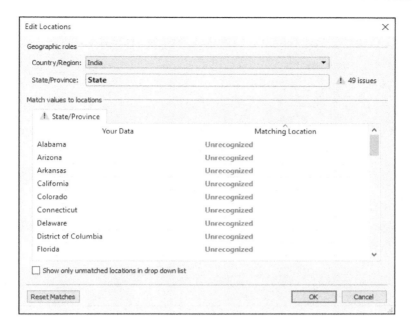

9. Notice the **Country/Region** dropdown. For me, it says **India**. This is because my system locale is set to **India**. However, our data field contains state-level information for the **United States**. So, let's change the country from **India** to **United States**. Refer to the following image:

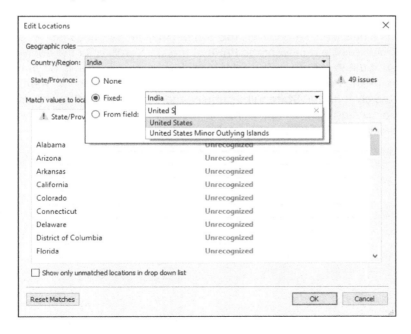

10. Once we select the country as **United States**, we'll get the following view:

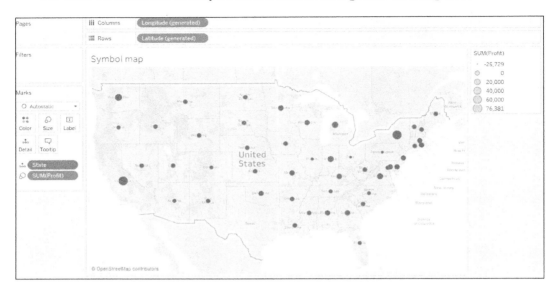

11. This is called the **Symbol map** in Tableau. Notice that the size of the bubbles/circles is different and we will see a size legend on the right-hand side of the chart that we can refer to. The inference is that the bigger the bubble size, the greater the **Profit**, and the smaller the size, the less the **Profit**. We will also see that the **Latitude (generated)** and **Longitude (generated)** fields have been automatically placed in the **Rows** and **Columns** shelf, respectively.

12. Now, as a next step, let's convert this Symbol map into a Filled map, where instead of having a bubble represent the **Profit** of the state, we'll color the entire state to represent the **Profit** value. The point to remember here is that, in a symbol map, we determine the **Profit** of the **State** based on the size of the bubble, whereas in a filled map, the color of that **State** will determine the amount of **Profit**. To create a Filled map, let us start by first duplicating the sheet by right-clicking on the sheet name and then selecting the **Duplicate sheet** option.

13. Next time we will rename this new sheet as **Filled map**.

14. We will then click on the **Show Me!** button and select the **Filled map** option. Refer to the following image:

15. Once we select the filled map, we'll get the following view:

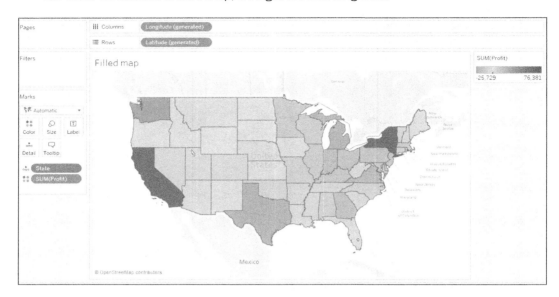

16. This is called the Filled map in Tableau. Notice the entire state is color-coded and the color legend on the right-hand side of the chart helps us understand the significance of the color range. In the preceding image, the Orange color indicates **Losses**, whereas the Blue color indicates **Profits**. Further more, the various shades of Blue and Orange indicate the intensity of **Gains** and **Losses**, respectively. Finally, to complete the visualization, let us get the **State** field in the label shelf. Refer to the following image:

How it works...

As mentioned previously, Tableau understands certain geographical roles.

The default logic in Tableau is that if the field name consists of common location names, such as country, state, city, zip code, post code, and so on, Tableau automatically identifies these fields as geographical fields. It will give these fields the previously discussed globe icon as a prefix and also automatically generate the **Latitude (generated)** and **Longitude (generated)** fields. The common location names identified by Tableau are typically the same as the geographical roles mentioned in the preceding link.

By default, Tableau will use the data from the online map provider. If we want to switch to the Offline mode, we can do so by selecting the **Offline** option from the **Map | Background Maps** menu.

In the case of the Offline maps, the image tiles that make up the map are stored in a cache along with our temporary Internet files. These temporary Internet files can be cleared manually at any time by simply deleting the temporary files from our browser. However, if we don't delete these manually, Tableau will clear them after about thirty days, after which it will then require us to reconnect and fetch an updated map. By doing this, Tableau makes sure that the map images that are being used don't become obsolete.

Apart from the default online and offline map options, Tableau also gives us the flexibility to use customized maps, by providing connectivity to either the **Web Map Servers (WMS)** or **Mapbox Maps**. This way, we can use custom maps, which can be specific to our industries. If we have access to a WMS provider or Mapbox maps, we can use these services by selecting either the **WMS Servers...** or the **Mapbox Map...** option by clicking on the **Add** button from **Map | Background Maps | Map Services...** in our toolbar.

To learn more about the usage of WMS Servers in Tableau, refer to `http://onlinehelp.tableau.com/current/pro/desktop/en-us/maps_mapsources_wms.html`.

To learn more about the usage of **Mapbox Maps** in Tableau, refer to `http://onlinehelp.tableau.com/current/pro/desktop/en-us/maps_mapsources_mapbox.html`.

As mentioned previously, Tableau reads the field name, and if it contains certain keywords such as state, city, country, zip code, and many more, and it will assume that the field is a geographical field. However, it may so happen that the field contains names of various cities, but the field name does not contain the word *city* in it. Instead it may be called, say, Location. In this case, Tableau will not consider this as a geographical field, and there won't be any Latitude (generated) and Longitude (generated) fields in the Measures pane. To convert this to a geographical field in order to create a map, we will have to assign a geographical role to the field. We can click on the dropdown or right-click on the field in the **Dimensions** pane and select the **Geographic Role** option, and then assign the relevant role. Refer to the following image:

Now, if we notice the **Region** field in our data, we will see the prefix *Abc* instead of the previously mentioned globe icon. This is because Tableau doesn't understand **Region** as a geographical role. However, if we wish to create a map from the **Region** field, we will have to right-click on the **Region** field in the **Dimensions** pane and select the **Create from... | State** option under **Geographic Role**. Refer to the following image:

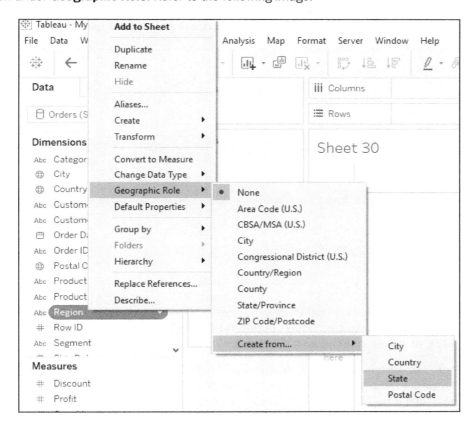

Once we do that, the prefix of the **Region** field will change from Abc to the globe icon similar to that of the **State** field or **City** field in the **Dimensions** pane. We can then use the **Region** field to create a map by simply getting the **Latitude (generated)** and **Longitude (generated)** fields in the **Rows** and **Columns** shelf, respectively. We can then drop the **Region** field from the **Dimensions** pane into the **Color** shelf, followed by dropping the **Sales** field from the **Measures** pane into the **Text** shelf. We can then convert the **Symbol map** to a **Filled map** by selecting the **Filled Map** option from the **Marks** dropdown. Refer to the following image:

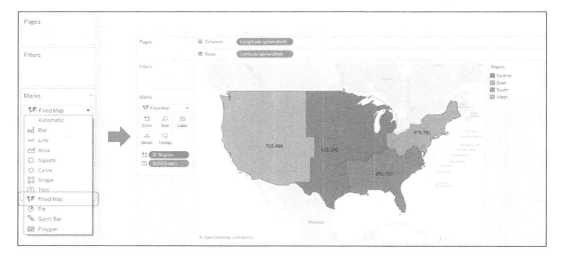

The preceding functionality was introduced in Tableau 10 and is referred to as **Custom Territories**. The other way to create the **Custom Territories** is by creating **Groups**, a functionality that we will learn about in the next chapter.

Further, there may be times, when the default mapping functionality in Tableau won't suffice and we may want to go beyond the roles that are predefined in Tableau. For example, let's say we have data for a retail chain. This retail chain may have various outlets that are spread across multiple locations within cities across various countries. The default mapping of Tableau may not be able to plot these outlets on the map since it doesn't have the necessary geographical role predefined. In this case, we may have to refer to an external source for these geocodes.

To do so, we'll need to Import Custom Geocodes in Tableau by creating a .csv file that contains the geocodes in the form of Latitude and Longitude. These Latitude and Longitude values will have to be stored as real numbers. This .csv should ideally be stored in a separate dedicated folder.

To import the Custom Geocodes, we will have to click on **Map | Geocoding | Import Custom Geocoding**. Refer to the following image:

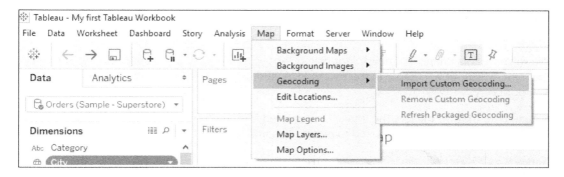

In this case, we will need to give the path of the folder which contains the `.csv` file. However, there are a couple of points to remember when using this approach:

▸   The `.csv` file must contain the **Latitude** and **Longitude** data.

▸   The **Latitude** and **Longitude** values must be stored as real numbers. We need to make sure to include at least one decimal place when specifying these values.

▸   Further more, we need to make sure that each geographical point has a unique geocode and that no two geographic points have the exact same geocodes.

▸   In most situations, the default map in Tableau will suffice, and the **Import Custom Geocodes** option may be very rarely used.

Using Background images

Tableau provides an option to display data on any given image. Typically, people use background images for displaying data on a custom map image. Even though Tableau allows us to use the default map options, background images can give us the flexibility to use our own custom images, which could be used as a special map. Background images need not necessarily be a custom map; instead it can be any image that corresponds to our data. For example, we may have data that corresponds to a floor plan of a building, or data that corresponds to a baseball game, which needs to be plotted on the baseball pitch, and so on. We can use background images to overlay that data on the actual floor plan of the building or on the baseball pitch image, to give more context.

To display the background image, we'll create an **XY axis Scatter Plot**. Each data point then has an *X coordinate* and a *Y coordinate*. The point to remember here is to have the right coordinates, as this is what will add precision to our view.

Getting ready

We will continue working in our existing workbook. For the following recipe, we will use a custom map image called `Custom Background Image.jpg`, which can be downloaded from `https://1drv.ms/i/s!Av5QCoyLTBpnhkNoaaBmncx0kM2K`.

We will save this image in a new folder called `Tableau Data Visualization Cookbook Extras`, which we will create in the following location: `Documents | My Tableau Repository`.

Please note that we will use the image downloaded from the preceding link and create a new dataset in Excel, which will be used to plot on this image.

How to do it...

1. Let us a new sheet in our existing workbook and rename it **Custom Background image**.

2. Also, open a blank Excel file and save it in the `Documents | My Tableau Repository | Datasources | Tableau Cookbook` data folder as Custom Background image data.

3. In this Excel file, we will create four columns, named **Region**, **Location**, **X axis**, and **Y axis**. We will fill in the data as shown in the following image. For now, we will enter the values only for the first row under the *X axis* and *Y axis* columns:

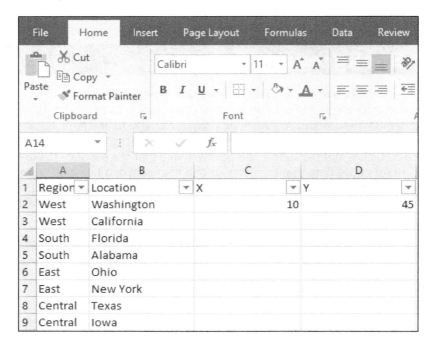

4. As mentioned previously, we will create an **XY** axis scatter plot for this recipe, which is why we have introduced two columns named *X* and *Y*. Now we will need the coordinates for each and every location in the Excel file. To begin with, we will put some values for the first row, which is *Washington*. Since, Washington appears in the top-left corner on the US map, we will give it the coordinates *X = 10* and *Y = 45*. We will then **Save** the Excel file.

5. We will then connect to this Excel file by pressing *Ctrl + D* on your keyboard. Once we have done that, we will get a new data source in the **Data** window and we will see the **Dimensions** and **Measures** of that particular data source.

6. Next, in the toolbar, we will select **Map | Background Images | Custom Background Image data**. Refer to the following image:

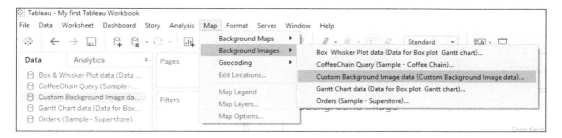

7. Once we do that, we will get a small pop-up window as shown in the following image:

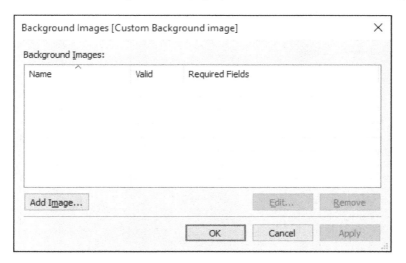

8. Click on the **Add Image...** option and we will see the following view:

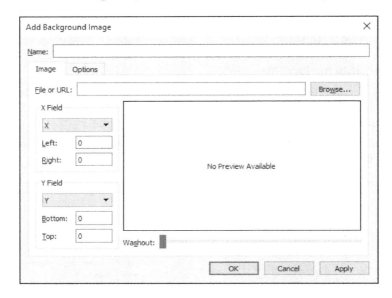

9. Make sure that the **X Field** dropdown has **X**, and that the **Y Field** dropdown has **Y**. We will then browse the `Custom Background Image.jpg` image file from the following location `Documents | My Tableau Repository | Tableau Data Visualization Cookbook Extras`. Once we do that, we will get the following view:

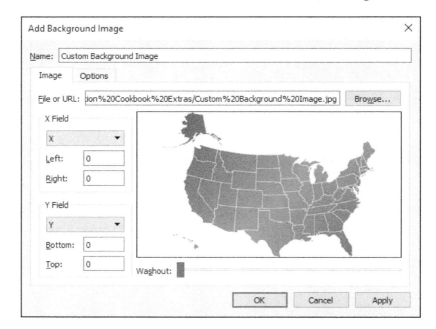

10. Enter values under the *X* and *Y* dropdown, as shown in the following image:

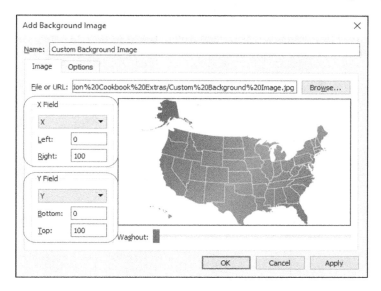

11. Let us **OK**. Here, we quickly need to make sure that the column that says **Valid** has **Yes** in it. **Yes** will essentially mean that we are good to go. Let's click **OK** once again and then drag the field *X* from the **Measures** pane and drop it into the **Columns** shelf, followed by dragging the field **Y** from the **Measures** pane and dropping it into the **Rows** shelf. We will get the following view:

12. Earlier, while calling the image, we entered values as 0 to 100 for both *X* and *Y* axes. However, in this view, the *X* and *Y* axes start from 0 but are not extending to 100; because of this, we are not getting the complete image. To get the complete image, edit the axes by right-clicking on each axis in the view and selecting the **Edit Axis** option. Refer to the following image:

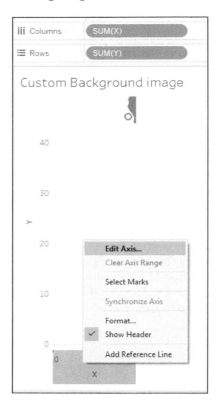

13. Once we do that, we will get the following view, where we will select the **Fixed** option and enter the values as 0 and 100 respectively:

14. We will do the same for the *Y* axis to get the following view:

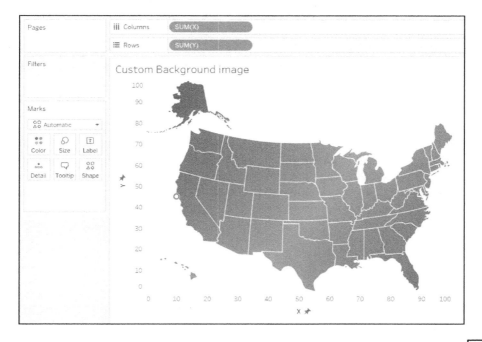

15. Now that we have the image in our view, it is time to plot the data. However, in the Excel file, we only have the data for the *X* and *Y* fields for **Washington**. We don't have the data for any of the other locations. Further more, the point for Washington is shown at the coordinate *(10, 45)*. However, this is not the right position for Washington. Refer to the following image:

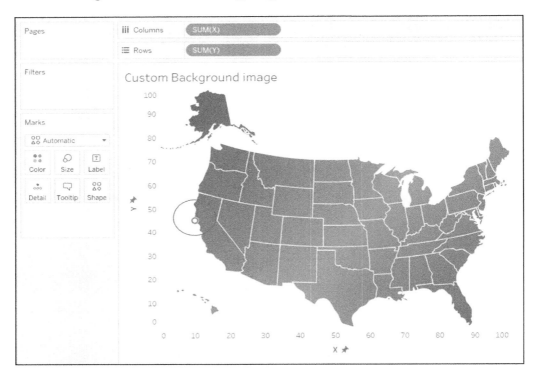

16. The reason why we did not fill in the data for columns **X** and **Y** is because we need to plot the locations at their correct position on the map. Now that we have the image, we can find the coordinates for each location with respect to the image coordinates, and feed it back into Excel. To do so, we will right-click on the Washington area on the image and select **Annotate | Point**. Since the area for Washington spans from approximately 15 to 25 on the *X* axis and 65 to 75 on the *Y* axis, we need to make sure that we click somewhere in the center of the area. This way we'll get values closer to what I have got. Refer to the following image:

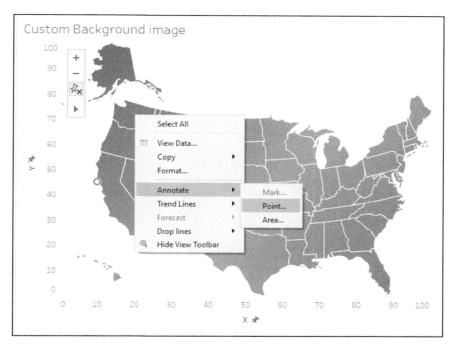

17. Once we do that, we see will a textbox, as shown in the following image:

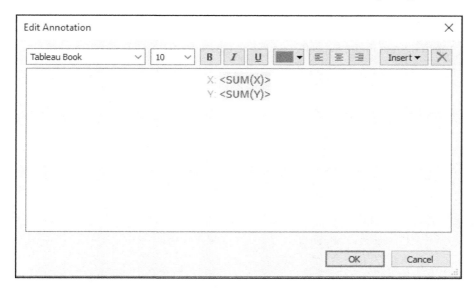

18. We will retain all the default settings and click **OK** to get the following view:

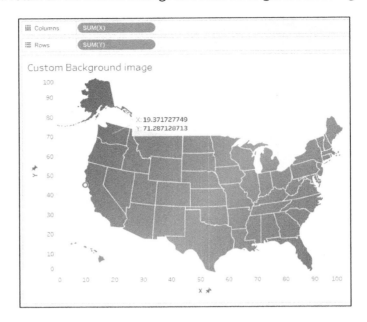

19. Now that we have the *XY* coordinates for Washington, we will update them in our Excel file. Using the same approach, we will find the *XY* coordinates for the rest of the locations as well. As mentioned earlier, our *X* and *Y* values may change depending on the exact point where we right-clicked and enabled the Annotations. After making these entries in the Excel file, save this file. Refer to the following image:

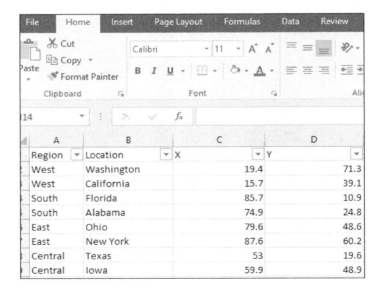

20. To maintain consistency, the updated Excel file can be downloaded from
   `https://1drv.ms/x/s!Av5QCoyLTBpnhkRaCtziJ7RmwErb`.

21. Next, in Tableau, in the **Data** window, let us right-click on the **Custom Background Image data (Custom Background Image data)** data source and select **Refresh**. Refer to the following image:

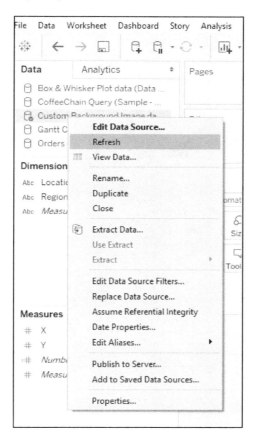

22. We will then drag **Location** from the **Dimensions** pane and drop it into the **Label** shelf. We can clear the annotations by right-clicking on the Annotation and selecting the **Remove** option. We will have to do so for each and every annotation. After we have removed all the annotations, click on the **Color** shelf and select the Black color. Once we are done with this, we will have the following:

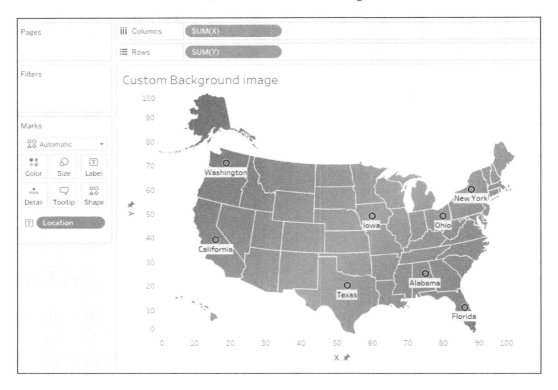

How it works...

When we are using the map as an image, the locations in our data may not perfectly fit to the areas on our map image, and these points may not be located exactly where they should be. Thus, in the preceding recipe, we followed a couple of steps to get the *X* and *Y* coordinates of these locations with respect to their position on our map image. This way, we were able to plot the locations on their respective positions on our image. There are a lot of other ways that we can use background images, and people have done some great stuff using background images in their Tableau views. Take a look at some of the visualizations that have been posted on the Tableau public gallery:

▶ https://public.tableau.com/profile/alchemists.#!/vizhome/
    HistoryofCricketWorldCupFinals/HistoryofCricketWorldCupFinals

- ▶ https://www.tableau.com/public/gallery/ncaa-court
- ▶ https://www.tableau.com/public/gallery/chelsea-manchester
- ▶ https://www.tableau.com/public/gallery/stairs-san-francisco

There are some informative articles on Tableau's website, which will help you understand the concept of using background images in more detail. Refer to the following links:

- ▶ http://onlinehelp.tableau.com/current/pro/desktop/en-us/bkimages.html
- ▶ http://kb.tableau.com/articles/knowledgebase/background-image-coordinates

There's more...

The primary focus of this chapter was to look into some of the advanced visualizations in Tableau. We saw how to create and use maps in Tableau. We also looked at various chart types, which can be used for comparing multiple measures. There is an additional chart, which can help us to compare two measures. This is called the **Bullet Chart**, and is typically used to do a **Plan versus Performance** analysis. We'll learn more about this chart when we talk about **Reference Lines** in Tableau.

4

Slice and Dice – Grouping, Sorting, and Filtering Data

In this chapter, we will focus on slicing and dicing our data, covering the following recipes:

- ▶ Sorting the data
- ▶ Creating a custom hierarchy
- ▶ Grouping the data
- ▶ Creating bins to bucket our data
- ▶ Creating and using filters
- ▶ Creating and using sets
- ▶ Creating and using context filters

Introduction

Now that we have seen how to create various chart types in Tableau, it is time for us to focus on how to add more value to our analysis by using the various methods of slicing and dicing the data, filtering our data to only look at the relevant data points, categorizing our data into groups to make better sense, and so on.

Sorting our data

To make more sense of the data, we need to slice and dice the data in various ways and also look at it from various angles.

Being able to sort the data in ascending, descending or even in a custom manual order will help us put the data into a certain specific order and categorize it better.

Let's say we have around 1,000 customers in our data. Just showing the customers in a random order may not be of much use to us. However, if we sort the customers in descending order by profit, we can see the most profitable customers at the top and the lowest profitable customers at the bottom. However, sorting these customers in ascending order by profit will give us lowest profitable customers at the top followed by the most profitable customers at the bottom.

An example of a manual sort could be sorting the regions in a specific way so that it reads **NEWS** (**North, East, West, and South**).

There are various ways of sorting the data in Tableau. Let us look at the steps in the following recipe.

Getting ready

We will continue working in the same workbook, My first Tableau Workbook, and will use the already connected **Orders** data from our Sample - Superstore.xlsx Excel file. Let us follow the steps in the following recipe to learn how we can sort the data in Tableau.

How to do it...

1. To begin with, let us first create a new sheet by pressing *Ctrl + M* on our keyboards and rename it as Sorting.

2. Since there are some new datasets that we have added in our workbook, let's make sure we select Orders (Sample - Superstore) to enable the **Dimensions** and **Measures** of that dataset. Once we do that, drag **Sub-Category** from the **Dimensions** pane and drop it into the **Rows** shelf, followed by dragging **Sales** from the **Measures** pane and dropping it into the **Columns** shelf. This will result in a bar chart as shown in the following screenshot:

3. In the preceding bar chart, we will see that the product sub-categories are listed in alphabetical order from A-Z. However, we will sort this in descending order by **Sales** by using the shortcut sorting option in the toolbar. Refer to the following image:

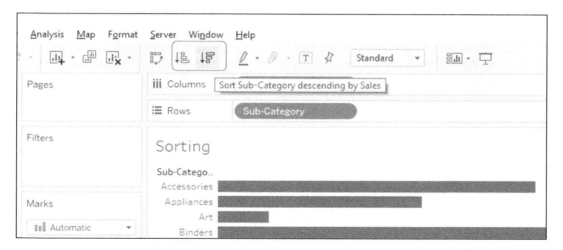

4. One is for the ascending sort and the other is for the descending sort. Let us click on the descending sort. Once we have selected the descending sort, we should see the view as shown in the following image:

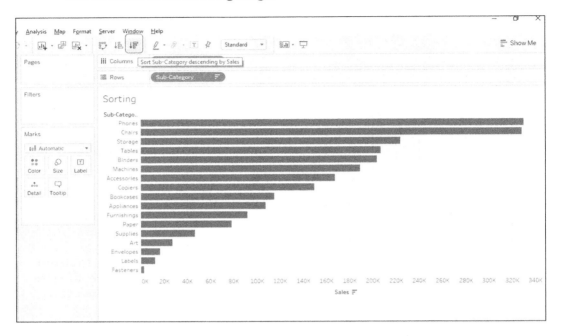

5. This is one way to sort the chart. Notice the Blue pill of **Sub-Category** in the **Rows** shelf; once the sorting is applied, we will see that the pill also has a **Sort indicator**. The other way to sort is by clicking on the axis. Refer to the following image:

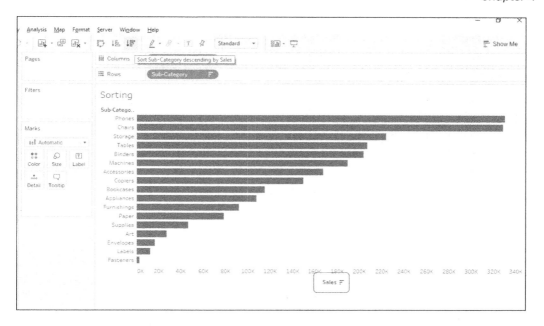

6. The preceding approach works perfectly well when there is a single measure. However, imagine having two measures. One on the axis and the other in the **Color** shelf. The problem with the above sorting method is that, even when we have two measures, this sorting method will only sort by the field that is placed on the axis. Let's look at this. On the same sheet, let's now get **Profit** from the **Measures** pane and drop it into the **Color** shelf. Refer to the following image:

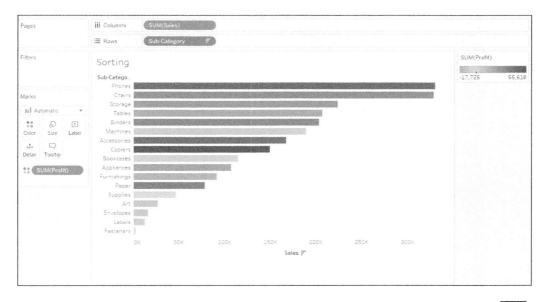

7. In the current view, the length of the bars indicates the amount of **Sales**, whereas, the color of the bars indicates the amount of **Profit**. Thus, the longer the bar, the larger the **Sales** figure; and the darker the blue the greater the level of **Profit**. Further, the bar chart is currently sorted in descending order of **Sales**. Imagine having to sort with respect to **Profit**. If we hover over the sorting icons in the toolbar, it will say **Sort Sub-Category ascending by Sales** or **Sort Sub-Category descending by Sales**. Thus, in order to sort by **Profit**, we will have to use another approach.

8. We will click on the drop-down menu of the Blue pill of **Sub-Category** in the **Rows** shelf and click on the **Sort...** option. Refer to the following image:

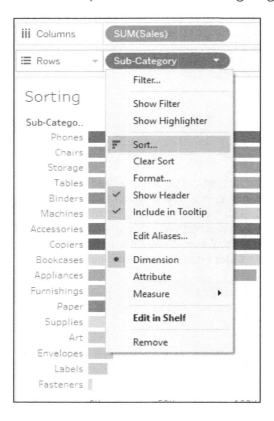

9. Once we do that, we will get to see the following view:

10. Notice that we also have a **Manual** sort option. However, since we need to sort our product **Sub-Categories** by **Profit**, we will select either the **Ascending** or the **Descending** option. In this instance, select the **Descending** option. Next, we will select the **Field** option and, from the dropdown, select **Profit** and keep the aggregation as **Sum**. Refer to the following image:

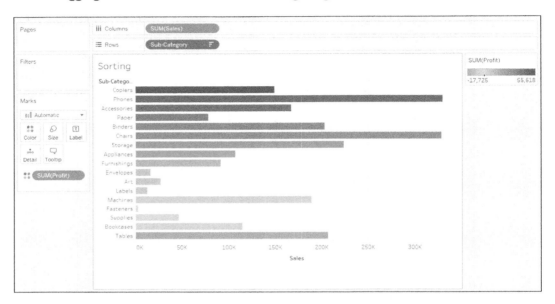

How it works...

The preceding view may not look sorted if we look at the length of the bars. However, if we look at the color of the bars, we will see that the bars are sorted by color which is **Profit**. So, the bar with highest **Profit** is dark blue in color which is right on the top. This is followed by bars that have lighter and lighter shades of blue which are then followed by shades of orange to indicate losses.

Another option to sort is from the **Dimensions** pane. If we select the **Default Properties** option by right-clicking on the **Dimensions** that needs to be sorted, then we will get a **Sort...** option. Refer to the following image:

If we set the sort order for a field in the **Dimensions** pane by using the **Default Properties** option, then it becomes the default sort order for the entire workbook whereas if we set the sort order for a field in the view, then the sort order applies only to the specific sheet view.

Creating a custom hierarchy

Using hierarchies is another way of slicing and dicing our data. This gives us the ability to be able to drill up and drill down into the data at various granularities. We have already seen an example of a default hierarchy in Tableau when we use any **Date** field.

When we get any **Date** field in either the **Rows** or **Columns** shelf, Tableau automatically aggregates it to the highest possible level. For example, if the date field includes multiple years, the default level is year. But, if the date field contains data for just one year but includes multiple months, then the default level is month.

In our data, if we get the **Order Date** field in the **Rows** shelf, then Tableau aggregates it at the Year level and gives us a field called **YEAR(Order Date)**. It also gives us the **+** button (expand button) so that we can easily break down the view by year, quarter, month, and so on. Refer to the following image:

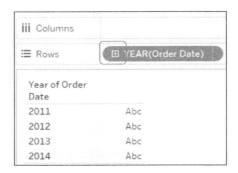

When Tableau identifies a field as a Date or Date/Time field, it creates the **Date** hierarchy by default. There could, however, be instances when we would want to create some custom hierarchies in Tableau. Let's say we have region, country, state, city, and so on. and we want to create a hierarchy with these fields to quickly drill through each level. In the following recipe, let's look at the steps to create a custom hierarchy in Tableau.

Getting ready

We will continue with the above stated example and create a custom hierarchy. We will use the fields **State**, **City**, and **Postal Code** from our already connected **Orders** data of the Sample - Superstore.xlsx dataset. We will continue working in our existing workbook. Let us go through the recipe to create a custom hierarchy.

How to do it...

1. Create a new sheet by pressing *Ctrl + M* on our keyboards. Rename this sheet Custom Hierarchy.

2. We will then click on the dropdown or right-click on the **State** field in the **Dimensions** pane and select the option of **Hierarchy | Create Hierarchy...**. Refer to the following image:

3. Once we do that, we will get an option for defining a **Name** for our hierarchy. Let us call it **Geographic Hierarchy**. Once we do that, we will get a new header in the **Dimensions** pane. Refer to the following image:

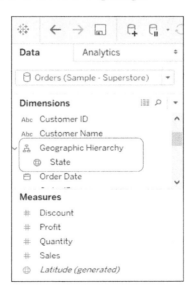

4. Next, we will right-click on the next field that will follow **State** in the **Hierarchy**. This is going to be the **City** field from the **Dimensions** pane. When we right-click on the **City** field, we will get option of **Hierarchy | Create Hierarchy...** or **Hierarchy | Add to Hierarchy**. Select the **Hierarchy | Add to Hierarchy | Geographic Hierarchy** option. Refer to the following image:

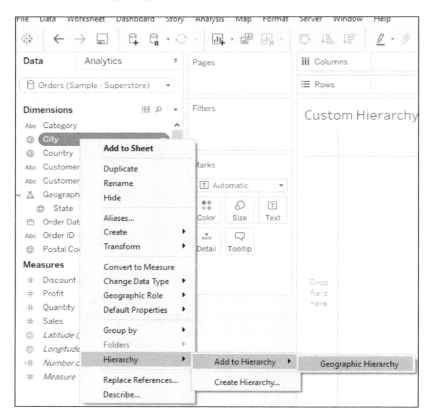

5. Repeat the process of **Add to Hierarchy** for **Postal Code** as well. This is how we create a **Custom Hierarchy** in Tableau. To use it, we will double-click on the **State** field from the **Dimensions** pane. This will automatically fetch the **Latitude (generated)** and **Longitude (generated)** fields into the **Rows** and **Columns** shelf respectively and also place the **State** field in the **Detail** shelf. This creates a geographic map at a State level. Then, we will drag **Sales** from the **Measures** pane and drop it into the **Size** shelf followed by dragging the **Region** field from the **Dimensions** pane and dropping it into the **Color** shelf. Refer to the following image:

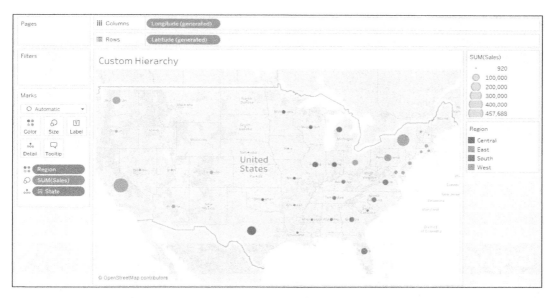

6. Further, in order to drill down, we will click on the **+** (expand) button on the Blue pill for **State** in **Detail** shelf. To drill up, we will click on the **-** (collapse) button.

How it works...

When we click on the **+** (expand) button on the Blue pill for **State** in the **Rows** shelf, we will drill down to the **City**. Now the **Blue pill** for **State** gets a **-** (collapse) button and the Blue pill for **City** gets a **+** button. This will happen for each drill-down level. One very important point to remember when creating hierarchies is to select the **Dimensions** in the order of how we want the hierarchy to drill down.

Another way to create hierarchies is by selecting multiple dimensions (*Ctrl + Select*) in the **Data** window, right-clicking and selecting the **Hierarchy | Create Hierarchy...**option. However, one may need to rearrange the Dimensions in the hierarchy when using this option. Refer to the following image:

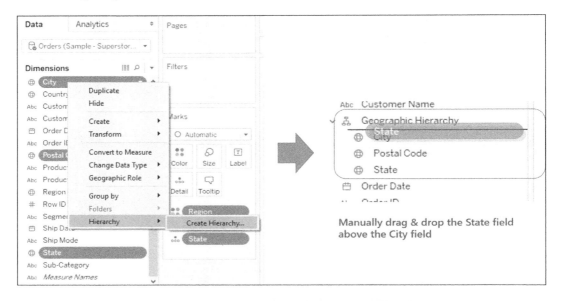

Grouping our data

Being able to group our data into higher categories is a very useful feature. The data that we connect to may not always have all the fields that are required for our analysis. There are times when we would have to go beyond what is available in the data and create some new fields either by doing some calculations or by using some default features. Imagine having data where we have state names, city names, and so on; but the region field has not been captured in the data. Now, there are going to be instances where we would need to do a region-level analysis. For example, we have state-wise sales but want to see how the sales are at a regional level. This information however, is not present in the data.

It's a good thing we have the **Grouping** feature in Tableau. We can create a group on the state names and club the relevant states into regions. Let us see how to create and use **Groups** in the following recipe.

Getting ready

We will continue working in our existing workbook and for the purpose of this recipe, we will use the **State** field from the **Orders** data of `Sample - Superstore.xlsx` data to create groups called **Sales Territories** for our business managers to look into. Let's see what steps are to be taken to create a Group.

How to do it...

1. Create a new sheet by pressing *Ctrl + M* and rename it `Groups`.

2. In the **Dimensions** pane, let us double-click on the **State** field and then get **Sales** from the **Measures** pane and drop it into the **Size** shelf. This will create a geographic map as shown in the following image:

3. Next we will right-click on the **State** field in the **Dimensions** pane and select the **Create | Group...** option. Refer to the following image:

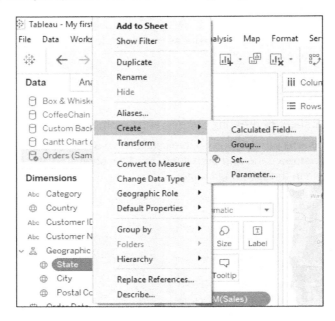

4. Once we do that, we will get the following view:

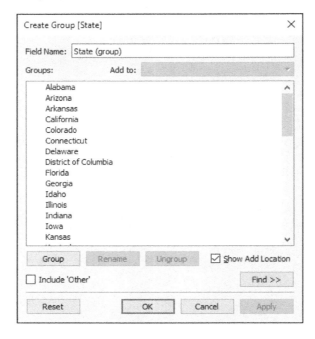

5. Let us give a name to this `Group`. Let us call it **Sales Territories** by typing the name in the **Field Name** input box at the top.

6. We will notice the **Find >>** button at the bottom-right corner. We can expand this section to see what further options are available for us to use. Refer to the following image:

7. Once we get the necessary type-in box, we will keep all the dropdown selections as they are and just type the word **New** in the type in box and make sure that we keep the bottom dropdown selection as **Contains** and then click on the **Find All** button. Please note that the type-in box is not case sensitive.

8. Once we do that, Tableau will give us a selection of all the members that contain the word *New* in it. We will then click on the **Group** button. Refer to the following image:

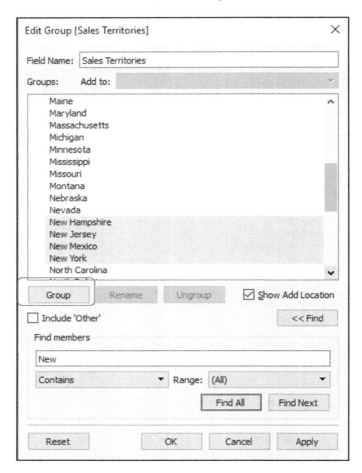

9. We will now get a **Group** called New Hampshire, New Jersey, New Mexico and one more. Let us rename it **Territory 1** by right-clicking on the new group or by clicking on the **Rename** button which is right next to the **Group** button. Once we do that, we will see a paperclip symbol:

10. Now, **New Hampshire, New Jersey, and New York** are all on the East side of the US map. However, **New Mexico** belongs to the West side of the US map. We need to remove it from our newly created group called **Territory 1:** right-click on **New Mexico** and choose the **Remove** option. Refer to the following image:

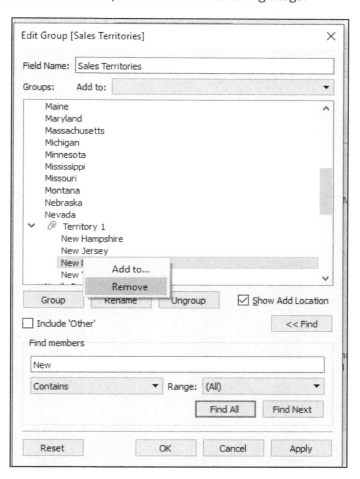

11. Further, let us add a few more states, such as Connecticut, Delaware, District of Columbia, Florida, Georgia, Maine, Maryland, Massachusetts, North Carolina, Pennsylvania, Rhode Island, South Carolina, Vermont, and Virginia to this **Territory 1** group by right-clicking on each one of the states in the preceding dialog box and selecting the option of **Add to...**. Refer to the following image:

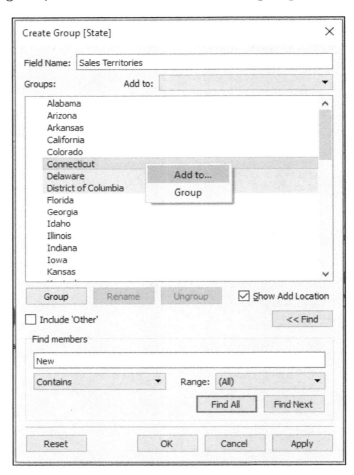

12. Let us add all those states to our group called **Territory 1**. Once we do that, we'll also create another group called **Territory 2** on states such as **Idaho**, Montana, Oregon, Washington and Wyoming. Similarly, we will create another group called **Territory 3** on states such as Arizona, California, Colorado, Nevada, New Mexico and Utah. This will give us three groups. To group the remaining states together, click on the checkbox which says **Include 'Other'**. Refer to the following image:

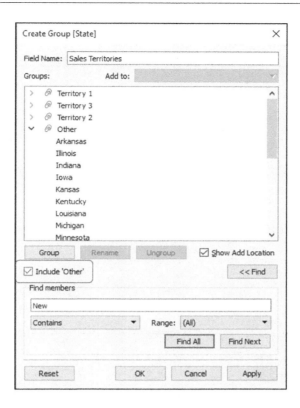

13. Once we do that, we get a group called **Other**. We will click on that group name and select the **Rename** option to call it **Territory 4**. Let us click on the **OK** button once we are done.

14. We will then see a new **Dimension** called **Sales Territories** in the **Dimensions** pane. Refer to the following image:

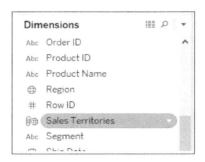

15. As a final step, let us drag and drop the **Sales Territories** field in the **Color** shelf. Refer to the following image:

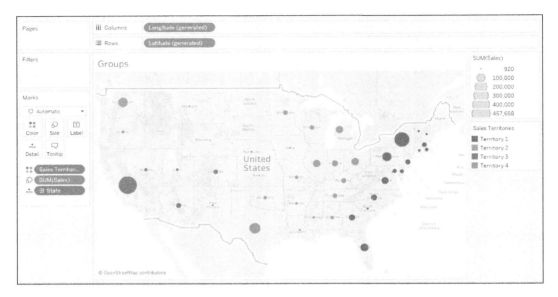

How it works...

This Group that we just created is now part of the **Dimensions** pane and is available for us to use across the entire workbook.

Another way of creating quick Groups is to select multiple marks in an already created view and selecting the Paper clip icon from the tooltip. Refer to the following image:

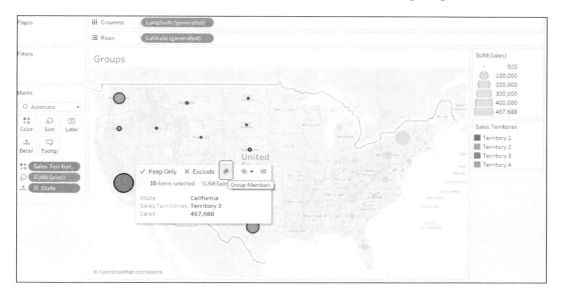

 Please note that we create Groups on data members within a field. That means multiple members of a field can be grouped together. However, multiple fields can't be grouped together.

The above-mentioned functionality of selecting multiple mark types on the view can further be extended to create what we call **Custom Territories** in Tableau. We've already seen a way of creating Custom Territories in the previous chapter. In this chapter, we'll now look at how to use Groups to create Custom Territories. In order to do so, we first create a filled map at state level and then visually group the **States** as shown in the following image:

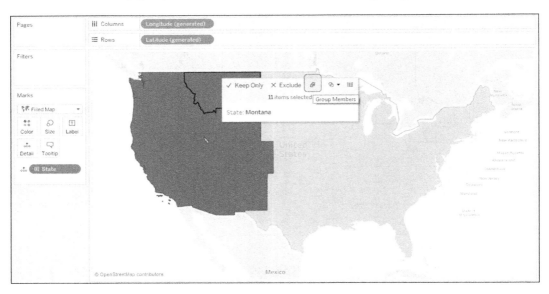

This action will result in creating an on-the-fly group called **State (group)** in the **Dimensions** pane. This new group will further be automatically placed into the **Color** shelf and our view will update as follows:

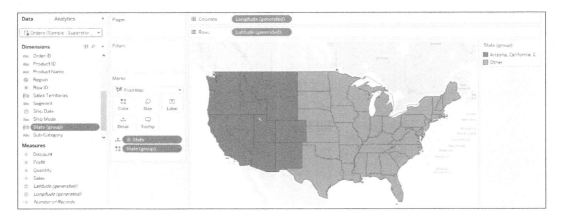

If we remove the **State** field from the **Detail** shelf, our view will update to give us a filled map at a **State (group)** level. Refer to the following image:

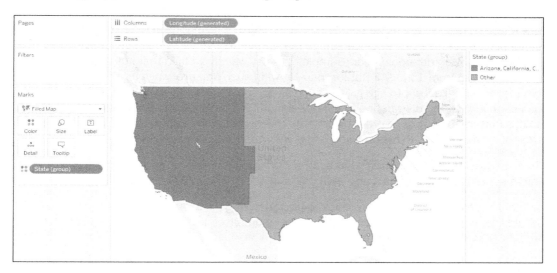

This functionality is referred to as the **Custom Territories**. Further, the color legend can be updated to read as **Zone 1** and **Zone 2** by right-clicking on the text and selecting the **Edit alias...** option. Refer to the following image:

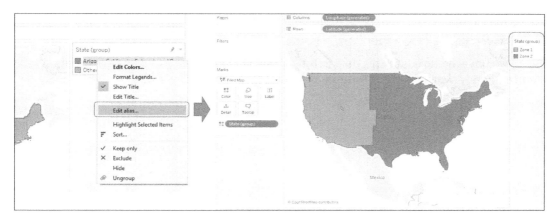

Creating bins to bucket our data

When we get fields such as sales, profit, discount, and many more in either the **Rows** or **Columns** shelf, it creates an axis. However, at times, it is important to organize these continuous measures into discrete groups rather than just showing the individual values for each and every data point. For example, let's say we have a field that holds the age of people ranging from 10 to 90. Rather than showing each and every age in the view, we can bin the individual ages into age groups such as 10 to 25, 26 to 40 and so on. This helps us get an idea of the distribution of the population. The range of this distribution is called a **Class Interval**. Further, in order to visualize this distribution of data, we use a graphical representation called **Histogram** which was first introduced by *Karl Pearson*.

Thus, in other words, **binning** is a process of dividing the entire range of quantitative values into a series of small intervals and then counting how many values fall into each interval.

Another example for creating bins could be for analyzing the sales performance where we would like to find out how many customers have purchased less than $500, between $500 and $1,000, between $1,000 and $1,500 and so on.

Getting ready

In the following recipe, we will see the steps to create a **Histogram**. We will continue working in the same Tableau workbook; however, we will use the **Box and Whisker Plot data** sheet from the `Data for Box plot & Gantt chart.xlsx` Excel data that we downloaded for recipes in *Chapter 3, Hungry for More Charts? Dig In!* from `https://1drv.ms/f/s!Av5QCoyLTBpnhkGyrRrZQWPHWpcY`.

Since we have already used this data in the current workbook, we should have the data source already available in our **Data** window. Refer to the following image:

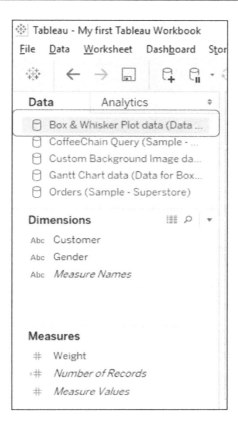

How to do it...

1. Let us create a new worksheet and rename it **Bins/Histogram**.

2. Select **Box & Whisker Plot data (Data for Box plot & Gantt chart)** data source in the **Data** window and we should see the relevant **Dimensions** and **Measures**.

3. Next, we will right-click on the **Weight** field in the **Measures** pane and select the **Create | Bins...** option. Refer to the following image:

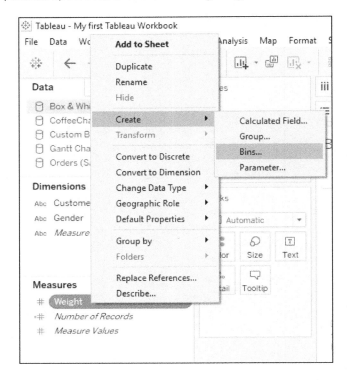

4. Once we do that, we will see a new dialog box as shown in the following image:

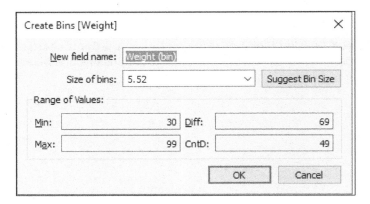

5. The size of the bins is basically the class interval and currently is set to 5.52. We will change that to 10 and click on **OK**. This will create a new dimension called **Weight (bin)**.

6. Next we will drag the newly created **Weight (bin)** field from the **Dimensions** pane and drop it into the **Columns** shelf.

7. Let us then drag **Customer** from the **Dimensions** pane and drop it into the **Rows** shelf. This will give us the list of customers. Refer to the following image:

8. Instead of all the individual customers, we need to show the **Count of Customers** in each weight bucket/bin and to do so, click on the dropdown of the **Blue pill** called **Customer** in the **Rows** shelf and select the option **Measure** and select the **Count (Distinct)** option. Refer to the following image:

9. Once we do that, we will get a view as shown in the following image:

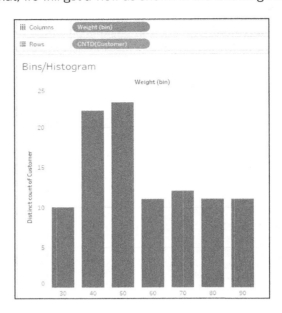

10. This chart, which looks like a **bar chart**, is actually called a **histogram**. We can enable the labels on the top of the bars/rectangles by clicking on the **Labels** shelf and enabling the **Show mark labels** option. Refer to the following image:

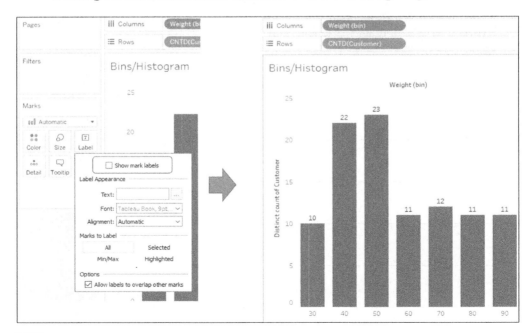

How it works...

In the preceding chart, the *X-axis* is made up of headers for each bin; each bin is a weight range; and the length of bar gives the count of customers in that weight range.

So, in the preceding chart, we can see that there are about ten customers in the weight bucket ranging from *30* to *39*.

People often confuse histograms with bar charts. The difference is that a histogram is created on continuous data (**Measures**), whereas a bar chart is created for categorical/discrete data (**Dimensions**).

Another way to creating a histogram in Tableau is to simply select the relevant measure in the **Measures** pane and select the **histogram** from the **Show Me!** button. Refer to the following image:

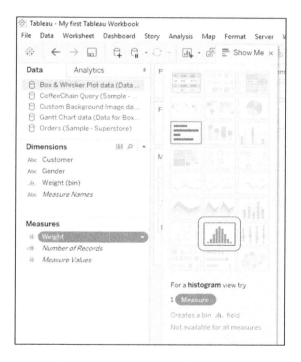

 When we bin a **Measure** we create a new **Dimension**. That's because we are creating discrete categories out of a continuous range of values. The bins that we create using the above methods, will result in creating equal size bins. If we want to create variable sized bins, then we can do so by creating calculations using either the **CASE** function or the **IF – ELSE** function, which we'll be looking at in the following chapters.

Creating and using filters

There are plenty of times when we want to narrow our focus on certain things in our view. This can be achieved by filtering the unnecessary data points. For example, we may have some products which are loss making and we want to focus only on those products or there are certain types of products that we want to use for our analysis. In such situations, we will use **Filters** in Tableau. We have a **Filters** shelf in Tableau and anything that needs to be filtered out will be placed on that shelf.

Let us see an example where we filter out the data.

Getting ready

For the following recipe, we will continue working in our existing Tableau workbook and we will now switch back to our **Orders** data from the `Sample - Superstore.xlsx` dataset.

How to do it...

1. Let us make sure that you have selected the **Orders (Sample - Superstore)** data source in the **Data** window. Once you've done that, create a new sheet and rename it to **Filters**.

2. Let us then drag **Sub-Category** from the **Dimensions** pane and drop it into the **Columns** shelf followed by dragging **Sales** from **Measures** pane and dropping it into the **Rows** shelf.

3. Once we have done that, we will get a bar chart. Next, let us drag the **Sub-Category** from the **Dimensions** pane again and this time drop it into the **Filter** shelf. We will get a pop up window as shown in the following image:

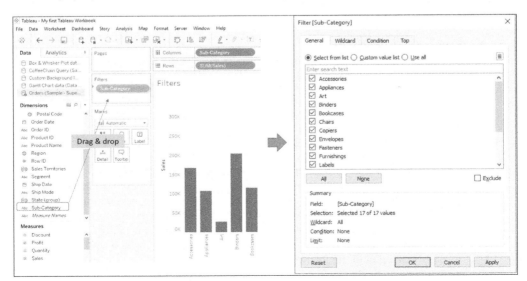

4. There are multiple tabs that are visible and we will continue with the **General** tab. From the list that is displayed, we will uncheck the first 2 **Sub-Categories**, that is, **Accessories** and **Appliances**. Clicking on **OK** will give us 15 Sub-Categories instead of the previously shown 17 Sub-Categories.

5. Next, let us drag **Profit** from the **Measures** pane and drop it into the **Filter** shelf. We will get a dialog box as shown in the following image where Tableau is primarily asking us about the aggregation that we want to filter, earning, do we want to filter **Sum of Profit** or **Average of Profit** and so on:

6. We will select the **Sum** option and then click on the **At Least** tab and type 0 in the type in box. Refer to the following image:

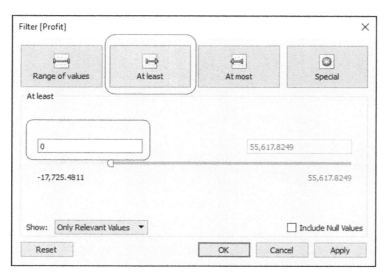

7. Keeping the rest of selection as it is, we will click **OK**. Once we do that, we will see that there are only 12 Sub-Categories out of the already filtered 15 Sub-Categories that are having positive **Profit** whereas the excluded Sub-Categories are loss making. Refer to the following image:

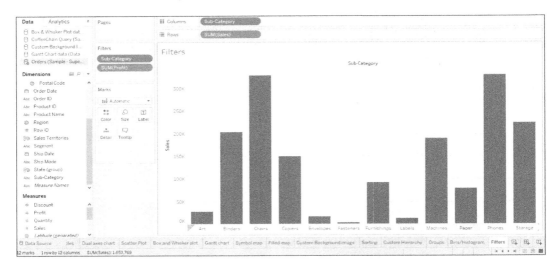

8. Using the preceding steps, we have now filtered the data but the end user doesn't have any control over changing the filters. For example, right now, we have filtered out the Sub-Categories that have negative **Profit**. However, our end user may only be interested in the loss making Sub-Categories. Thus, we need to give the flexibility to change the filter to the end user and to do so, we need to show the filter to the end user by clicking on the dropdown arrow of **Sub-Category** in the **Filter** shelf and selecting the option which says **Show Filter**. Let us do the same for **SUM(Profit)** in the **Filter** shelf. Refer to the following image:

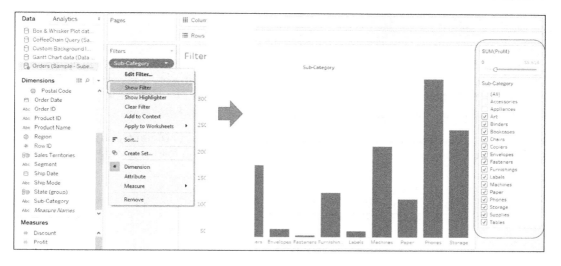

9. Currently the filter is a multi-select filter and a slider. We can change these by clicking on the dropdown arrow for the Filter and selecting from the various options available. Refer to the following image:

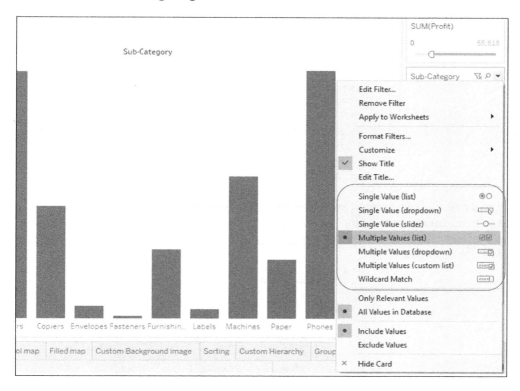

How it works...

Once we show the filter to the end user, the end user can change the filters and slice and dice the data as required. Further, in the preceding recipe, we saw that the way Tableau works with **Dimensions** on the **Filter** shelf versus **Measures** on the **Filter** shelf is very different and hence the options that we get when we drop a **Dimensions** on a **Filter** shelf will vary as against the options that we get when we drop a **Measure** on the **Filter** shelf.

Even though dates are referred to as **Dimensions**, they are special **Dimensions** and when called on the **Filter** shelf, the options will appear as shown in the following image:

The filters that we have created are restricted to the current worksheet and are at times referred to as **Local filters**. In the upcoming chapters, we will see how we can extend these filters to affect multiple worksheets on a **Dashboard** or even across the entire data source or multiple data sources.

Another way of filtering data is by selecting multiple marks from the view and selecting either the **Keep Only** or **Exclude** option from the **Tooltip**. Refer to the following image:

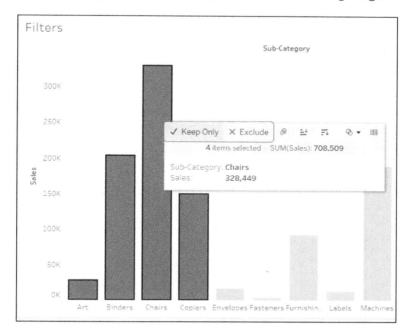

There is a lot more to filtering in Tableau and to read more about Filters, refer to `https://onlinehelp.tableau.com/current/pro/desktop/en-us/filtering.html`.

Creating and using sets

The filters that we created in the previous recipe were created on the fly and are not available for later use, meaning each time we want to use the 12 product Sub-Categories that were shown as an output in the previous recipe, we will have to recreate the filters all over again. This becomes cumbersome and it would be great if we could save the output of the filtering conditions and simply drag the new field whenever we need to analyze it rather than repeating all the steps that we followed in the previous recipe. Luckily, we have **Sets** in Tableau to do this for us.

I like to call Sets as Pre-computed filters which can be used for the creating a sub-set of the data and/or saving the filters for later use.

Getting ready

To create Sets, we will continue working in the same workbook and use the `Orders` data from the `Sample - Superstore.xlsx` dataset for the following recipe.

How to do it...

1. Let us create a new sheet and rename it to `Sets`.

2. We will then on the dropdown or **right-click** on the **Customer Name** field in the **Dimensions** pane and select the option **Create | Set...**. Refer to the following image:

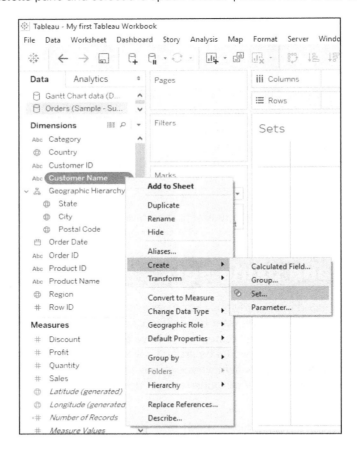

3. We will then get a new dialog box which looks similar to that of the **Filters** in the previous recipe. We will switch to the **Top** tab.

4. In the **Name** input box, let us type **Top 5 customers by Sales**. This is the name of our **Set**.

5. Next, let us select the **By field:** option and keep **Top** in the dropdown.

6. Then we will type 5 and select the field **Sales** in the next dropdown and keep the aggregation as **Sum**. Refer to the following image:

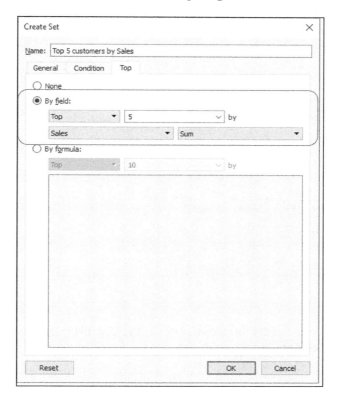

7. Once we click on **OK**, we will see a new pane called **Sets** just below the **Measures** pane. This pane basically stores all the **Sets** that we will create. Currently, we have created only one set which is visible there. Let us drag and drop it into the **Rows** shelf. This action will result in an output as **In** and **Out**. Refer to the following image:

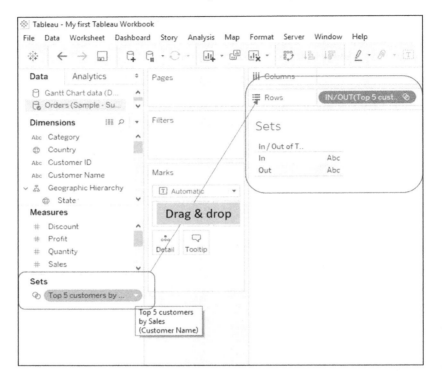

8. We will then click on the dropdown arrow of the Blue pill in the **Rows** shelf and select the **Show Members in set** option. Refer to the following image:

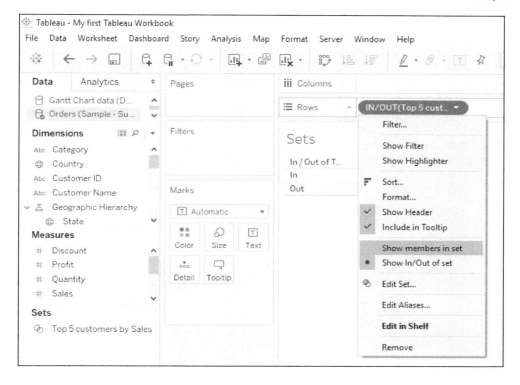

9. Doing this will give us the names of our **Top 5 customers by Sales**. You'll notice that when we select this option, the set will automatically get placed in the **Filter** shelf.

10. As a next step, let us drag **Sales** from the **Measures** pane and drop it into the **Columns** shelf. Refer to the following image:

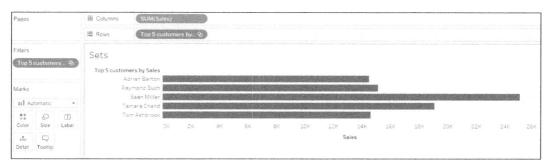

How it works...

As mentioned earlier, **Sets** are like pre-computed filters. However, we can decide whether we want to use the Set as a Filter or use it for categorizing our data. By default, the Set acts as an **In / Out** set where it creates two headers: **In** and **Out**. These are like True (included in the result) or False (excluded from the result) values where if we put the **Customer Name** next to the Set in the **Rows** shelf, it will categorize **Customer Name** into two groups: customers that are **In** the Set, that is, customers who are among the Top 5 customers by Sales list, or customers that are **Out** of the **Set**, that is, customers who are not among the Top 5 customers by Sales list. Refer to the following image:

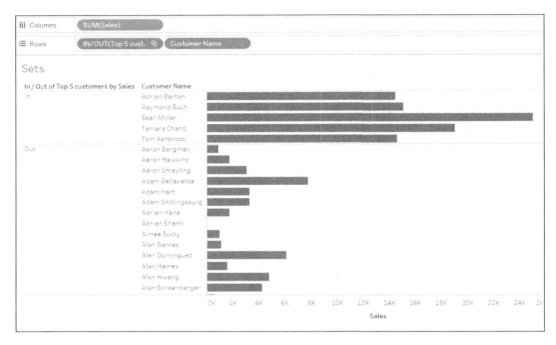

In this case, there is nothing that is getting filtered out. All the customers are shown and they are simply clubbed under either the **In** or the **Out** header. However, when use the option as **Show Members in set**, we are only getting the names of the customers that are part of the Set. The rest of the customers are filtered out.

Further, we can also create two sets and combine them. For example, we can create one set as **Top 100 customers by Sales** and another set as **Bottom 100 customers by Profit**. Refer to the following image:

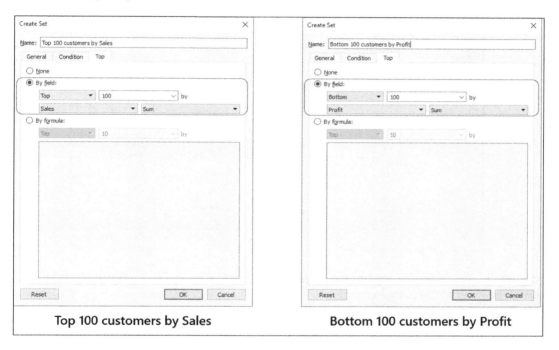

Top 100 customers by Sales   **Bottom 100 customers by Profit**

Once we have these two sets, we can **Combine** them by doing an *Ctrl + Select* and then right-click to select the option of **Create Combined Set...**. Refer to the following image:

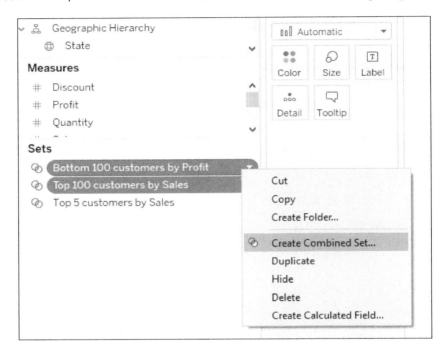

We will then see a new dialog box that shows the multiple ways in which we can combine our two Sets. Refer to the following image:

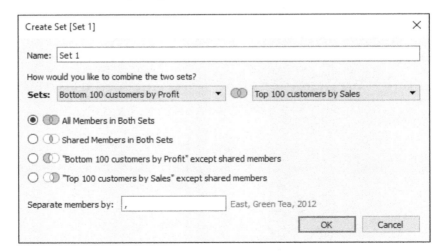

The options of combining two sets are as follows:

- **All Members in Both Sets**: In this case, the combined set will contain all of the members from both sets.

- **Shared Members in Both Sets**: In this case, the combined set will only contain members that exist in both sets. This is a kind of *Intersection* of two sets.

- **Except Shared Members**: In this case, the combined set will contain all members from the specified set that don't exist in the second set. These options are equivalent to subtracting one set from another. For example, if the first set contains Adam, Peter, and Silvia and the second set contains Silvia and Donna, then combining the first set except the shared members would contain just Adam and Peter, as Silvia is removed since she exists in the second set as well.

Creating and using context filters

By default, each and every filter in Tableau will access all the records in our data source without taking into consideration the other filters. It means that these filters are computed independently of each other. However, we may want to set one or more categorical filter as context filters for the view.

For example, we have a **Filter/Set**, which gives us the Top five customers by Sales. Now this Set gives us the Top 5 customers from the entire data set. However, when we get another filter, let's say **Region**, then we expect Tableau to give us the Top five customers for the selected Region. But, because these filters are independent, Tableau still gives us the Top five customers from the entire data set and if it doesn't find a record of any customer from the Top five list in a particular region, then it will simply remove that name from the list. This is because Tableau doesn't understand that the Top five Filter/Set needs to be based on the output of Region filter.

A context filter is like an independent filter and any other filters that we create will be dependent filters. These dependent filters will then process only the data that passes through the context filter.

Getting ready

We will use the preceding example to create and use the **Context Filter**. We will continue working in our existing workbook and will continue using the `Orders` data of `Sample - Superstore.xlsx`.

How to do it...

1. Let us create a new sheet and rename it **Context Filter**.

2. We will the drag **Customer name** from the **Dimensions** pane and drop it in the **Rows** shelf followed by dragging **Sales** from the **Measures** pane and dropping it into the **Columns** shelf. We will get a view as shown in the following image:

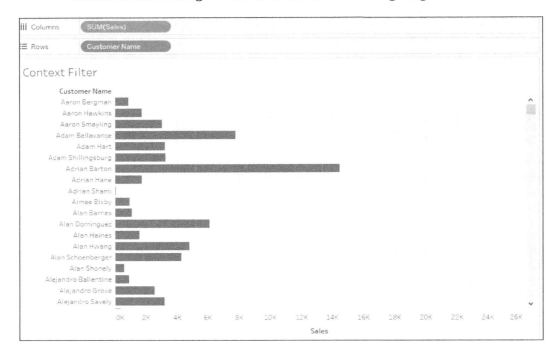

3. Next drag **Customer name** from the **Dimensions** pane again but this time, we will drop it in the **Filter** shelf.

4. We will select the **Top** option in the **By field:** section. Type 5 and keep **Sales** and **Sum** in the dropdown as it is. Refer to the following image:

5. This is similar to what we did in the previous recipe where we created a Set to do the exact same thing. The steps mentioned above help us achieve the same objective using another the **Filter** approach. Next, let us right-click on **Region** in the **Dimensions** pane and select the **Show Filter** option:

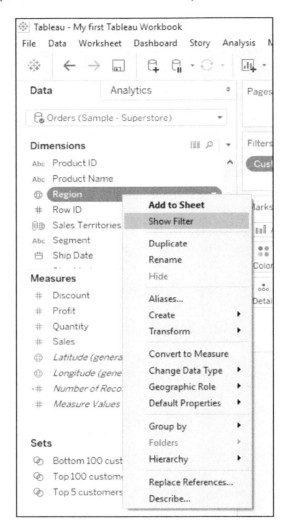

6. From the **Region** filter, let us select only the **South** region. You'll see the view update to show only four names. Refer to the following image:

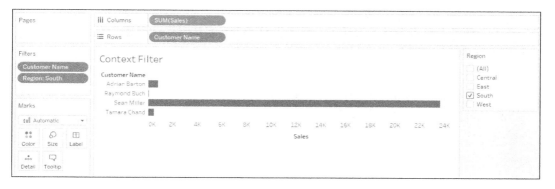

7. Our preliminary condition was to show **Top 5 Customers by Sales**. Since the **South** region is giving only four names, does that mean that **South** region does not have more than four customers? This does not seem right. Since both the filters are computed independently, Tableau gives us the Top five customers from the entire data set and since it does not find any record of Tom Ashbrook in the **South** region; he is eliminated from the list shown in our view. Thus, the list that we see is basically the list of **Top Five Customers by Sales** for the entire dataset and who are also present in the **South** region. However, we are interested in finding out the **Top Five Customers by Sales** in **South** region. In order to get that, let us click on the dropdown of the **Region** field in the **Filter** shelf and select the option of **Add to Context**. Refer to the following image:

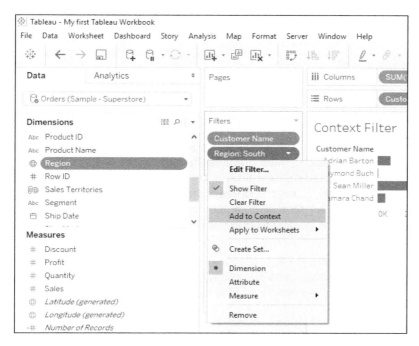

8. Once we do that, the Blue pill for the **Region** filter will become gray in color and it will automatically be shifted above the **Customer Name** filter. Refer to the following image:

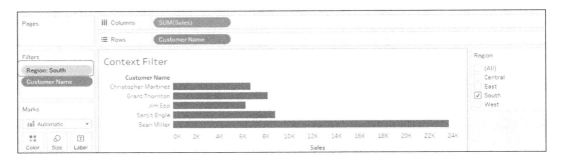

9. Now, even though the earlier selection of **Region** filter is still showing **South**, our view however has been updated to give us exactly five **Customer Names**. Thus, whichever Region we select henceforth in this quick filter, the graph will always show us exactly five **Customer Names**, that is, the top 5 for the selection. Refer to the following image:

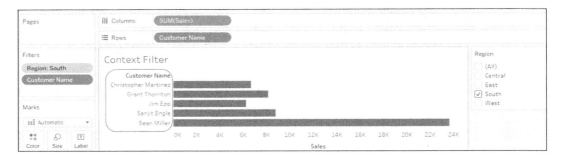

How it works...

In the preceding recipe, we displayed the Top 5 customers by creating a **Filter**. We could have also used the **Set** that we had created previously to find out the Top five customers. Further, in the preceding recipe, we used **Context filter** along with a **Filter**. We can also use it with **Sets**. The point to remember here is that the **Context filter** will take precedence over the rest of the filters and the other filters will then be computed on the basis of the **Context filter**. Further, we can have more than one Context filter in our view.

 Context filters can help us improve the performance of our workbook. However, if our data set is heavily indexed, context filters may actually result in slower query performance.

5

Adding Flavor – Creating Calculated Fields

In this chapter, we will be covering the following topics:

- ▸ Creating string calculations
- ▸ Creating arithmetic calculations
- ▸ Creating date calculations
- ▸ Creating logic calculations
- ▸ Using Sets in calculations
- ▸ Understanding Table Calculations
- ▸ Understanding Level of Detail (LOD) Calculations
- ▸ Understanding INCLUDE LOD
- ▸ Understanding EXCLUDE LOD
- ▸ Understanding FIXED LOD
- ▸ Understanding how to create and use Parameters

Introduction

In the previous chapter, we saw how to slice and dice our data. In this chapter, we will focus on creating calculated fields in Tableau to give us more flexibility and power. We will also learn how to make use of some predefined calculations and how one can change the scope and direction of these calculations to in turn affect the final result. We will then learn how to empower the end user by giving them the flexibility to pass values, which can then be called in the outcome by creating parameters.

Understanding how to create and use Calculations

When working with data, we may come across situations where we may want to go beyond what is available from our data. There are times when the fields available in our data won't be enough to fulfill our requirements. For example, our data may have fields such as Selling price and Cost price. However, we may want to find out how much profit we made. Also, we may want to conditionally format our view to highlight losses. In these cases, it makes sense to create computed fields on the data fields and use them in our analysis.

On a broad level, we will classify our calculations into four categories as follows:

- String Calculations

- Arithmetic Calculations

- Date Calculations

- Logic Calculations

In order to create a calculated field, we can click on the dropdown or right-click on any **Dimension** or **Measure** and select the option of **Create | Calculated Field...**. Refer to the following screenshot:

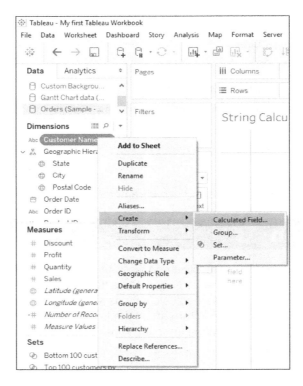

Another option to create a calculated field is from the toolbar. Select **Analysis | Create Calculated Field...**. Refer to the following screenshot:

One more option to create a calculated field is by clicking on the dropdown from the **Dimensions** pane and then selecting the option of **Create Calculated Field...**. Refer to the following screenshot:

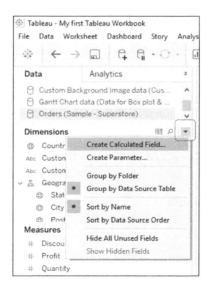

Once we select any of the previously mentioned options, we will get a new dialog box, as shown in the following screenshot:

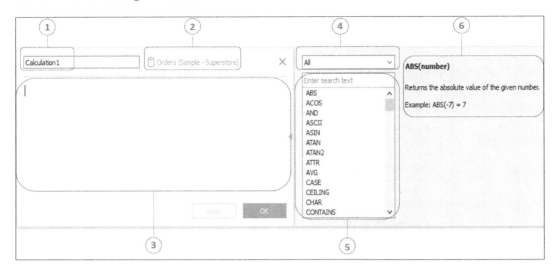

The preceding screenshot shows the calculation dialog box. The top section is where we give a name to our calculation *(ref. annotation 1)*. The next highlighted section *(ref. annotation 2)* is the data source that we are currently connected to. The type in box *(ref. annotation 3)*, is the place where we will type our calculation or formulae. We can either drag and drop our fields from the **Dimensions** or **Measures** pane or simply start typing the field name and Tableau will auto suggest to help us pick up the relevant field. The next highlighted section *(ref. annotation 4)* is the list of various types of calculations such as number, string, date, logical, type conversion, and so on. Now, when we select the type of calculation as String from this list, then we will get the list of all the Functions classified as string functions in the list below, *(ref. annotation 5)*. The highlighted section *(ref. annotation 5)*, is basically the list of all the Functions that are available in Tableau. We will build our calculation logic using functions from this list. However, in order to use a particular function, we need to use it in the right syntax and that syntax is made readily available to us in the highlighted section labeled as *(ref. annotation 6)*. When we select any particular Function, then we will get to see the syntax of that Function, an explanation as to what that Function does, along with an example in the highlighted section labeled as *(ref. annotation 6)*. This is more of a quick help section to understand more about each function in terms of what it does, how to use it, and examples to give better clarity about using that function.

When we create a calculated field, then depending on the output, the calculated field will either be a **Dimension** or a **Measure**.

Also, any calculated field in Tableau will be shown with **=** as a prefix icon. This helps us quickly differentiate between the fields that are coming from our data and the fields that are computed in Tableau.

Having said that, when we connect to any data, by default we will see a field called **Number of Records** with **=** as a prefix icon. As mentioned in earlier chapters, this is a default pre-computed field that shows us the number of records that we are dealing with after we have connected to our data.

Now that we know how to create calculated fields in Tableau, let's get to actually creating different types of Calculations.

 Please remember that all the calculations that we create in Tableau will stay in the Tableau workbook and will not be written back to your database. By default, Tableau Desktop is a *read-only* tool with no write back functionality.

Creating string calculations

There are times when we are required to do some manipulations on fields that are stored as strings. Typical calculations that we may do on strings are as follows:

- Concatenating separate strings into a single string or separate a string into smaller substrings
- Changing the letter case (upper case to lower case and vice versa)
- Extracting parts of the string to find certain substrings or find the position of a particular character or trim the string from a particular point

In the following recipe, let's do some string manipulations to create new calculated fields.

Getting ready

For the following recipe, we will use the **Customer Name** field from the **Orders** sheet from `Sample - Superstore.xlsx` data and we will continue working in the same workbook, `My first Tableau Workbook`.

Let us get started by creating a fresh new sheet.

How to do it...

1. Let us create a new sheet by pressing *Ctrl + M* and rename it **String Calculation**.

2. We will then drag the **Customer Name** field from the **Dimensions** pane and drop it into the **Rows** shelf. We will get a long list of 793 Customers, as shown in the following screenshot:

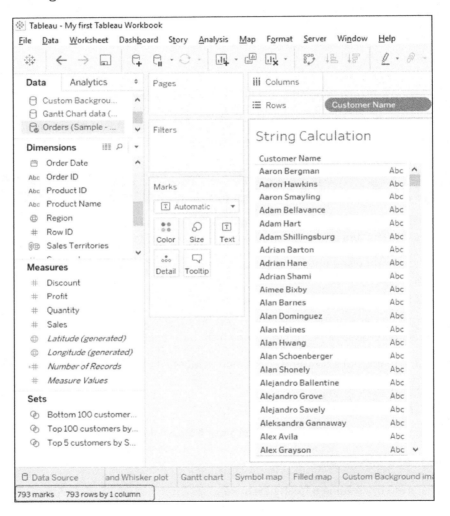

3. The **Customer Name** field returns a name per Customer. Next, let us right-click on the **Customer Name** field in the **Dimensions** pane and select the **Transform | Split** option. This action will result in two new **Dimensions** being created called **Customer Name - Split 1** and **Customer Name - Split 2**. Refer to the following screenshot:

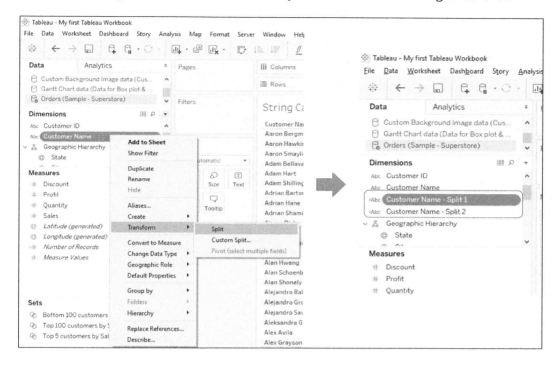

4. These two new calculations are actually the substring of the original field and if we pull these new fields in the view, we will see that **Customer Name - Split 1** is giving us **First Name of the Customer** and **Customer Name - Split 2** is giving us **Last Name** of the **Customer**. Thus, as a next step, we will rename **Customer Name - Split 1** as **Customer First Name** and **Customer Name - Split 2** as **Customer Last Name** by clicking on the dropdown or right clicking on each of the new fields in the **Dimension** shelf and selecting the **Rename** option. Also, if we look carefully, both these new fields are shown with **=Abc** as a prefix icon, which indicates that these are computed fields in Tableau and are of the string datatype. In order to understand what logic is being used to generate these fields, we will click on the dropdown or **right click** on these fields in the **Dimensions** pane and select the **Edit...** option. Once we do that, we will get to see the formula used by Tableau. Refer to the following screenshot:

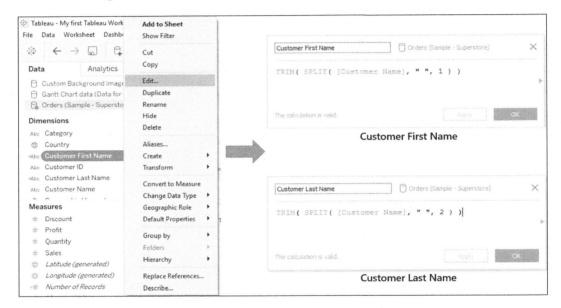

5. What Tableau did when we used the Split function, is that it auto-computed two calculated fields for us. Now, let us see how we can use these new calculations. Let us drag the **Customer First Name** field by dragging it from the **Dimensions** pane and dropping it into the **Rows** shelf. Make sure to place it before the **Customer Name** field, which is already present in the **Rows** shelf. Refer to the following screenshot:

6. When we do that, we get to see that there are three customers with the first name Aaron, three customers with the first name Adam, and so on.

7. Next, let us remove the **Customer Name** field from the **Rows** shelf. When we do that, we will notice that the number of rows now reduces from 793 to 338. Check the status bar. Refer to the following screenshot:

8. This is because Tableau will always give us unique records. Once we remove the Customer Name field, first names such as Aaron and Adam become unique.

9. Next, let us extend this recipe to further understand how to concatenate Strings. Let us drag the **Customer ID** field from the **Dimensions** pane and drop it into the **Rows** shelf, right next to the **Customer First Name** field. We will now see the number of rows increases to 793. This is because each **Customer ID** is unique to each **Customer Name**.

10. As a next step, we will now concatenate the **Customer First Name** and **Customer ID** field to create a single field called **Concatenated string**. To do so, we will right click on the **Customer First Name** field and select **Create Calculated Field...**. Let us name this calculation as **Concatenated string**.

11. There is no default function for concatenation in Tableau. However, concatenation is nothing but addition. So, we will use the **+** operator by typing it from our keyboard, followed by dragging the **Customer ID** field from the **Dimensions** pane and dropping it into the calculated field dialog box. Refer to the following screenshot:

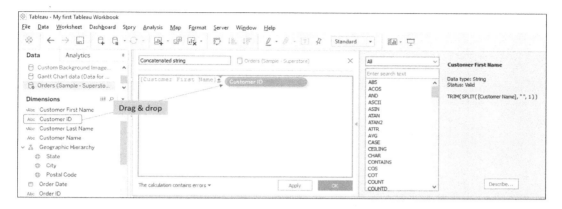

12. When we are done fetching the **Customer ID** field into the calculation box, we will see the following text, which in the preceding screenshot reads as **The calculation contains errors** and then is changed to **The calculation is valid**. Refer to the following screenshot:

13. So, our calculation as of now reads *[Customer First Name]+[Customer ID]*.

14. Let us click **OK** and we will find our new calculated field in the **Dimensions** pane. Let us drag this new calculated field and drop it into the **Rows** shelf, just right after our existing fields, to get a view as shown in the following screenshot:

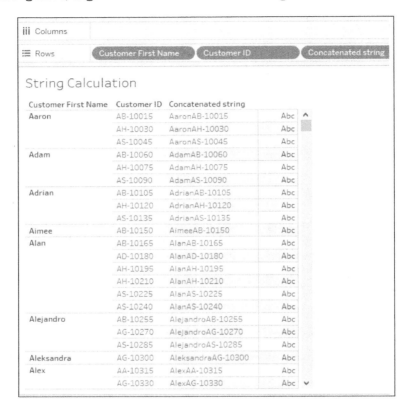

How it works...

In the preceding recipe, we did two things. Firstly, we used the **Split** function in Tableau to extract part of the entire string to get a substring that gave us two new calculations called **Customer First Name** and **Customer Last Name**. Since this was a shortcut functionality that was quickly available, we used the same. However, the exact same formula that Tableau has auto-computed for us could also have been written from scratch in the **Create Calculated Field...** window.

Next, after we got the **Customer First Name** and **Customer Last Name** fields, we then concatenated the **Customer First Name** and **Customer ID** field using a **+** operator to create a single field called **Concatenated string**.

Now, the **Customer ID** field in our data is alphanumeric and Tableau is treating it as a String data type. However, imagine if the **Customer ID** field had numeric values, Tableau would treat it as an Integer data type. In that case, if we tried concatenating the **Customer First Name** and **Customer ID** fields using a **+** operator, Tableau would throw an error that would prohibit us from adding a String field (**Customer First Name**) and an Integer field (**Customer ID**).

In order to resolve this kind of data type mismatch issue, we can simply do a **Type Conversion** on **Customer ID** and convert it into String. We could use the STR() function and our calculation would be updated as *[Customer First Name]+STR([Customer ID])*.

To understand the various String functions available in Tableau, please refer to http://onlinehelp.tableau.com/current/pro/desktop/en-us/functions_ functions_string.html.

Creating arithmetic calculations

In the previous recipe, we looked at String manipulations. In this section, let us focus on manipulations on numbers. However, before we move to arithmetic calculations, we must first understand the difference between aggregated and disaggregated measures. To elaborate on this, let us see an example. The two formulae are *SUM(Profit) / SUM(Sales)* and *SUM(Profit / Sales)*.

The question is, whether these two formulae will give the same result or will they give different results?

From what we have learnt in school, we know that the **Bracket operations** or **Parentheses** will be computed first. We know this methodology as **PEMDAS** (**Parentheses, Exponents, Multiply, Divide, Add**, **Subtract**). Since many people tend to say brackets instead of parentheses and orders instead of exponents, it is also referred to as **BODMAS** (**Brackets, Orders, Divide, Multiply, Add, Subtract**) or **BEDMAS** (**Brackets, Exponents, Divide, Multiply, Add, Subtract**).

Based on this knowledge, we can clearly say that the output of the previously listed formulae will be different.

In the first formula, which is *SUM(Profit) / SUM(Sales)*, the way the formula will be executed is as follows:

1. Compute **SUM(Profit)**.
2. Compute **SUM(Sales)**.
3. Divide **SUM(Profit)** by **SUM(Sales)**.

However, in the second formula, which is *SUM(Profit / Sales)*, the execution will be as follows:

1. Divide Profit by Sales (that is, divide transactional Profit by transactional Sales).
2. SUM(Profit divided by Sales) (that is, sum up all the transactional output values from the previous step).

To put this in a more simplistic way, in the first calculation, the individual measures are first aggregated by doing a summation of all the rows of Profit and all the rows for Sales and the aggregated Profit is then divided by the aggregated Sales. However, in the second calculation, each and every single transactional Profit value is first divided by the respective transactional Sales and then added up.

Let us actually try this example out in Tableau to gain more perspective.

Getting ready

As usual, let us continue with our existing workbook by creating a new worksheet. We will use the **Profit** field and **Sales** field from the **Orders** sheet from `Sample - Superstore.xlsx` data. As stated in the preceding example, we will divide Profit by Sales in two ways using the formulae listed previously. Let us get started.

How to do it...

1. Let us create a new sheet by pressing *Ctrl + M* and rename it **Arithmetic Calculation**. We will then drag the **Sub-Category** field from the **Dimensions** pane and drop it into the **Rows** shelf.

2. Next, let us double-click on **Profit** from the **Measures** pane. Followed by double clicking on **Sales** from the **Measures** pane. Once we have done that, we should get the following view:

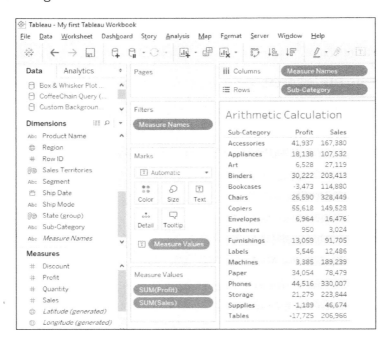

3. We will now create a new calculated field by right clicking on the **Profit** field and selecting the option of **Create Calculated Field...**.

4. Let us name this Calculation as **Profit Margin-disaggregated**. The formula that we will type is as follows: *SUM([Profit] / [Sales])*.

5. Making sure that we aren't missing any brackets or parentheses, we will check for any error messages. If it says **The calculation is valid**, we will click **OK**.

6. We will now look for this new field in the **Measures** pane and double click on it. Our view will update, as shown in the following screenshot:

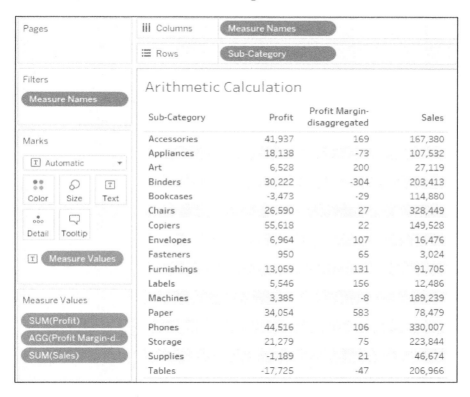

Sub-Category	Profit	Profit Margin-disaggregated	Sales
Accessories	41,937	169	167,380
Appliances	18,138	-73	107,532
Art	6,528	200	27,119
Binders	30,222	-304	203,413
Bookcases	-3,473	-29	114,880
Chairs	26,590	27	328,449
Copiers	55,618	22	149,528
Envelopes	6,964	107	16,476
Fasteners	950	65	3,024
Furnishings	13,059	131	91,705
Labels	5,546	156	12,486
Machines	3,385	-8	189,239
Paper	34,054	583	78,479
Phones	44,516	106	330,007
Storage	21,279	75	223,844
Supplies	-1,189	21	46,674
Tables	-17,725	-47	206,966

7. We will rearrange the display of **Measures** in the view by dragging **AGG(Profit Margin-disaggregated)** and placing it after the **SUM(Sales)** field in the **Measure Value** shelf just below the **Marks** card. Refer to the following updated screenshot:

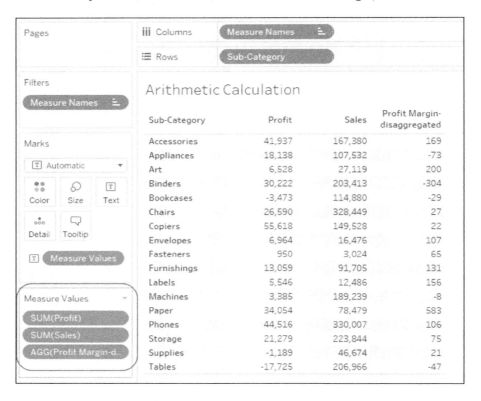

8. If you look closely, the second row, that is, **Appliances**, has **Profit** of **18,138** and **Sales** of **107,532**. When we divide this **Profit** value by the **Sales** value, the output should be **0.17**. However, we are getting an output as **-73**. This is strange from two perspectives. Firstly, how can division of two positive numbers return a negative value? Secondly, we are dividing a smaller number by a larger number and hence should get a decimal value.

9. If we look carefully in the **Measure Values** shelf, the original fields are called **SUM(Profit)** and **SUM(Sales)**. Whereas in our calculation, which is **SUM([Profit] / [Sales])**, we are asking Tableau to compute a **Profit** divide by **Sales** for each transaction and then add it up at each **Sub-Category** level. Whereas, what we actually wanted to do was to divide **SUM(Profit)** for each Sub-Category and divide it by **SUM(Sales)** for that **Sub-Category**. Thus, we will create another calculated field and name it **Profit Margin-aggregated**.

10. The formula will be: *SUM([Profit]) / SUM([Sales])*. We will click **OK** and then call this new field in the view by double clicking on it. The view will be as shown in the following screenshot:

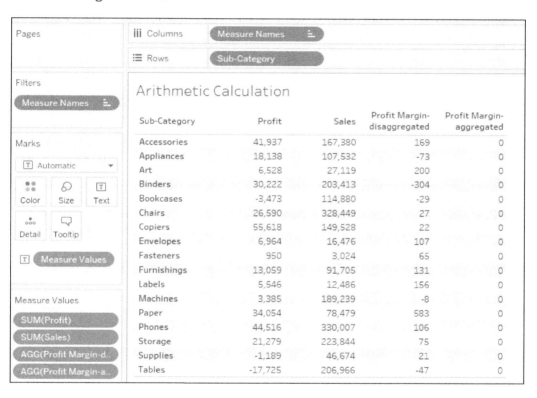

Sub-Category	Profit	Sales	Profit Margin-disaggregated	Profit Margin-aggregated
Accessories	41,937	167,380	169	0
Appliances	18,138	107,532	-73	0
Art	6,528	27,119	200	0
Binders	30,222	203,413	-304	0
Bookcases	-3,473	114,880	-29	0
Chairs	26,590	328,449	27	0
Copiers	55,618	149,528	22	0
Envelopes	6,964	16,476	107	0
Fasteners	950	3,024	65	0
Furnishings	13,059	91,705	131	0
Labels	5,546	12,486	156	0
Machines	3,385	189,239	-8	0
Paper	34,054	78,479	583	0
Phones	44,516	330,007	106	0
Storage	21,279	223,844	75	0
Supplies	-1,189	46,674	21	0
Tables	-17,725	206,966	-47	0

11. Once we do that, we will notice that all the displayed values are zero. This is because even though the output is a decimal number, Tableau by default rounds it off to the closest integer. Thus, in order to change the format, we will click on the dropdown of the **Profit Margin-aggregated** field in the **Measure Values** shelf and select the **Format** option. Once we do that, we will get a **Format** section on the left-hand side, just where we earlier had our **Dimensions** and **Measures** pane. Refer to the following screenshot:

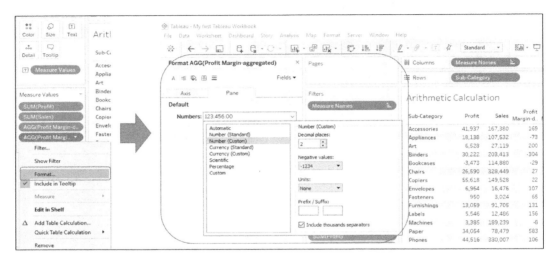

12. In the **Format** section from the **Numbers** dropdown, we will select the **Number (Custom)** option. Our view will then update, as shown in the following screenshot:

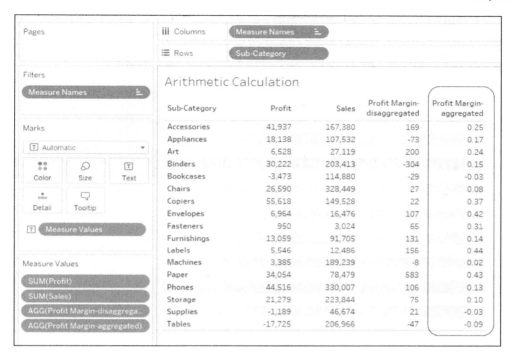

Sub-Category	Profit	Sales	Profit Margin-disaggregated	Profit Margin-aggregated
Accessories	41,937	167,380	169	0.25
Appliances	18,138	107,532	-73	0.17
Art	6,528	27,119	200	0.24
Binders	30,222	203,413	-304	0.15
Bookcases	-3,473	114,880	-29	-0.03
Chairs	26,590	328,449	27	0.08
Copiers	55,618	149,528	22	0.37
Envelopes	6,964	16,476	107	0.42
Fasteners	950	3,024	65	0.31
Furnishings	13,059	91,705	131	0.14
Labels	5,546	12,486	156	0.44
Machines	3,385	189,239	-8	0.02
Paper	34,054	78,479	583	0.43
Phones	44,516	330,007	106	0.13
Storage	21,279	223,844	75	0.10
Supplies	-1,189	46,674	21	-0.03
Tables	-17,725	206,966	-47	-0.09

How it works...

In the **Profit Margin-aggregated** calculation, we are asking Tableau to first compute a **SUM([Profit])** for each **Sub-Category** and compute **SUM([Sales])** for the same **Sub-Category** and then divide the two, whereas, as explained earlier in the **Profit Margin-disaggregated** calculation, we are dividing transactional **Profit by transactional Sales** for every record that is contributing to a particular **Sub-Category**. These transactional values are then added up at the **Sub-Category** level.

Also, notice both the calculations in the **Measure Values** shelf. We will see **AGG** as a prefix and it stands for **Aggregated**. Since we are using **SUM** in both the calculations, it is **Aggregated**. By default, all the fields will be aggregated in Tableau.

The point of this whole exercise was to clarify the difference between a field, say **Profit**, and an aggregated field, say **SUM(Profit)**, and how this can make or break our calculations. We need to remember that when we say just **Profit**, we are referring to the transactional **Profit** and when we say **SUM(Profit)**, we are referring to the **Aggregated Profit**.

In case we wish to turn off the default aggregation properties of Tableau for a particular sheet, then we can do so by unchecking the **Aggregate Measures** option from **Analysis** in the toolbar. For more information on **aggregating** and **disaggregating data**.

Creating date calculations

Working with Dates is an essential part of any analysis. However, it can also be tricky and messy at times depending how dates are stored in the databases and what manipulation we need to do on them. Typical analysis on Dates is to find out Sales trends over a period of time or what the year over year growth has been. For a customer centric organization, Date calculations will be useful for understanding the customer's buying patterns. Taking this point ahead, let us do some calculations to find out the First purchase date and the Last purchase date of customers. We will then use the Last purchase date to find the out how long it has been since the customers last purchased from us.

Let us see how this can be done in the following recipe.

Getting ready

For this recipe, we will work on the Order Date field and the Customer Name field from the **Orders** sheet of `Sample - Superstore.xlsx` data. We will continue working in our existing workbook. Let's get started with the recipe.

How to do it...

1. Let us create a new sheet by pressing *Ctrl + M* and rename it **Date Calculation**.
2. We will start by dragging **Customer Name** from the **Dimensions** pane and dropping it into the **Rows** shelf. Next, we will right click and drag the **Order Date** field from the **Dimensions** pane and drop it into the **Rows** shelf, just right after the **Customer Name**. Let us make sure to select the **MDY(Order Date)**:

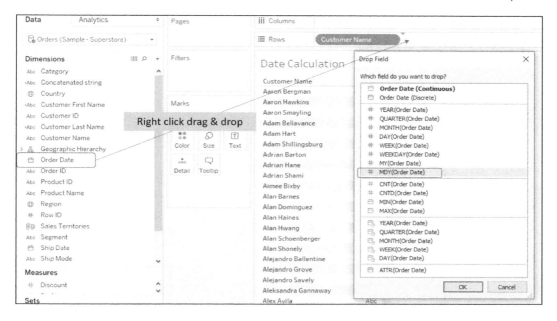

3. This action will give us the actual dates on which the Customer has placed an order with us. However, instead of looking at all the transaction dates of a Customer, it would be great if we can quickly find the First purchase date and the Last purchase date of these customers. Now, to do so, let us right click on the **Order Date** field in the **Dimensions** pane and select the option of **Create Calculated Field....** Let us name this calculation as **First purchase date**.

4. **First purchase date** is the date when the customer made their first transaction and to find this **First purchase date**, we will take the Minimum of **Order Date**. Thus, our formula will be *MIN([Order Date])*.

5. Similarly, the **Last purchase date** is the date when the customer made their last transaction and to find this **Last purchase date**, we will take the Maximum of **Order Date**. Thus, our formula will be *MAX([Order Date])*.

6. Refer to the following screenshot:

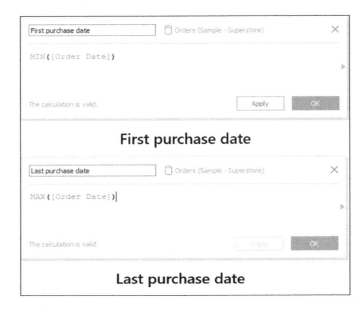

First purchase date

Last purchase date

7. Now that we have both these calculations ready, let us use them in our view. We will find these calculations in the **Measures** shelf. Let us drag and drop the **First purchase date** and **Last purchase date** into the **Rows** shelf. Also, let us remove the **MDY(Order Date)** pill from the **Rows** shelf. Our view will be updated, as shown in the following screenshot:

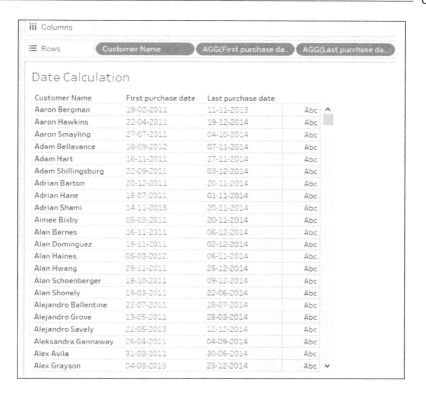

8. Now that we have the **First purchase date** and the **Last purchase date** of the customers, let us also find out how long it has been since the customers last purchased from us. Now, what we want is essentially the difference in days between the customer's last purchase date and today. However, the data that we are using has information only till December 31, 2014. So, if we take the difference between the last purchase date and today, we will get huge difference in days, which won't make sense. However, we can tweak the logic a little and try to find out how long it has been since the customers last purchased from us as of December 31, 2014 instead of today. To do so, let us create a new calculated field and name it **Days since last purchase**.

9. We will use the DATEDIFF function in Tableau. The formula is *DATEDIFF('day', [Last purchase date], #2014-12-31#)*.

10. Refer to the following screenshot:

11. After clicking **OK**, we will drag this new calculation from the **Measures** pane and drop it into the **Columns** shelf. The view will be updated, as shown in the following screenshot:

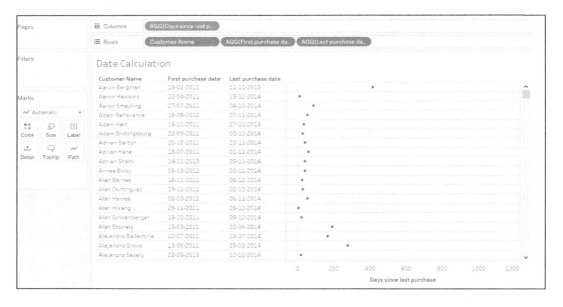

12. Let us convert this chart to a bar chart by selecting the **Bar** option from the dropdown in the **Marks** card. Refer to the following screenshot:

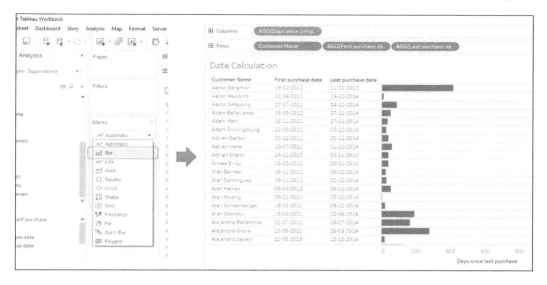

13. For the last and final step, let us sort the customers in descending order by **Days since last purchase**, using the shortcut option from the toolbar, and let us also enable the filter of **Days since last purchase** by clicking on the dropdown of **Days since last purchase** from the **Column** shelf and selecting the **Show Filter** option. Refer to the following screenshot:

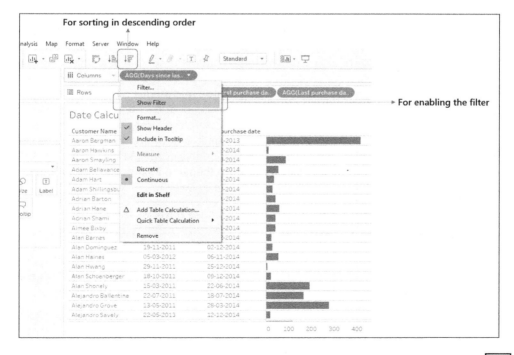

14. Once we do that, let us also quickly enable the labels on the bars by selecting the **Show Mark Labels** option in the toolbar. Refer to the following screenshot:

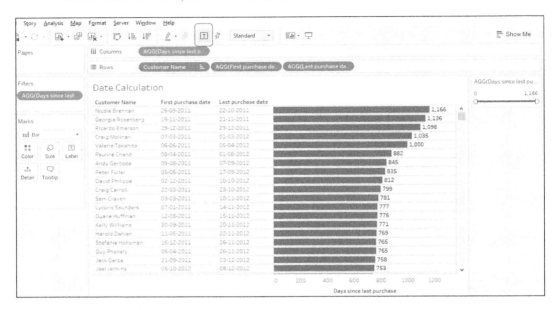

How it works...

In the preceding recipe, we created two calculations: the **First purchase date** and the **Last purchase date**. We created both the calculations from scratch by using the **Create Calculated Field...** option on the **Order Date** field. However, as an alternate approach, we could have only created the **First purchase date** calculations from scratch by using the **Create Calculated Field...** option on the **Order Date** field and then duplicated and modified the same to get the **Last purchase date**. In order to use the alternate approach of duplicating and then modifying the existing calculation, all we had to do was to right click on the **First purchase date** field and then select the **Duplicate** option, which would result in a new calculated field called **First purchase date (copy)**. We could then simply right click on this copy field and select the **Edit...** option and change the name from **First purchase date (copy)** to **Last purchase date** and modify the Formula from *MIN([Order Date])* to *MAX ([Order Date])*.

After finding the **First purchase date** and the **Last purchase date**, we then created another calculation called **Days since last purchase** by using the DATEDIFF function in Tableau. This DATEDIFF function helps us specify the date part, which essentially helps us compute the difference in two dates in terms of years, months, days, and so on. In the preceding recipe, we fixed our end date as December 31, 2014. Thus, in the preceding recipe, we can see that it has been 1,166 days since Nicole Brennan has last purchased from us as of December 31, 2014.

Currently, we are seeing a long list of all the customers. However, if we want to narrow our focus on let's say only the customers whose last purchase date with us has been more than 30 days or more than 60 days or maybe even more than 365 days as of 31st December 31, 2014, then we can use the filter control to get a list of only the relevant customers.

Tableau offers a wide variety of Date functions. To understand more about these, refer to `http://onlinehelp.tableau.com/current/pro/desktop/en-us/functions_ functions_date.html`.

Creating logic calculations

In the previous recipes, we have looked at different calculations such as string, arithmetic, and date calculations. In this section, we will focus on the Logic statements. These are typically **IF....ELSE** statements or **CASE** statements.

Imagine having to conditionally format your data to highlight products having actual sales less than the target value. In order to address this requirement, we need to make use of Logic statements. These logic statements will execute a certain expression once a condition is met or else it will execute another expression.

Let's get started with Logic statements in Tableau.

Getting ready

Let's take an example where we will try to conditionally color code/highlight the product Sub-Categories that are having Sales less than 100K. We will use the fields from the **Orders** sheet of `Sample - Superstore.xlsx` data and as usual, continue working in our existing workbook. Let's see how we can achieve the previously stated objective.

How to do it...

1. Let us create a new sheet by pressing *Ctrl + M* and rename it `Logic Calculation-IF...ELSE`.

2. We will first drag and drop the **Sub-Category** field into the **Columns** shelf, followed by dragging and dropping the **Sales** field into the **Rows** shelf. This will result in a vertical bar chart, as shown in the following screenshot:

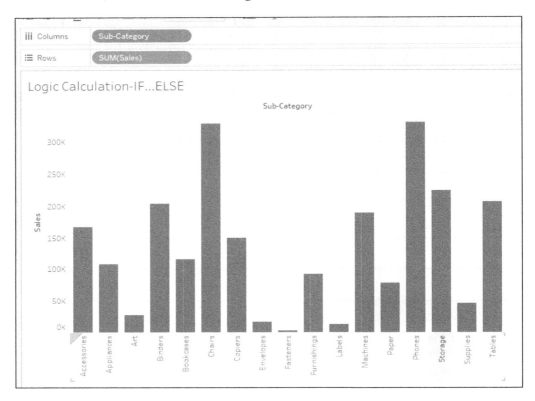

3. Now, for conditionally highlighting Sub-Categories having Sales below 100K, we will create a new calculated field called **Is Sales < 100K?** and we will type the following formula: *IF [Sales] < 100000 THEN 'Below 100K' ELSE 'Above 100K' END*.

4. Let us then click on **OK**. This new calculated field can now be found in the **Dimensions** pane. Now, in order to color code the bars, we will get this new field in the **Color** shelf in the **Marks** card and once we do that, we will get the following view:

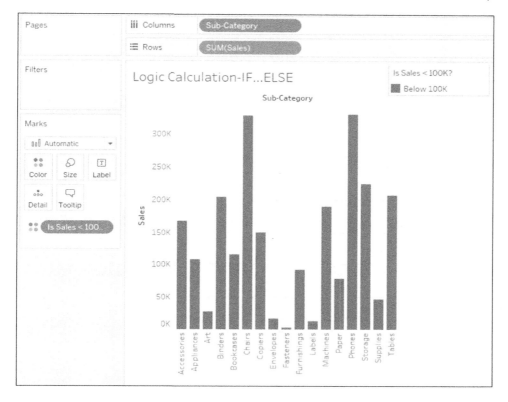

5. The view looks the same as it was earlier. However, if we notice closely, we will see a **color legend** that says **Below 100K**. This is strange as we can clearly see that there are plenty of Sub-Categories having Sales above 100K. For example, **Accessories, Appliances, Binders, Bookcases, Chairs**, and so on. Clearly, there is something amiss. So, let us revisit our calculation by right clicking on the **Is Sales < 100K?** calculation in the **Dimensions** pane and selecting the **Edit...** option.

6. Once we do that, we will see that our calculation says *IF [Sales] < 100000 THEN 'Below 100K' ELSE 'Above 100K' END*. However, if we look at our *Y axis*, by referring to the **Rows** shelf, then we will see that it is showing **SUM(Sales)**. This is exactly what we had seen earlier, that is, difference between **Sales** and **SUM(Sales)** or difference between disaggregated and aggregated fields. Thus, when we say Sales, we are referring to the transactional Sales and if we look at our raw data, we will see that each transactional Sale is less than 100K. So, let us quickly modify our formula and change it to *IF SUM([Sales]) < 100000 THEN 'Below 100K' ELSE 'Above 100K' END*.

7. Refer to the following screenshot:

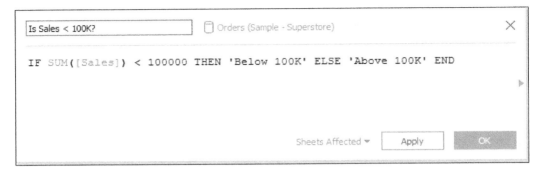

8. Once we click **OK**, we will see that our view is faded out. Refer to the following screenshot:

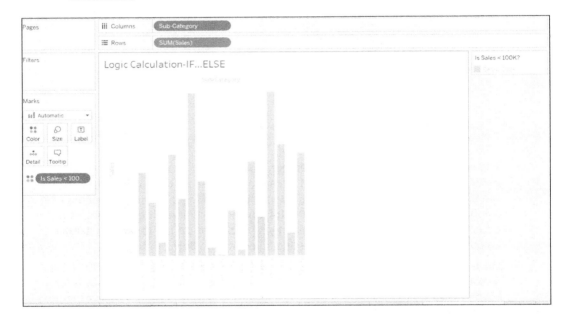

9. This is because we have changed the properties of our calculation. The calculation was previously a **Dimension**, but since we are aggregating the calculation by using **SUM**, it becomes a **Measure**. Thus, let us drag the **Is Sales < 100K?** field from the **Measures** pane and drop it into the **Color** shelf. Once we do that, we get the view, as shown in the following screenshot:

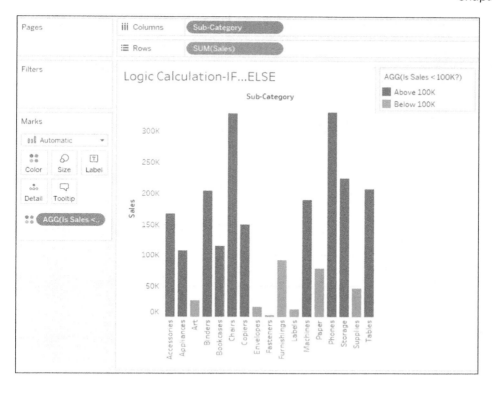

10. So, in the current view, all the orange bars are Sub-Categories having **Sales** below 100K and all the blue bars are Sub-Categories having **Sales** above 100K.

11. In the preceding calculation, we had only two conditions and hence an **IF...ELSE** function worked. However, in case we have multiple conditions then the **IF...ELSE** function will have to be extended to an **IF...ELSEIF** function. Let us quickly look at one example of an **IF...ELSEIF** function by duplicating the existing sheet and renaming it **Logic Calculation-IF...ELSEIF**.

12. Let us then create a new calculated field called **Sales bins** and the formula will be as follows:

```
IF SUM([Sales])<100000 THEN '<100K'
ELSEIF SUM([Sales])>=100000 AND SUM([Sales])<=200000  THEN
'100K-200K'
ELSE '>200K'
END
```

13. Let us click **OK** and then get this field into the **color** shelf. Our view will then update, as shown in the following screenshot:

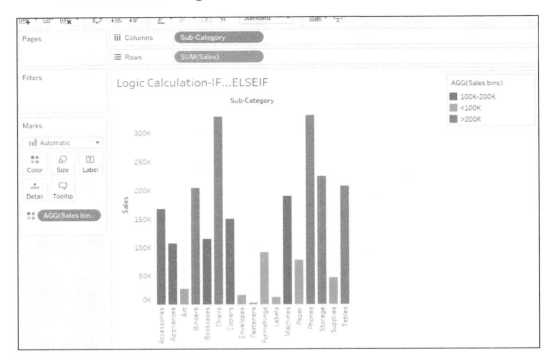

How it works...

In the preceding recipe, we saw how to use the **IF...ELSE** function as well as the **IF...ELSEIF** function. An important point to remember is the difference between **ELSEIF** and **ELSE IF**. In the latter case, another **IF** statement will be computed within the first **IF** statement.

Another important point to remember is that every **IF** function that we use needs to be terminated using an **END** function and hence, in the latter case, there will be two **END** functions as we are starting another **IF** statement within the first.

Also, when we used the **IF...ELSEIF** function, we used an **AND** operator. Some of the other operators that can be used are **OR**, **NOT**, and so on.

To know more about the **Operators**, please refer to http://onlinehelp.tableau.com/current/pro/desktop/en-us/functions_operators.html.

To know more about **Logical functions**, please refer to `http://onlinehelp.tableau.com/current/pro/desktop/en-us/functions_functions_logical.html`.

 Please note that neither the Functions nor the Operators are case sensitive in Tableau. Only the data fields are case sensitive. For example, *sales* and *Sales* will be treated as two different fields in Tableau.

Using sets in calculations

In the previous chapter, we learnt what Sets are and how to create and use them. We saw an example of **Top 5 customers by Sales**. When we use this set, we can either use it as **IN/OUT**, which is a Boolean output, and which when used in our view, will give us two **In** and **Out** headers, or we can use it as **Show Members in Set**, which will only give us the names of our top five customers and filter the rest of the customers.

Now, what if we don't want to filter any customer, but instead group the customers who don't belong in the top five set (that is, the **Out** customers) under one header called **Others**? So, what we essentially want to show is the names of the top five customers by sales, that is, all the **In** customers and the rest of the customers to be grouped as **Others**.

Since we already have a set that gives us the customers belonging to the top five list and which customers do not belong to that list, we will use this set and achieve our objective. This is one example of how we can use a Set in the calculation.

Let us see how this can be done.

Getting ready

For this recipe, we will use our **Set** named **Top 5 customers by Sales**, which we created in the previous chapter. As discussed, we will use this set to show the names of the top five customers and group the rest of the members as **Others**. Since we already have created the set on the `Sample - Superstore.xlsx` data, we will continue using the same dataset and create a new sheet in our existing workbook.

Let's get started.

How to do it...

1. We will begin by creating a new sheet and rename it **Sets in Calculation**.

2. We will then right click on the **Set** named **Top 5 customers by Sales** from the **Sets** pane (just below the **Dimensions** and **Measures** pane) and select the option of **Create Calculated Field...**.

3. Let us name this calculation **Top 5 + Others** and type *IF [Top 5 customers by Sales] THEN [Customer Name] ELSE 'Others' END*.

4. Refer to the following screenshot:

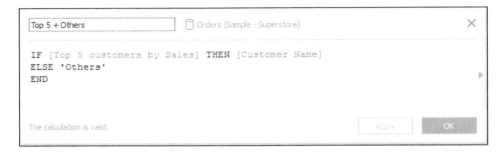

5. Let's click on **OK** and then drag this new calculated field from the **Dimensions** pane and drop it into the **Rows** shelf followed by dragging and dropping the **Sales** field in the **Text** shelf. Refer to the following screenshot:

6. For the final finishing touch, let us sort this view in a way that **Others** is shown at the very bottom of the list. We can use the ascending sorting option from the toolbar. Refer to the following screenshot:

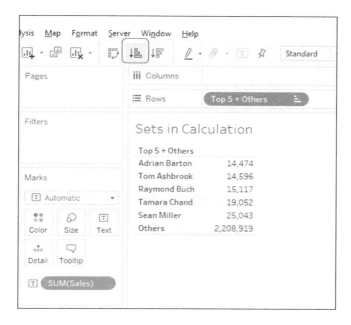

How it works...

What we saw was one example of using a **Set** in a calculation field. The logic that we used was fairly simple. All that we did was use a **Logic** statement, which basically tested whether the Customer was **In** the set or **Out** of the set. If the condition was true, then we fetched the names of the customers, or else we created a label called **Others**.

Understanding Table Calculations

Table calculations are one of the advanced levels of calculations available in Tableau. They are also one of the most powerful features of Tableau. The reason for calling them **Table Calculations** is because we can define the **scope** and **direction** of the calculation based on the table/view.

To elaborate this point further, let's take a look at an example. See the following screenshot:

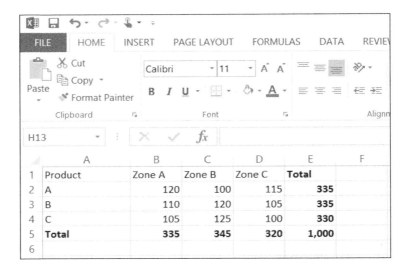

The preceding screenshot shows the value of three products sold across three zones. The information is arranged in a crosstab manner where the zones are placed in the columns and products are placed in the rows. Also shown are the Row Totals, that is, totals for each product across all the zones and Column Totals, that is, totals for each zone across all the products and finally we also have the Grand Total, which is the total for the entire view, that is, across all products and across all the zones.

Now, if we want to show percentages instead of just looking at the absolute numbers, we would have to do a simple calculation, where we would divide each value with the total value. However, the dilemma is that there are three different total values and each division will give us separate results, so which total value do we use?

Well, the answer depends completely on the business question. So, say the questions were as follows:

- What percentage of sales is contributed by each product in a particular zone?
- What percentage of sales is contributed by each zone for a particular product?
- What is the percentage of total sales for each product in each zone?

For the preceding set of questions, and the way the table is currently structured, that is, zones in columns and products in rows, we would use the **Column Total**, **Row Total**, and **Grand Total**, respectively.

Now, imagine swapping the Rows and Columns. Refer to the following screenshot:

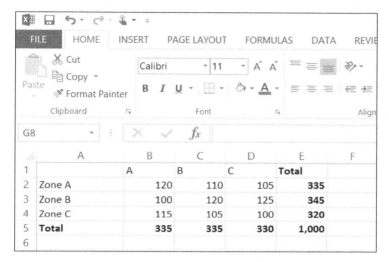

The screenshot shows products as columns and zones as rows. In this case, our selections of total would change. We will use Row Total for the first question, Column Total for the second, and finally the Grand Total for the third question.

Thus, we have seen how certain calculations will have to be modified depending on the way the table or the view is structured.

Now that we have understood this example, let us recreate a similar view in Tableau and understand **Table calculations** in a bit more detail.

Getting ready

We will use the **Sales**, **Region**, and **Category** field from the **Orders** sheet of `Sample - Superstore.xlsx` data for the following recipe. Let us get started.

How to do it...

1. We will begin by creating a new sheet and renaming it **Table Calculations-percent of total**.

2. Let us then drag the **Category** field from the **Dimensions** pane and drop it into the **Rows** shelf. Followed by dragging the **Region** field and dropping it into the **Columns** shelf.

3. Next, let us drag and drop **Sales** into the **Text** shelf.

4. Once we do that, let us then make sure to enable both the **Row Totals** as well as **Column Totals** from the **Analysis** tab in the toolbar or the **Analytics** pane. Refer to the following screenshot:

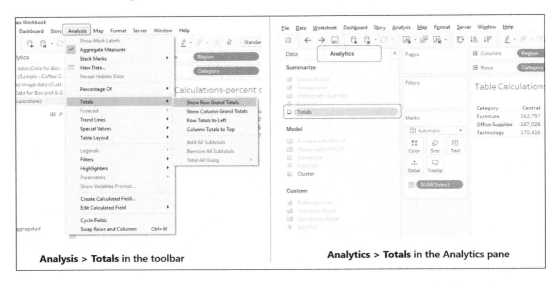

Analysis > Totals in the toolbar

Analytics > Totals in the Analytics pane

5. After enabling the totals, our view will be updated, as shown in the following screenshot:

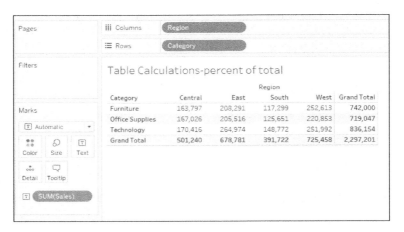

Table Calculations-percent of total

Category	Central	East	South	West	Grand Total
Furniture	163,797	208,291	117,299	252,613	742,000
Office Supplies	167,026	205,516	125,651	220,853	719,047
Technology	170,416	264,974	148,772	251,992	836,154
Grand Total	501,240	678,781	391,722	725,458	2,297,201

6. Let us now click on the dropdown of the green pill in the **Text** shelf, which is basically our **SUM(Sales)**. Let us select the option that says **Quick Table Calculation**. Refer to the following screenshot:

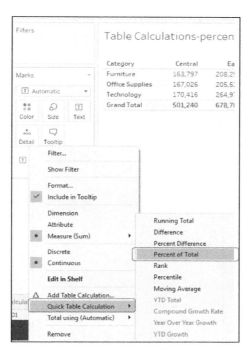

7. We will then select the **Percent of Total** option and once we do that, we will get a view as shown in the following screenshot:

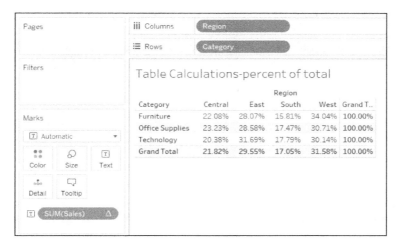

8. Now, the view does show some percentages, and if we notice carefully we are getting 100 percent for each row. That means that the percentages are computed using the **Row Total** and it answers the question of *What percentage of sales is contributed by each Region for each Product Category?*

9. Also, notice the **SUM(Sales)** green pill in the **Text** shelf. We will see a small triangle or delta symbol. This is basically an indicator that a **Table Calculation** is being used. Let us again click on the **SUM(Sales)** in the **Text** shelf and this time select the **Compute using** option. Refer to the following screenshot:

10. We will see that by default, the **Table(Across)** option is selected and hence we are getting the **Row Total**. If we select the **Table(Down)** option, we will get the **Column Total**. Refer to the following screenshot:

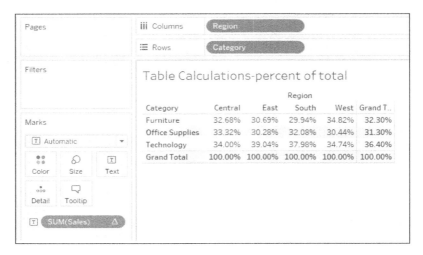

11. Also, if we select the **Table** option under **Compute using**, it will give percentages out of the **Grand Total**. Refer to the following screenshot:

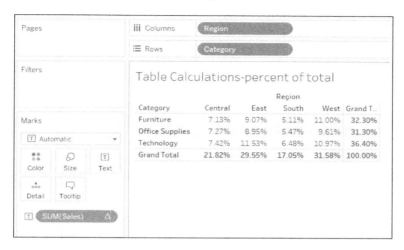

How it works...

In the preceding recipe, we saw how to create and use a **Quick Table Calculation**. The reason why they are called **Quick** is because they are readily available and the reason why they are called **Table Calculations** is because we can change the scope and direction of the calculation.

Also, if we double click on the Green pill in the **Text** shelf, which is called **SUM(Sales)**, then we can actually see the formula that is being used by Tableau in order to execute the output. Refer to the following screenshot:

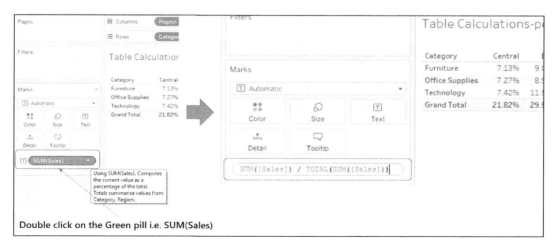

Double click on the Green pill i.e. SUM(Sales)

The **Quick Table Calculation** option does computations on the fly; however, if we want to save this calculation for later use, then we can do so by pressing *Ctrl* on our keyboards and dragging and dropping the Green pill from the **Text** shelf into the **Measures** pane. Refer to the following screenshot:

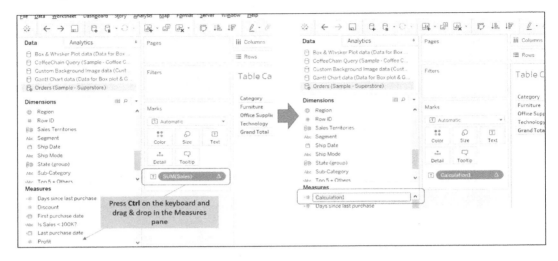

We can then name this calculation as **Percent of Total Sales**. Once we do that, we will see that the Green pill in the **Text** shelf, which was earlier called **SUM(Sales)**, will now be called **Percent of Total Sales**.

What we saw in the preceding recipe was a quick and easy way to get a **Table Calculation**. There are certain calculations that are required quite often in business and these are made readily available to us in the form of **Quick Table Calculations** in Tableau. We can either make use of these pre-defined and pre-computed calculations by clicking on the field and selecting the **Quick Table Calculations** option, or we can even create them from scratch by creating a calculated field and then selecting the **Table Calculation** option from the dropdown. This will populate the list of all the **Table Calculation** functions available in Tableau. Refer to the following screenshot:

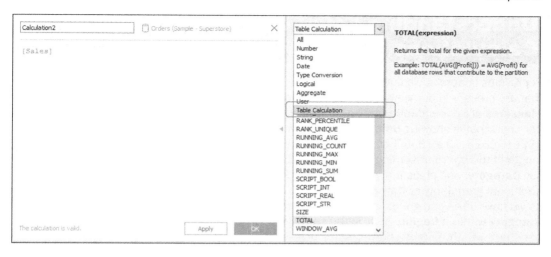

Refer to `https://onlinehelp.tableau.com/current/pro/desktop/en-us/ functions_functions_tablecalculation.html` link to know more about the **Table Calculations** in Tableau:

There is also an interesting article that gives a couple of examples of Table Calculations. The article even has the options to download the packaged workbooks for one's perusal. The link to the article is `http://www.tableau.com/table-calculations`.

Another important link to refer to is `http://onlinehelp.tableau.com/current/ pro/desktop/en-us/calculations_tablecalculations_understanding_ addressing.html`. This gives a detailed explanation on the **direction** and **scope** or as we call it in Tableau, the **Addressing** and **Partitioning** of the **Table Calculation**.

The preceding links will help us understand more about Table calculations. However, to know more about all the various functions that are available with Tableau, please refer to `http:// onlinehelp.tableau.com/current/pro/desktop/en-us/functions.html`.

Understanding Level of Detail (LOD) Calculations

In previous chapters, we learnt about how our **Measures** are dependent on the **Dimensions** that are present in our view. These **Dimensions** act as independent variables, whereas the **Measures** are dependent on those **Dimensions**. For example, imagine having a horizontal bar chart that is showing **Sales** across **Region**. Since our **Orders** sheet of `Sample - Superstore.xlsx` data has four regions, we will get a bar chart showing four bars and the length of the bar representing the sales across regions. Now, if we get another **Dimension**, say **Category**, and place it right after the **Region** field in the **Rows** shelf, we will add an additional granularity of **Category** into the view and now instead of 4 bars, we will get 12 bars as we have three categories in our data and at this point, the **Sales** will be computed for each **Category** within a **Region**. Also, in the same view, if we remove **Region**, then we will have a bar chart with three bars showing sales across categories without any regional granularity.

What this means is that when we add a **Dimension** into the view or remove a **Dimension** from the view, we are essentially adding or removing certain granularity from our view. In the versions prior to version 9.0 of Tableau, we had to make sure that the necessary **Dimensions** are kept in the view to maintain that granularity. However, with the **Level of Detail** (**LOD**) calculations we can add the granularity that we want without having to call the necessary Dimensions in the view. This can also work if we wish to remove a certain granularity as well. In other words, LOD calculations help us set the level of detail that we want for a particular field regardless of what is in the view.

There are three different types of LOD calculations, and they are as follows: **INCLUDE**, **EXCLUDE**, and **FIXED**:

- ▶ **INCLUDE**: Computes values using the specified dimensions in addition to whatever dimensions are present in the view

- ▶ **EXCLUDE**: Computes the values by omitting the dimensions from the view's level of detail

- ▶ **FIXED**: Computes values using the specified dimensions without reference to any other dimensions in the view

We will take a look at all three functions in the following recipes. However, before getting into these functions, let us revisit our recipe of table calculations where we saw an example of calculating the percent of total. Now, depending on what percentages we wanted to see, we changed the direction of our calculation to either give us percentage with respect to the Row Total, or with respect to the Column Total, or with respect to the Grand Total. In that case, when we wanted to show the percentage with respect to the Grand Total, we simply changed the direction of our table calculation to **Table** instead of **Table (across)** or **Table (down)**. This worked out well, but imagine having another view with different set of dimensions where we need to do the same exercise of showing percentages with respect to the **Grand Total**. In this case too, we will first have to design our view, make sure that we don't change the same, and then do a table calculation on the measure and make sure that the scope and direction of this table calculation is well defined. If we decide to use table calculations, then we will have to do this exercise every time for all the different views where we wish to show the percentage with respect to the Grand Total, and this can be cumbersome. So, the question is that instead of having to compute the Grand Total on the fly every time, is it possible for us to maybe have the Grand Total pre-computed and saved for later use? This can be achieved by using the **Level of Detail** (**LOD**) calculations in Tableau. Let us see how this objective can be achieved using LOD calculation.

Getting ready

Let us use the same example as that of our Table calculation recipe, where we used the **Sales**, **Region**, and **Category** fields from the **Orders** sheet of `Sample - Superstore.xlsx` data. Let us get started.

How to do it...

1. We will begin by duplicating the sheet called **Table Calculations-percent of total** and renaming it **LOD-percent of total**.

2. Let us then remove the **Percent of Total Sales** calculation from the **Text** shelf.

3. We will then right click on the **Sales** field in the **Measures** pane and select the **Create | Calculated Field...** option. Let us call this calculation **LOD-Percent of Total Sales** and type *SUM([Sales])/SUM({SUM([Sales])})*.

4. Refer to the following screenshot:

5. Let us click **OK**. Now, if we double click on this calculation and get it in the view, we will see some decimal numbers, as shown in the following screenshot:

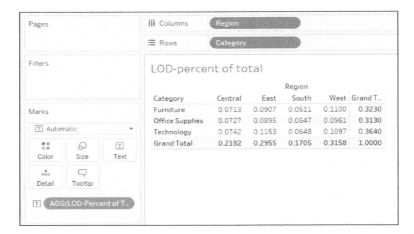

6. Now, let us convert these decimals numbers to percentages, and to do so, let's right click on **LOD-Percent of Total Sales** in the **Measures** pane and select the **Default Properties | Number format...** option. We will select the **Percentage** option with two decimals. Refer to the following screenshot:

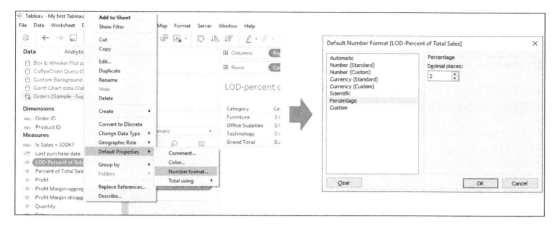

7. Once we do that, our view will update to show the exact same percentages as that of what we saw in the Table calculation recipe. Refer to the following screenshot:

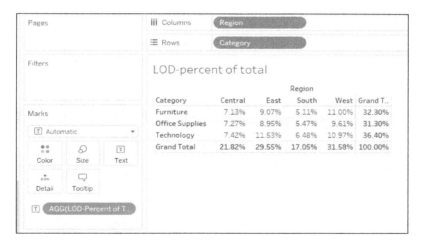

How it works...

Table calculations are performed on the fly in Tableau after the data is already fetched in the view, thus making them dependent on the table structure. This means that if we add or remove any dimension from our view, the table calculation will not give us the same values as it was before adding or removing that new dimension. However, in the case of LOD calculations, the computation happens independent of our view.

In the preceding recipe, we are essentially dividing our sales with the total sales; however, instead of using the `TOTAL()` function, which is a table calculation, we are using the *SUM({SUM([Sales])})*. What this does is that it computes the total sales regardless of what Dimensions we have in the view.

The *SUM([Sales])* returns sales for each category in each region, whereas the *SUM({SUM([Sales])})* returns the total sales of the entire data source.

All LOD calculations are written within the curly brackets and one needs to start the LOD calculation using the opening curly bracket and terminate the calculation using the closing curly bracket.

Understanding INCLUDE LOD

As mentioned earlier, the **INCLUDE LOD** expression, computes values using the specified dimensions in addition to whatever dimensions are present in the view. These expressions are most useful when including a dimension that is not part of our view as the results are computed at a lower granularity than the visualization's level of detail.

The syntax of using an INCLUDE LOD expression is *{ INCLUDE [Dimension] : aggregate expression}*.

The preceding syntax shows how one can use an INCLUDE expression for a single dimension, however, if there is more than one dimension that we want to include in our calculation, then the syntax can be modified as *{ INCLUDE [Dimension1], [Dimension2], [Dimension3] : aggregate expression}*.

Let us see how we can use the INCLUDE LOD expression in the following recipe.

Getting ready

Let's use the **Sub-Category** and **Sales** fields from the **Orders** sheet of `Sample - Superstore.xlsx` data.

How to do it...

1. Let us create a new sheet by pressing *Ctrl + M* and rename it `INCLUDE LOD`.

2. Let us then drag **Sub-Category** from the **Dimensions** pane and drop it into the **Rows** shelf.

3. We will then create a new calculation called **Average Sales** and the formula will be *AVG([Sales])*.

4. Let us drag the **Average Sales** field from the **Measures** pane and drop it into the **Text** shelf. Our view will update, as shown in the following screenshot:

5. Next we will create another calculation called **Include Region-Average Sales** and we will type the formula as *AVG({INCLUDE [Region]:SUM([Sales])})*.

6. We will click **OK** and then double click on the new calculated field to fetch it into our view. Our view will then be updated, as shown in the following screenshot:

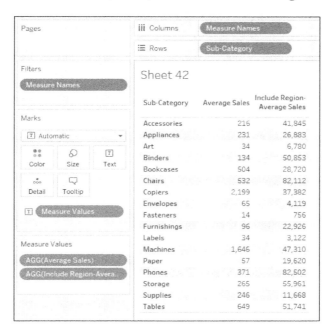

How it works...

In the preceding recipe, we created two calculations called **Average Sales** and **Include Region-Average Sales**. The first calculation, that is, **Average Sales** looks at the sum of sales for all records under each sub category and then takes an average at a sub-category level.

However, the second calculation, that is, **Include Region-Average Sales** looks at the sum of sales at region level even though the region is not part of our view and then takes an average at a sub category level.

To know more about INCLUDE LOD, refer to `https://onlinehelp.tableau.com/ current/pro/desktop/en-us/calculations_calculatedfields_lod_include. html`.

Understanding EXCLUDE LOD

The **EXCLUDE LOD** expression is just the opposite of the INCLUDE LOD expression. As mentioned earlier, EXCLUDE LOD computes the values by omitting the dimensions from the view level of detail and it is most useful when excluding a dimension as the results are computed at a higher granularity than the visualization's level of detail.

The syntax of using the **EXCLUDE** LOD expression is *{ EXCLUDE [Dimension] : aggregate expression}*.

The preceding syntax shows how one can use an EXCLUDE expression for a single dimension; however, if there is more than one dimension that we want to include in our calculation, then the syntax can be modified as *{ EXCLUDE [Dimension1], [Dimension2], [Dimension3] : aggregate expression}*.

Let us see how we can use the EXCLUDE LOD expression in the following recipe.

Getting ready

Let us use the **Category**, **Sub-Category**, and **Sales** fields from the **Orders** sheet of `Sample - Superstore.xlsx` data.

How to do it...

1. Let us start by duplicating the previous sheet, that is, **INCLUDE LOD** and let us rename it as `EXCLUDE LOD`.

2. Let us then drag the **Category** field from the **Dimensions** pane and drop it just before the **Sub-Category** field in the **Rows** shelf.

3. As a next step, let us remove the **Include Region-Average Sales** and the **Average Sales** fields from the view. We will then drag the **Sales** field from the **Measures** pane and drop it into the **Text** shelf.

4. We will then create a new calculated field called **Exclude Subcategory-Sum of Sales** and the formula will be *SUM({EXCLUDE [Sub-Category]:SUM([Sales])})*.

5. Let us click **OK** and then double click on the new calculated field to fetch it into our view. Our view will then be updated, as shown in the following screenshot:

How it works...

In the preceding recipe, **Exclude Subcategory-Sum of Sales** excludes the granularity of the sub-category even though it is part of the view and computes the sum of sales at the category level.

To know more about EXCLUDE LOD, refer to `https://onlinehelp.tableau.com/current/pro/desktop/en-us/calculations_calculatedfields_lod_exclude.html`.

Understanding FIXED LOD

The **FIXED LOD** expression, computes values using the specified dimensions without reference to any other dimensions in the view. These expressions are most useful when fixing a dimension regardless of what is and what is not part of our view. In this case, the results are computed at a granularity that is independent of the fields used in the visualization's level of detail.

The syntax of using FIXED LOD expressions is *FIXED [Dimension] : aggregate expression}*.

The preceding syntax shows how one can use a FIXED expression for a single dimension; however, if there is more than one dimension that we want to include in our calculation, then the syntax can be modified as *{FIXED [Dimension1], [Dimension2], [Dimension3] : aggregate expression}*.

Let us see how we can use the FIXED LOD expression in the following recipe.

Getting ready

Let us use the **Customer Name** and **Order Date** fields from the **Orders** sheet of `Sample - Superstore.xlsx` data to find out how we can compute the first purchase date of a customer regardless of what else is in the view.

How to do it...

1. Let us create a new sheet by pressing *Ctrl + M* and rename it as `FIXED LOD`.

2. Let us drag **Customer Name** from the **Dimensions** pane and drop it into the **Rows** shelf. We will then right click and drag the **Order Date** field from the **Dimensions** pane and drop it right after the **Customer Name** field into the **Rows** shelf.

3. We will then select the **MDY(Order Date)** option. This will give us all the dates when a particular customer purchased from us.

4. Next, let us find the **First purchase date** of each of these customers. In our previous recipes, we have already created a **First purchase date**. Let us drag that field and drop it into the **Rows** shelf, just after the **MDY(Order Date)** field. This will give us the exact dates of what is shown in the **MDY(Order Date)** column, instead of giving us one date per customer, which is the **First purchase date** of that customer.

5. This is because our **First purchase date** calculation is simply taking a minimum of **Order Date** as the formula that we used earlier, which was *MIN([Order Date])*.

6. Now if we remove the **MDY(Order Date)** field from the view, we will get one date, that is, their first purchase date per customer. However, in the current view that isn't happening. So, if we want to retain the current view and still be in a position to show one date, that is, their first purchase date per customer, then we will create a new calculated field and name it **First purchase date fixed @ customer**. The formula will be {FIXED [Customer Name]:MIN([Order Date])}.

7. After clicking **OK**, let us right click and drag the **First purchase date fixed @ customer** field from the **Dimensions** pane and drop it into the **Rows** shelf. Let us select the **MDY(First purchase date fixed @ customer)** option. Our view will update, as shown in the following screenshot:

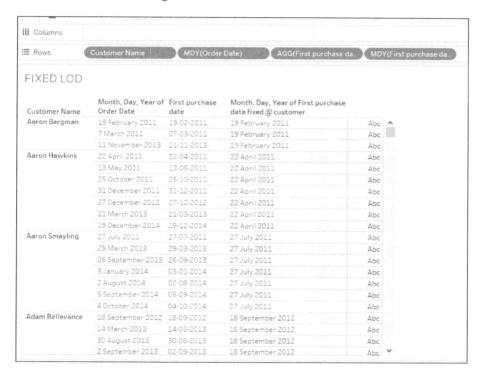

How it works...

In the preceding recipe, when we get the **First purchase date** calculation, it takes into consideration all the granularity that is there in the view and hence we get the exact dates as of the **MDY([Order Date])**. Whereas, when we created **First purchase date fixed @ customer**, we essentially made Tableau take the minimum **Order Date** at a customer level by ignoring all the dimensions in the view.

To know more about **FIXED** LOD, refer to https://onlinehelp.tableau.com/current/pro/desktop/en-us/calculations_calculatedfields_lod_fixed.html.

Understanding how to create and use Parameters

Being able to create custom calculations is a very useful functionality of any tool. It gives the user an immense flexibility and power to do a lot of things. However, there are times when we would want to go beyond the calculations that are based on static hard coded conditions. So, for example, in the **Logic statement** that we saw earlier, we had hard coded the **Sales Target** value to **100K**. Now the problem is that as we continue with our business, the 100K target may soon become redundant and the calculations will soon have to be revisited. Plus, hard coding the Target at the development stage may not be a good idea as the end user may have some different values in mind. In this case, it makes sense to have the option where, the end user can pass certain values at the viewing level.

To address the preceding requirement, we will use the **parameter** functionality provided by Tableau. **Parameters** are controls that can be given to the end user to dynamically modify values and/or replace the constant values in calculations. Thus, rather than manually editing the calculation and all its dependent calculations, we can use a **parameter**, which will ensure that when we select or enter the value in the **parameter**, all the calculations that are using the parameter will update accordingly.

Now that we have understood what **Parameters** are, let us explore them in detail and see how we can create and use them.

Getting ready

Let us see how to create and use parameters in the following recipe. We will continue with our existing `Sample - Superstore.xlsx` data source. Let's get started.

How to do it...

1. Let us first create a new sheet and rename it **Parameters**.

2. Let us right click on the **Set** named **Top 5 customers by Sales** and select the **Duplicate** option. We will then right click on the duplicated **Set**, which is called **Top 5 customers by Sales (copy)** and select the **Edit Set...** option. Let us rename the set as **High sales customers**.

3. We will then click on the **Top** tab and keep most of the things as they are except for the dropdown, which has number 5. Let us click on that dropdown and see what options we get. Refer to the following screenshot:

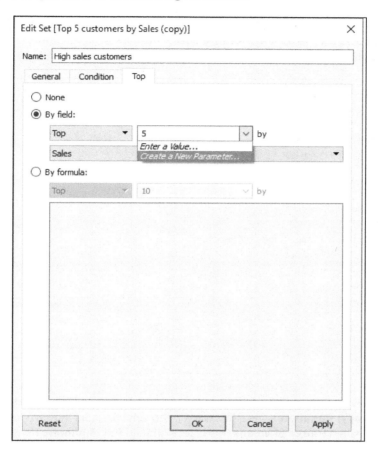

4. When we do that, we get to see two options; one is to **Enter a Value....** This obviously will be a hard-coded value and the next is to **Create a New Parameter...** which is going to be dynamic. So, essentially, if we **Enter a value**, say 10, then we will get our Top 10 customers by sales, whereas if we create a parameter, then we will be giving the control to the end user to select the number of customers that they want to see. So, let us select the option of **Create a New Parameter....** Once we do that, we will get the following view:

5. Let's call this **Parameter** as **Count of customers** instead of **Top 5 customers by Sales (copy) Parameter**. Also, let us keep the selections as they are for all except the section called **Range of values**. Here, let's change the **Minimum:** from 1 to 5 and **Maximum:** from 100 to 25. Let's also select the **Step size:** checkbox and change the values from 1 to 5. Refer to the following screenshot:

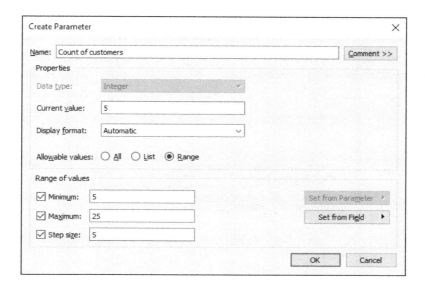

6. Let's click on **OK** and our set will look as follows:

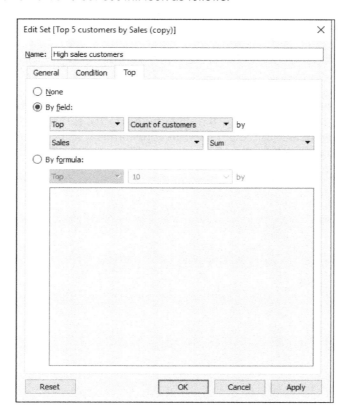

7. Let's click **OK** once again and then let's drag and drop this new set in the **Rows** shelf and we will change it from **IN/OUT** to **Show Members in Set**.

8. Next, let's add the **Sales** field in the **Columns** shelf and our view will be updated, as shown in the following screenshot:

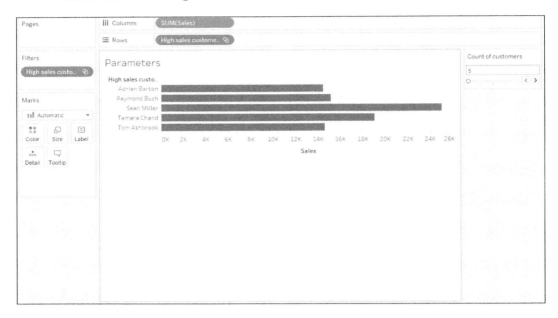

9. Notice the slider on the right-hand side of the sheet; this is the **Parameter** that we have just created. If we change the slider from 5 to 10, our view will update and give us 10 names instead of the 5 names that are currently visible. In other words, it will give us the names of the top 10 customers who are having high sales. Refer to the following screenshot:

10. This is how we can create and use a **Parameter** in the **Filters / Sets**. Now, as a next step, let's create another **Parameter** and use it in the **Calculated** field. For this, let us click on the dropdown of the **Dimensions** pane and select the option of **Create Parameter...**. Refer to the following screenshot:

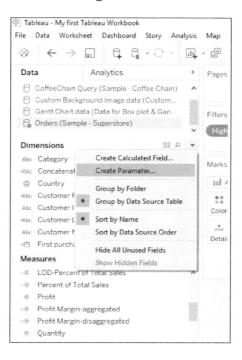

11. Once we do that, we will get a view as shown in the following screenshot:

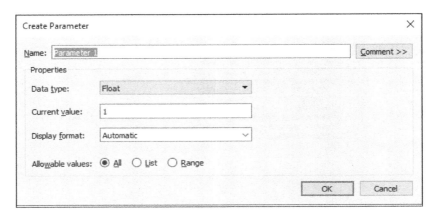

12. Let us call this **Parameter** as **Sales Target**. Since we want the user to enter integer values as **Sales Target**, we will change **Data Type** to **Integer**. Keeping the rest of the selection as is, we will click **OK**.

13. Next, we will create a new calculated field called **Sales Performance**, which will be used to highlight the Customers with **Sales** below the value defined in the **Sales Target parameter**. Our formula will look as follows:

```
IF SUM([Sales]) < [Sales Target] THEN 'Below Target'
ELSE 'Above Target'
END
```

14. Refer to the following screenshot:

15. Let's fetch this new calculated field and drop it into the **Color** shelf. Now, when we created the **Sales Target Parameter**, the **Current value:** was predefined as 1. This has now become the current **Sales Target**. Since each and every Customer in the view is having **Sales** above 1, everything is shown as **Above Target**.

16. This should change based on what we enter in the **Sales Target Parameter**. However, the problem is that there is no place to enter the value. The **Parameter** isn't available for us to use yet. In order to make the **Parameter** visible to the user, we will have to right click on the **Parameter** in the **Parameter pane**, which is on the left-hand side bottom corner of the Tableau workspace, just under the **Sets pane** or **Measures pane** and select the option to **Show Parameter Control**. Refer to the following screenshot:

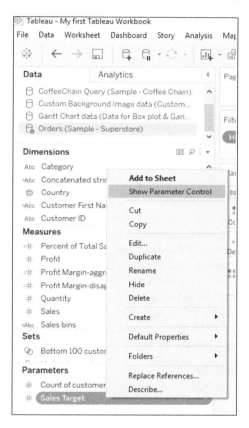

17. Once we do that, we will get a **Type In** box on the right-hand side section of the workspace where we will change the value from 1 to 15,000 and see how that affects our view. Refer to the following screenshot:

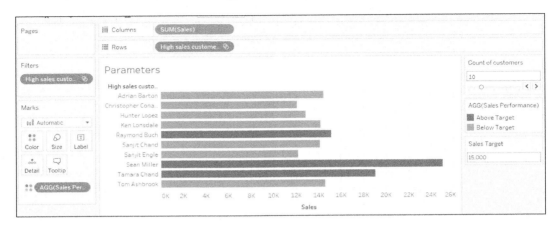

How it works...

In the preceding recipe, Orange indicates **Sales** below target and blue indicates **Sales** above target. We also saw two examples of **Parameters**. Since **Parameters** are not called from the data source, but instead are created on the fly in Tableau, they don't have any relationship with the data source fields and hence will not affect any field or any view on their own. In order to make them useful, we need to call them in our view. It is of no use to create a **Parameter** and not call it in our view. In the preceding recipe, we called the **Parameter** in a **Filter** or a **Set** as well as in a **Calculated field**. We can also call **Parameters** in **Bins** to make the bin size flexible as well as in **Reference Lines** (we will discuss reference lines in future chapters).

There are three types of **Parameter** controls available in Tableau and these will help us specify how the **Parameter** can accept values. They are as follows:

- ▸ **All**: Provides a simple type-in field
- ▸ **List**: Provides a list of possible values for us to select from
- ▸ **Range**: Allows us to select values within a specified range

The availability of these **Parameter** control options is determined by the data type that is specified. For example, an integer parameter can accept **All** values, or a **List**, or even a **Range**, whereas a string parameter can only accept **All** values or a **List**, but does not support a **Range**.

We have already seen the **All** and **Range** parameter control in the preceding recipe. When we select the **List** parameter control as an option, then we must specify the list of values. The left column, which is labeled as **Value**, is where we type the value and the right column, which is labeled as **Display As** in the display alias. The display alias shows the values that the end user can see in the **Parameter**. Refer to the following screenshot:

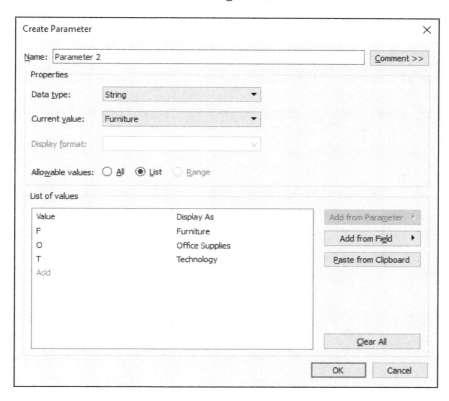

Now, instead of typing the values and the display alias, we can also copy and paste a list of values by selecting the option of **Paste from Clipboard**, or we can also add the members of a field as the list of values by selecting the **Add from Field** option. However, we need to remember that even though we have the option of **Add from Field**, the **Parameter** will still be static in nature. This means that the **Parameter** will not dynamically update itself if a new entry is made in the field that we have used to create the **Parameter**. As of now, the **Parameters** are static in nature, and will not update automatically even if the backend data source updates.

As of now, the **Parameters** are available as a single select option, meaning we cannot select multiple values at a time. We can only have one value at a time. For example, if we want to have a **Parameter** from which we can enter or select a minimum threshold value and a maximum threshold value, then we will have to create two **Parameters**, one which will help us enter the minimum value and the other which helps us enter the maximum value.

Parameters can be used in many ways to give us immense flexibility. One interesting way to use Parameters is to swap the dimensions or measures on the fly or change the view on the fly. Refer to the following links to know more:

- `https://onlinehelp.tableau.com/current/pro/desktop/en-us/parameters_swap.html`
- `http://onlinehelp.tableau.com/current/pro/desktop/en-us/help.htm#changing-views-using-parameters.html`

6
Serve It on a Dashboard!

In this chapter, we will cover the following recipes:

- ▶ Combining multiple visualizations into a dashboard
- ▶ Using the filter action
- ▶ Using the highlight action
- ▶ Using the URL action

Introduction

In all the previous chapters, we've created various visualizations and all these visualizations are either individual charts or analysis. Individual charts or analytics provide specific and limited information, like a single piece of a larger puzzle. As we put the pieces together, a larger picture takes shape. This is what we do on a dashboard. A dashboard is a collection of several worksheets and their supporting information put together to convey a broader perspective. A dashboard allows us to facilitate interactivity between individual worksheets, provides a unified view to present or to compare a variety of information and disseminate this information in a structured and fluent manner.

Combining multiple visualizations into a dashboard

A very important yet often neglected aspect of dashboard design is its ability to communicate information in a seamless and coherent manner; without this, a dashboard becomes nothing more than a series of unrelated views and scattered information.

In order to make the dashboard more holistic and useful, it needs to be designed with a specific purpose in mind. Different people in an organization will need different slices of information and each resulting dashboard should be aligned to this specific purpose. For example, a CXO will typically want to look at a higher or macro level of information that gives him a pulse of the overall health of the business, whereas a marketing head would want to look at a more granular perspective, of say his customer segmentation and transactional behavior, in order to plan a more effective marketing strategy.

To create and use dashboards in Tableau, let us follow the recipe given here.

Getting ready

In order to create a dashboard, first create a few worksheets. We will continue using data from the Orders sheet from the Sample - Superstore Subset .xlsx file and we will continue working in the same workbook, My first Tableau Workbook. Let's get started with the creation of dashboard by first building some worksheets.

How to do it...

1. Let us create a new worksheet and name it as Sales distribution by Region. We will create a pie chart here by selecting the **Region** field from the **Dimensions** pane and then selecting the **Sales** field from the **Measures** pane using *Ctrl + Select*.

2. Once we are done with the selection, select the **Pie charts** option from **Show me!**. Refer to the following screenshot:

3. After creating the pie chart, we will create another worksheet and name it **Sales distribution by State**. Here, we will create a map by selecting the **Sales** field from the **Measures** pane and the **State** field from the **Dimensions** pane. Then select the **Symbol Maps** option from the **Show Me**.

4. Next, let us drag the **Region** field from the **Dimensions** pane and drop it into the **Color** shelf. Then increase the size of the bubbles by moving the slider which appears when we click on the **Size** shelf. Refer to the following screenshot:

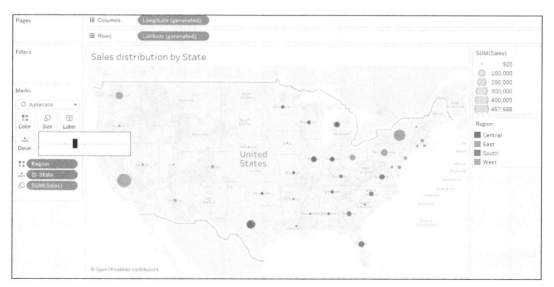

5. Next, create one more worksheet and name it **Sales distribution by Region and Category**. For this sheet, we will drag the **Region** field and put it into the **Columns** shelf, followed by dragging and dropping the **Category** field into the **Rows** shelf and **Sales** into the **Columns** shelf.

6. We will then right-click on the **Order Date** field in the **Dimensions** shelf and select the option of **Show Filter**. Our view should be as shown in the following screenshot:

7. Now that we have three worksheets, let us put them together on a dashboard. In order to create a dashboard, we need to select the **Dashboard | New Dashboard** option from the toolbar or click on the tab which is right next to the sheet tab. Refer to the following screenshot:

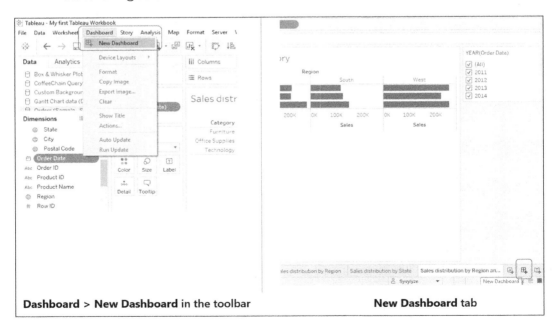

Dashboard > New Dashboard in the toolbar   **New Dashboard** tab

8. Once we do that we will get a blank canvas as shown in the following screenshot:

9. This blank canvas is where we will create our dashboard. What we see on the left-hand side, are all the worksheets that we have created so far in this workbook. Refer to the following screenshot:

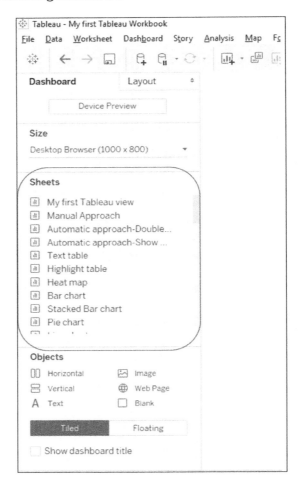

10. To begin with the dashboard, we will first rename the dashboard from `Dashboard 1` to `My first Tableau Dashboard`. If we see any scroll bars, we can then simply adjust the dashboard size from **Desktop** to **Automatic**. Refer to the following screenshot:

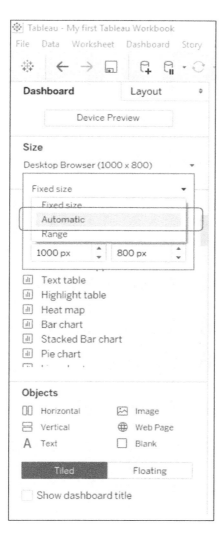

11. Next, we will get the three new sheets that we have created earlier in this recipe. In order to get these sheets on the dashboard, we can either drag the sheet names from the left-hand side or we can double-click on them. When we double-click, Tableau will automatically place the sheets. However, when we drag and drop the sheets manually, we can place them as desired by dropping them wherever we see the grey tile. Refer to the following screenshot:

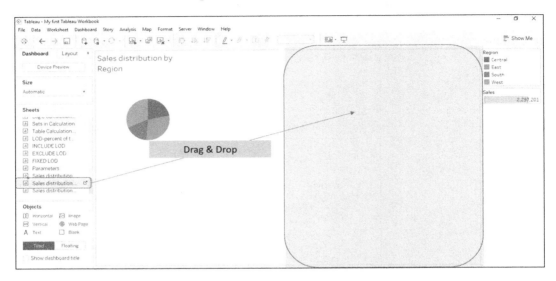

12. Once we get all three sheets that we created earlier, our dashboard will look as shown in the following screenshot:

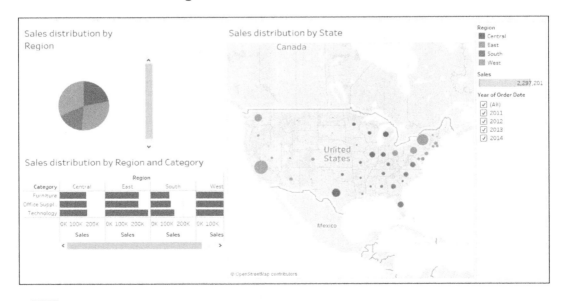

13. Once we are done placing the sheets, we can again re-arrange them. In the preceding image, we see that the bar chart needs more horizontal space and hence we will move the map and try to align it in the top section of the dashboard where we have the pie chart. This way we will get more horizontal space for the bar chart. Refer to the following screenshot:

14. This is how we can combine multiple visualizations into a dashboard. However, let us give it some finishing touches. Notice how the pie chart has a scroll bar. This leaves a lot of blank space on the dashboard. The same goes for the bar chart. There is plenty of blank space below the bar chart. This makes the dashboard look a little messy. In order to remove these blank spaces, we will have to make the chart fit in the space that has been allocated to it. To do this, select the pie chart sheet on the dashboard and select the option of **Entire View** from the dropdown which is available in the toolbar. Refer to the following screenshot:

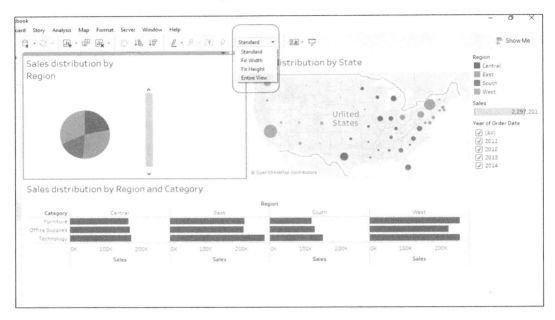

15. Let's do the same for our bar chart and the dashboard will now look like the image in the following screenshot:

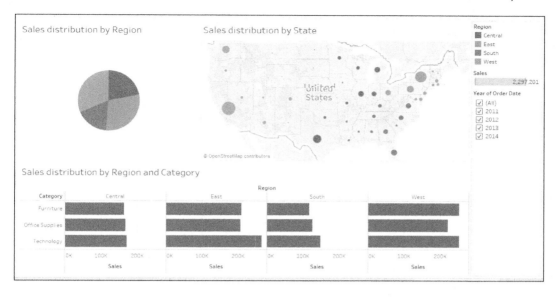

16. Also, if you notice, the **Dashboard** tab is called **My first Tableau Dashboard**. However, there is no title to our dashboard. In order to get a title for our dashboard, we will have to enable the **Show dashboard title** checkbox at the bottom left corner of the screen from the left-hand side menu. Refer to the following screenshot:

17. When we do that, we will get the title for the dashboard. By default, the dashboard title is the same as the **Dashboard** tab name. Refer to the following screenshot:

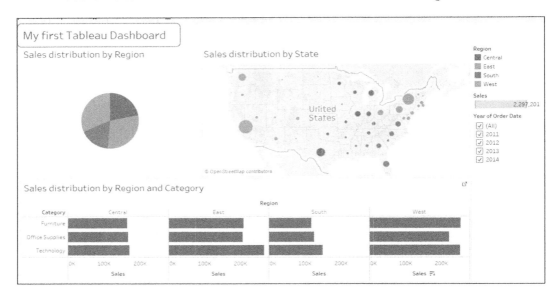

18. We can change the title of our dashboard by double-clicking on the title text or selecting the **Edit Title....** option which is available when we select the title and click on the dropdown of the gray border. Refer to the following screenshot:

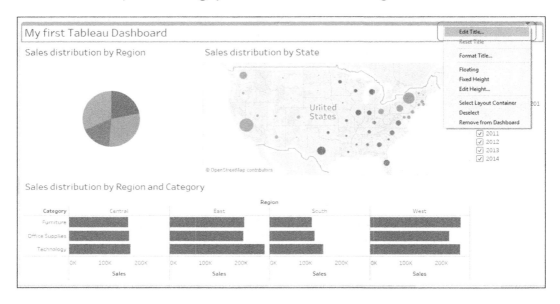

19. When we edit the title, we get the option as shown in the following screenshot:

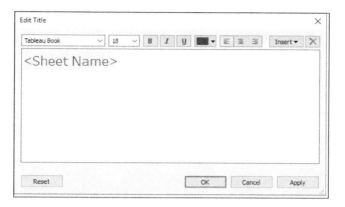

20. Let's change the title and call it **Sales distribution dashboard**. We will also keep the title centre aligned. Once we do that, our dashboard will be as shown in the following screenshot:

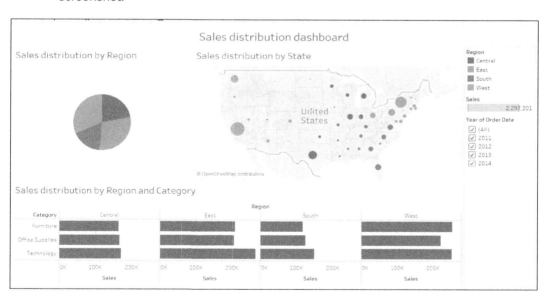

21. Just like the dashboard title, we can similarly edit our sheet title. In the current view, the font of sheet titles is a little big, so let's reduce the size of these sheet titles by keeping the font type the same and reducing the font size to 10. Once we do that, our dashboard will look like the following screenshot:

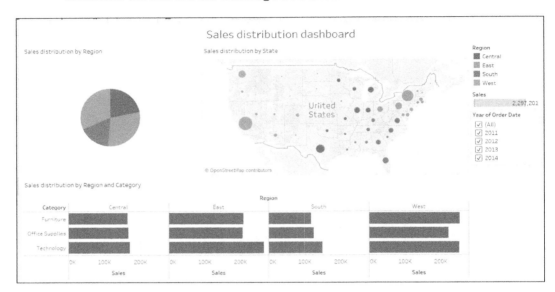

22. There are a lot of cosmetic changes that can be done in order to make the preceding dashboard aesthetically more appealing. We will consider these formatting options later. Moving ahead, now that we have the desired visualizations in place, let's add some images. Typically, logos in the form of images are used to brand the dashboard. We will select the **Image** option from the left-hand side section of our Tableau screen by either double-clicking on it or by dragging and dropping it to a desired location on the dashboard. Refer to the following screenshot:

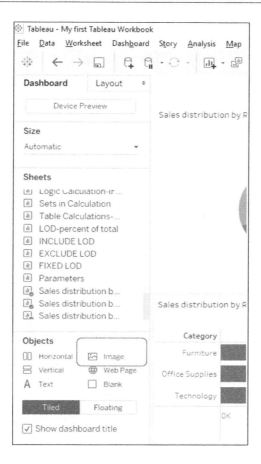

23. Once we do that, we will be asked to browse the desired image file from our desktops/laptops. In this recipe, we will be using the image called `Image for Tableau dashboard.png` that has been uploaded on the following link: `https://1drv.ms/i/s!Av5QCoyLTBpnhkmdeOQ54NAUkB97`.

24. We can download this image and save it in a new folder called `Tableau Data Visualization Cookbook Extras` that we'll create in `Documents\My Tableau Repository`. We can use this image in the dashboard so that it now looks like the following screenshot:

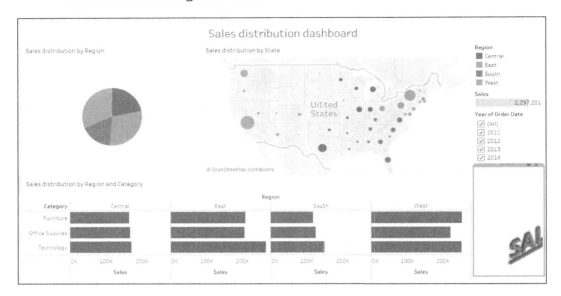

25. You may notice that the image is not completely visible. In order to rectify that, we'll click on the drop-down menu of the gray border surrounding the image and select the **Fit image** and **Center image** options. Refer to the following screenshot:

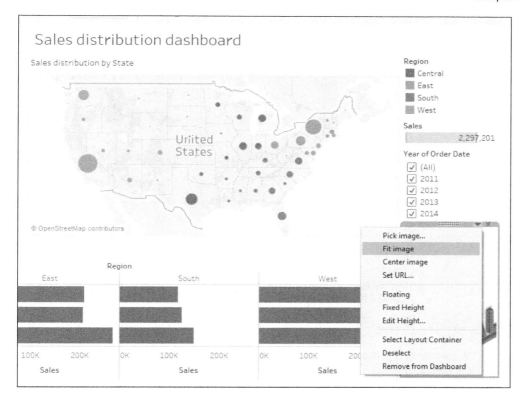

26. Once we do that, the view will look like the following:

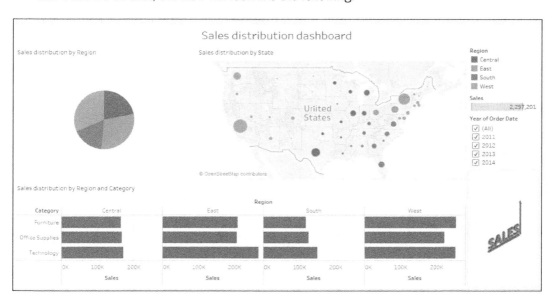

27. In the preceding dashboard, the image appears to be floating. In order to align it properly and place it at the right-hand side bottom section, simply get a **Blank** and place it between the image and the filter. Refer to the following screenshot:

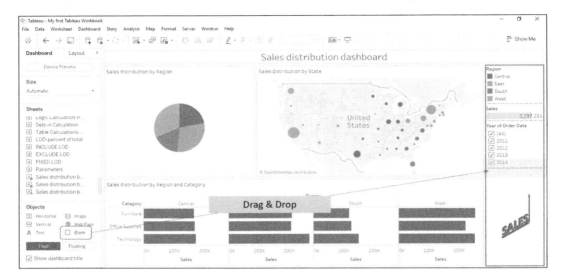

28. Once we drop the **Blank** in the highlighted grey area/tile, our dashboard will update as shown in the following screenshot:

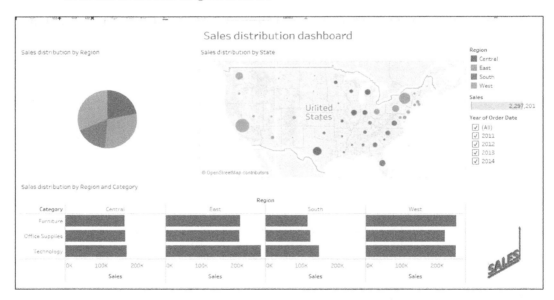

29. Next, if we click on the **Year of Order Date** filter, we will see that it only affects the bar chart. This is because the filter was created locally for that sheet. To make this filter applicable to all the worksheets on the dashboard, click on the dropdown from the gray border that appears when we select the filter and select the option of **Apply to Worksheets**. Refer to the following screenshot:

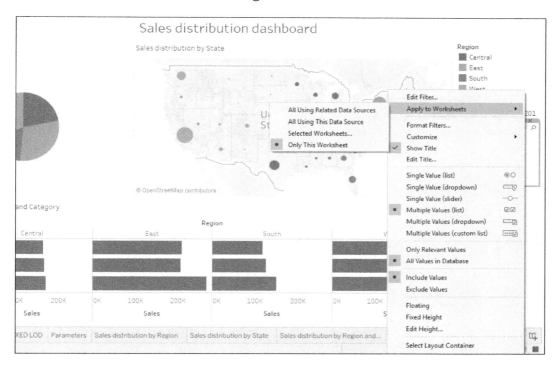

30. Select the **Selected Worksheets...** option and, after we have done that, we will be given an option to select the worksheets that we wish to apply the filter to. Select all the sheets. Refer to the following screenshot:

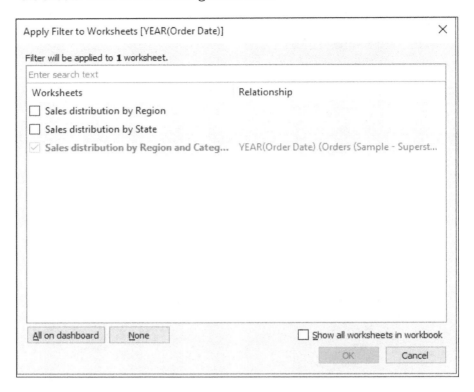

31. Click **OK** and then use the filter and you'll see that all the sheets on the dashboard are now filtered.

How it works...

In the preceding recipe, we saw how to combine multiple visualizations into a dashboard, align them and format them to a certain extent.

When we get any particular worksheet on the dashboard, all the filters, **Color** legends, **Size** legends, **Shape** legends, and so on that are part of that worksheet, are by default fetched onto the dashboard and these can be removed from the dashboard if required.

Another important thing that we saw in the preceding recipe, was how to add images and blanks to our dashboard. The section which has the option of **Images**, also has various other options like **Blank**, **Text**, **Web Page**, and so on. These are referred to as dashboard objects in Tableau. These dashboard objects are explained here:

> ▸ **Horizontal**: The **Horizontal** object adds a horizontal layout container. This container will accommodate all the views or objects horizontally. Further, the widths of these views or objects will be automatically adjusted to equally fill the width of the container.

> ▸ **Vertical**: The **Vertical** object adds a vertical layout container. This container will accommodate all the views or objects vertically. Further, the heights of these views or objects will be automatically adjusted to equally fill the height of the container.

> ▸ **Text**: The **Text** object allows us to add a text box to our dashboard. This text box can contain instructions, descriptions, important notes and so on.

> ▸ **Image**: As seen in the previous recipe, the **Image** object allows us to add static image files to our dashboard. These could be logos, descriptive images and so on.

> ▸ **Web Page**: The **Web Page** object allows us to embed a web page into our dashboard. We will take a closer look at this object later in the chapter.

> ▸ **Blank**: As seen in the preceding recipe, the **Blank** object allows us to add blank areas to our dashboard. This is helpful for creating a perfect layout and for aligning our views and dashboard objects.

Just below the section of dashboard objects, there are two options called **Tiled** and **Floating**. These are the layout options for our views or objects.

When we get our views or objects on the dashboard, these will by default be arranged into a single layered grid which is the tiled layout.

However, when we want these views or objects to overlap, then we can change the layout to **Floating**. A tiled object can later be changed to **Floating** by clicking on the drop-down menu in the grey border surrounding the object and selecting the **Floating** option. Refer to the following screenshot:

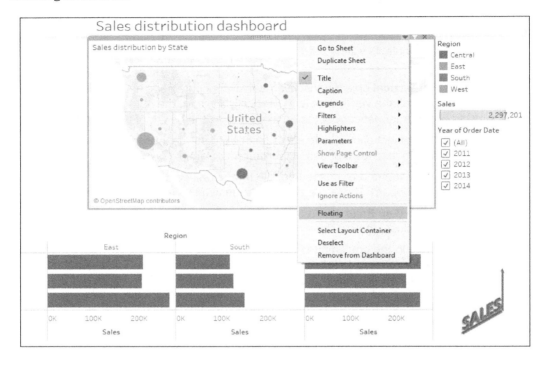

One more important point to remember about dashboards is the dashboard size. In the preceding recipe, we saw how to change the dashboard size. Depending on our screen resolutions, many of us may get vertical or horizontal scroll bars when creating a dashboard, or many of us may even get a lot of grey space. This is because, the dashboard is by default set to fit a desktop which is 1,000 pixels by 800 pixels. We can change the size by using the drop-down menu as seen earlier in the recipe.

Lastly, we also saw how to apply a filter to more than one sheet on the dashboard. When we click on the drop-down menu of the **Filter**, we get an option of **Apply to Worksheets** as seen in steps number 30 and 31 of the preceding recipe. When we select this option, we further get four options to choose from. These are as follows:

▶ **All Using Related Data Sources**: Using this option allows us to apply the filter to all the worksheets that use the related data sources as their primary data source. This filter will automatically be applied to the relevant existing worksheets that are part of the workbook. Further, when we create any new worksheets that use the related data source going forward after using this option, then the filter will automatically be applied to those new worksheet as well.

- ▸ **All Using This Data Source**: Using this option, we can make the filter affect all the worksheets in the workbook that connect to the same data source. In other words, this is a **Global filter** that affects all the worksheets that are using the same data source as that of the filter.

- ▸ **Selected Worksheets...**: This option allows us to select the sheets that should be affected by the filter. Using this option, we can extend the filter's functionality to more than one worksheet. These worksheets can be either part of the same dashboard, across other dashboards, or just plain individual worksheets that may or may not be part of any dashboard.

- ▸ **Only This Worksheet**: This option allows the filter to only make changes to the sheet in which it was created. In other words, this is a **Local filter** that affects only the sheet where it was created.

There's more...

In the previous recipe, we saw how to combine multiple visualizations on a dashboard. There are altogether three charts which convey the following:

- ▸ What is the **Sales** distribution across **Regions**?
- ▸ What is the **Sales** distribution across **States**?
- ▸ What is the **Sales** distribution for **Product Categories** across **Regions**?

What we currently have on the dashboard are visualizations that answer these business questions. However, what if we have to find out the **Sales** distribution of the **Product Categories** in a particular **State**. We already have the visualization which gives us **Sales** distribution by **Region** and **Category**. If we were able to click on a desired **State** from the **Map** which is **Sales** distribution by **State** and drill down to the bar chart which is **Sales** distribution by **Region** and **Category**, then that would help us answer our question. This can be achieved in Tableau with the help of actions.

Actions are another very important and powerful functionality of Tableau which allows us to add context and interactivity to our data and helps us create reactive components. We can use these actions to filter one view based on the selection from another view or to highlight certain results in our view to get our end user's attention. We can also link to web pages, files, and other Tableau worksheets.

An action can be applied at a worksheet level or at a dashboard level. When working on worksheets, we can create actions by navigating to **Worksheet | Actions...** from the toolbar. Refer to the following screenshot:

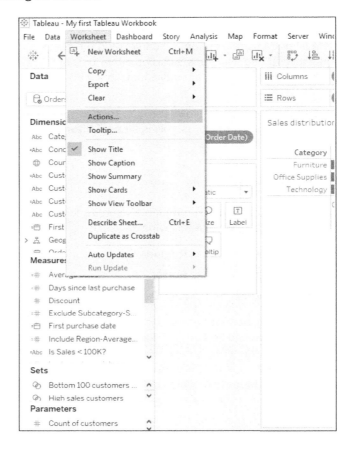

Further, when working on a dashboard, we can create actions by navigating to **Dashboard | Actions...** from the toolbar. Refer to the following screenshot:

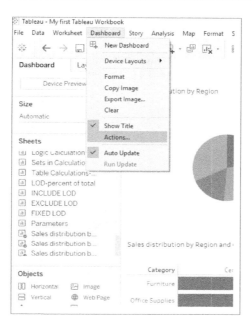

There are three types of actions in Tableau and they are as follows.

▸ Filter action

▸ Highlight action

▸ URL action

Let us look how to enable interactivity by creating and using these actions in detail in the following sections.

Using the filter action

As the name suggests, this action will help us drill down from a master view to show related and more detailed information in one or more target sheets. For example, drilling down to show relevant **States** by selecting a particular **Region** and further drilling down to show relevant cities by selecting a particular **State** from the filtered view. This kind of a structured drill down is often referred to as guided analytics. Let us understand how to create and use filter actions in Tableau.

Getting ready

We will use the already built dashboard for this recipe. We will begin by duplicating this dashboard and then creating the filter action to drill down from **Sales distribution by Region** sheet to **Sales distribution by State** as well as **Sales distribution by Region and Category** sheet. Let's get started.

How to do it...

1. Begin by right-clicking on the **Dashboard** tab which says **My first Tableau Dashboard** and selecting the **Duplicate Sheet** option. Refer to the following screenshot:

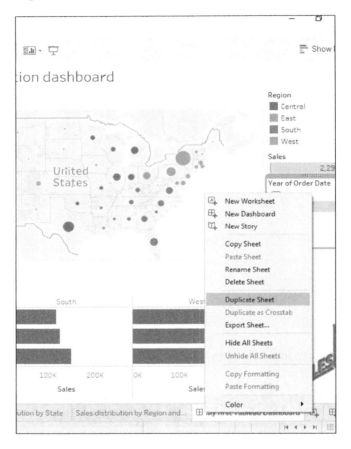

2. Rename this dashboard as `Dashboard for Filter Action`.

3. Next, we will create actions by navigating to the **Dashboard | Actions....** option from the toolbar. We will be offered the option as shown in the following screenshot:

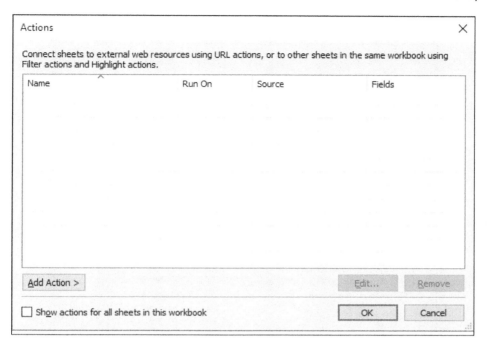

4. Next, click on the **Add Action >** button and select the **Filter...** option. Refer to the following screenshot:

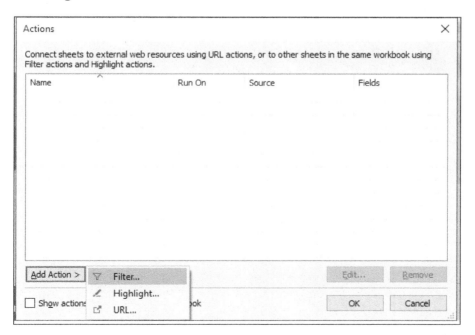

5. Once we do that, we will get the view as shown in the following screenshot:

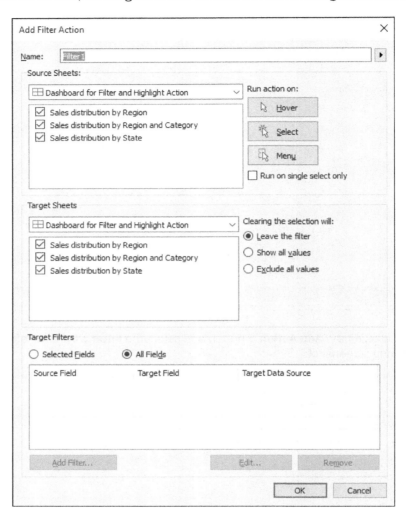

6. Name this action `Region filter`. In the **Source Sheets:** selection, we will keep the selection from the drop-down menu as it is and then uncheck everything except the **Sales distribution by Region**. In the **Target Sheets** selection, we will do a similar thing, except we will keep everything and instead only uncheck the **Sales distribution by Region**. From the **Run action on**: selection, click on the **Select** option and our updated action will be as shown in the following screenshot:

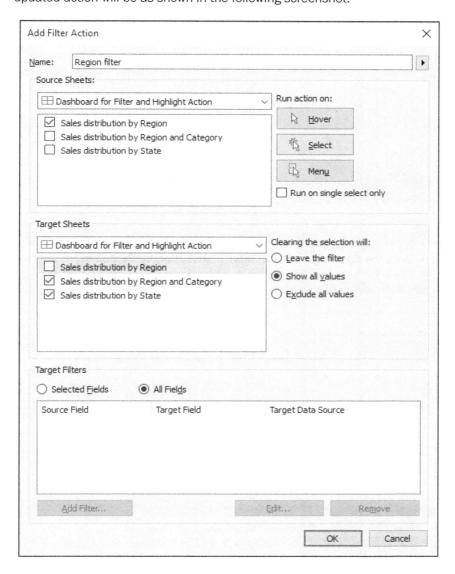

7. When we click **OK**, we will get to see the view as shown in the following screenshot:

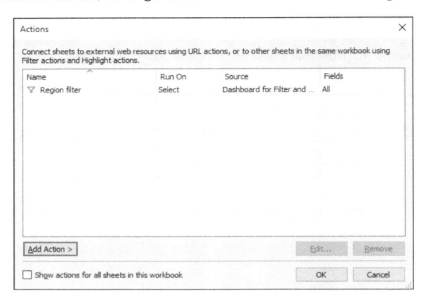

8. Click **OK** to return to the dashboard. Now, click on the orange slice of the pie which represents the **East** region in the **Sales distribution by Region** sheet and see the other two sheets update accordingly to show the relevant information for the **East** region. Refer to the following screenshot:

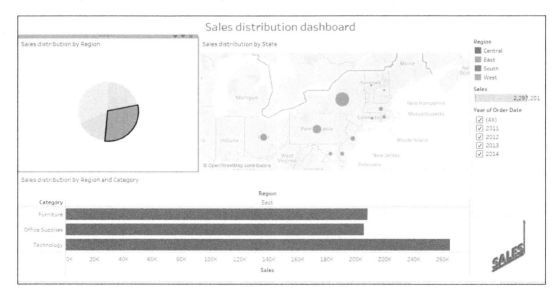

9. In order to clear the filter, we can click in the white area of the `Sales distribution by Region` sheet or click again on whatever is currently selected or simply just press *Esc*.

How it works...

For any action to work, we need to specify a source and a target for that action. The source is where the action is created and the target is where the action will show the effect. We can have multiple source sheets and multiple target sheets as well.

The drop-down list that is available for the source and target selection can be used to either select a source sheet or data source. When we select a data source, we will get the list of individual sheets that should act as our source sheet.

Further, we can run the action by giving the user the following options:

▸ **Hover**: This will enable the action by simply hovering over a mark in the view.

▸ **Select**: We will have to click on a mark in the view to run the action.

▸ **Menu**: We can either activate the action by selecting the action from the right-click menu or by selecting the action that appears in the tooltip when we click or hover over a particular mark. Refer to the following screenshot:

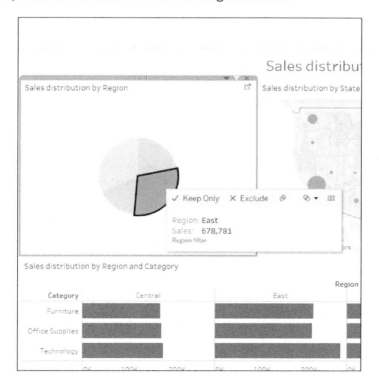

Just below the **Run action as**: section, there is a section which says, **Clearing the selection will**:. There are three option available which are explained here:

- ▶ **Leave the filter**: Once the filter is cleared, this option will leave the filter on the target sheets. Even after the filter is cleared, the target sheets will still show the last filtered results.

- ▶ **Show all values**: Once the filter is cleared, this option will restore the original view of the target sheets by including all values.

- ▶ **Exclude all values**: Once the filter is cleared, this option will clear the complete view of the target sheets by excluding all values. These cleared sheets will only be visible when we select a mark from the source sheet.

Next, when we want to run the action from a specific mark on the source sheet, then we can specify the same in the bottom section of the action which says **Target Filters**. This section has an **Add Filter** dialog box which helps us add a filter to the target sheet based on a specific field. This filter will only include values that match the target field and the source field. For example, we have `Sales distribution by Region and Category` sheet. If we use this sheet as a source of the filter, then it will give us an output which will be for a combination of a particular **Region** and **Category**. Let's say we click on a bar which represents **Furniture** as **Category** and **Central** as **Region**. The filter action in this case, will update our target sheets to show information for **Furniture Category** and **Central Region**. However, this may not be the case always. We already have a `Sales distribution by Region` sheet, which is being used to filter the desired **Regions**. Whereas, we currently don't have the option for selecting only the categories. In this case, we can use the **Target Filters** option, where we use the **Selected Fields** option then click on the **Add Filter** button at the bottom left corner and define **Category** as **Source Field** and **Target Field**.

Read more about filter actions by referring the following link:

`http://onlinehelp.tableau.com/current/pro/desktop/en-us/actions_filter.html`.

Further, one last but important point to know is that we can also auto-generate a filter action by clicking on the dropdown of the gray border of the source sheet and selecting the option of **Use as Filter**. Refer to the following screenshot:

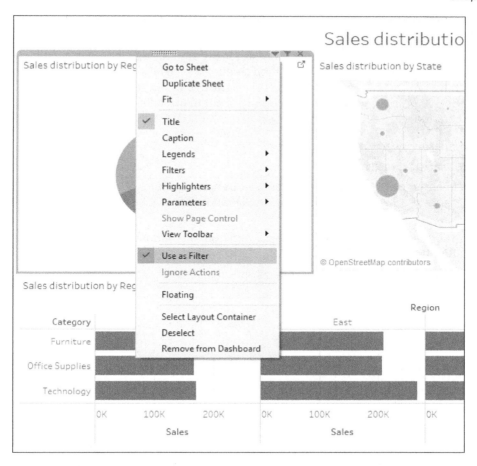

Using the highlight action

In the previous recipe, we saw the filter action which basically filters the view based on the selection. However, if you don't wish to filter the view but instead just draw attention to certain marks that are of interest, then a great way to do so is to simply color them and dim the rest. This is what we use highlight actions for. As the names suggests, this action highlights the marks based on a certain selection while dimming the other marks. This way we can draw attention to the points of interest while being able to compare them with the other marks as well.

Let us see how to create and use a highlight action.

Getting ready

We will use the already built dashboard for this recipe. We will begin by duplicating the `My first Tableau Dashboard` and then creating the highlight action from `Sales distribution by Region` sheet to `Sales distribution by State` as well as `Sales distribution by Region and Category` sheet to highlight only the selected region. Let's get started.

How to do it...

1. In order to create a highlight action, let us first duplicate the **Dashboard** tab which says `My first Tableau Dashboard` and rename it as `Dashboard for Highlight Action`.

2. Then select **Dashboard | Actions....** and from the **Add Action >** button select the **Highlight...** option.

3. Once we do that, the view will be as shown in following screenshot:

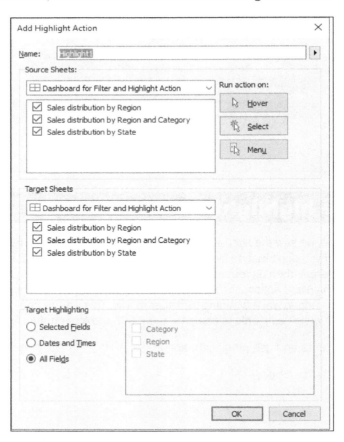

4. Name this action `Region highlight`. In the **Source Sheets:** selection, we will keep the selection from the dropdown as it is and then uncheck everything except the **Sales distribution by Region**. In the **Target Sheets** section, we will do a similar thing except we will keep everything and instead uncheck the **Sales distribution by Region**. From the **Run action on**: section, we will click on the **Menu** option and our updated action will be as shown in the following screenshot:

5. When we click **OK**, we will get to see the view as shown in the following screenshot:

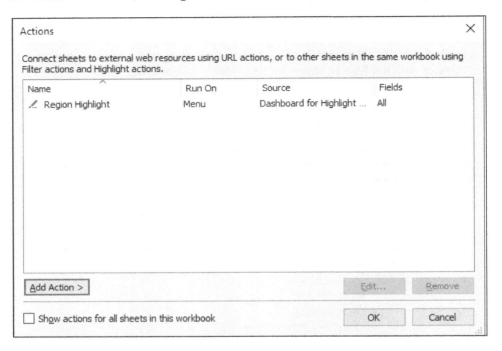

6. Click **OK** and return to our dashboard. Now we need to remember that the highlight action is available on the **Menu** option.

7. Now, in order to enable the highlight action, we will first have to click on the link which appears in the tooltip when we hover over any **Region** on the pie chart. However, if the link doesn't appear in the tooltip , then we can enable it in our tooltip by first selecting the `Sales distribution by Region sheet` and then clicking on the **Worksheet | Tooltip...** option in the toolbar and then selecting the **On Hover – Show tooltips on hover** option from the dropdown. Refer to the following screenshot:

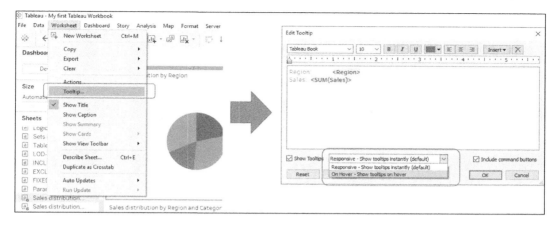

8. Once we are done with this, we can see a link when we hover over any **Region** in the
   `Sales distribution by Region` sheet. Refer to the following screenshot:

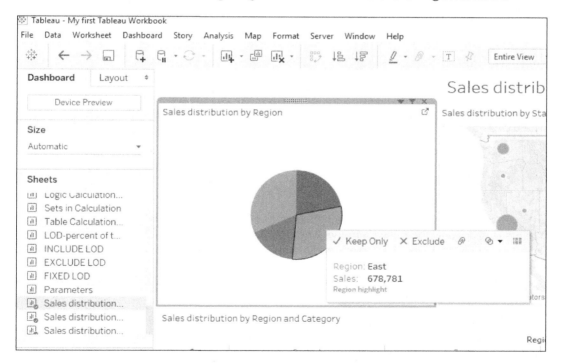

9. Enable the highlight action by clicking on this link in the tooltip which appears when, let's say, we hover over the orange slice which is the **East** region. Once we do that, we will see the see the view as shown in the following screenshot:

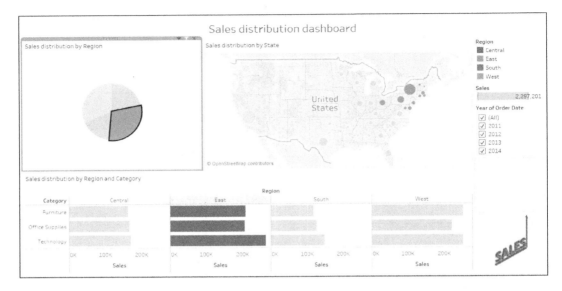

10. Notice how the map highlights the orange colored bubbles, whereas, in the bar chart, since there is no color used, it just highlights the pane for the **East** region.

11. Now, in order to clear this action, we can click in the white area of the `Sales distribution by Region` sheet or just press *Esc* on our keyboards.

How it works...

The difference between filter and highlight actions is that the filter action will update the target sheets to show only the relevant marks whereas the highlight action will update the target sheets to show each and every mark and highlight only the relevant marks and dim the rest.

In the highlight action, we saw a section labeled **Target Highlighting**. This has three options which are as follows:

▶ **Selected Fields**: When we use this option, the marks in the target sheets will be highlighted based on the selected fields in the source sheet and these marks will only be highlighted when the marks in the target sheets are the same as the selected ones that are selected in the source sheets.

▶ **Dates and Times**: When we use this option, the marks in the target sheet will be highlighted only when the date and time of the marks in the target sheet and the date and time of the selected marks in the source sheets are the same.

▶ **All Fields**: When we use this option, the marks in the target sheets are highlighted when they match the marks selected in the source sheet. This is like an **Include all** option where all fields are considered while trying to find a match.

Highlight actions can also be auto-generated from a **Color** legend or from the highlight option in the toolbar. Refer to the following screenshot:

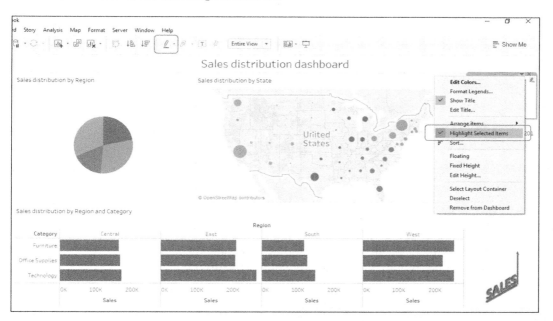

Another way of highlighting any mark is to use the **Highlighters** feature in Tableau. It basically gives an input box where we can search for data points by typing the words or selecting from a drop-down list. In the preceding example, if we enable this functionality for **Region**, then we will get an input box saying **Highlight Region** and when we type a region, Tableau will highlight that region. To enable this, we can select a sheet on the dashboard or go to a sheet and select the **Analysis | Highlighters** option from the toolbar. Refer to the following screenshot:

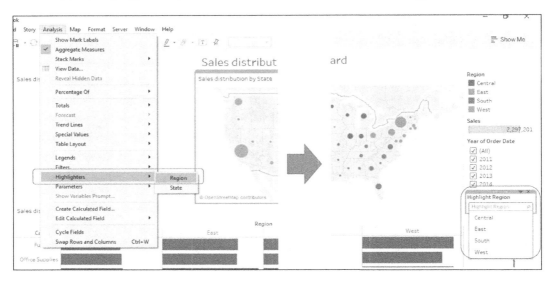

Read more about the highlight action by referring to the following link: `http://onlinehelp.tableau.com/current/pro/desktop/en-us/actions_highlight.html`.

Using the URL action

There are times when we would want to access more information about data that maybe hosted outside our data source. This information could either be on a web page, file, or other web-based resources that are outside of Tableau. To access these from our Tableau workbook, we will need to create hyperlinks. These hyperlinks can be created using a URL action. Thus, a URL action is a hyperlink that points to a web page, file, or other web-based resources that are outside of Tableau.

Further, we can pass values and replace the field values in the URL to make the link more relevant to our data. Let us follow the recipe that is given here, to understand the URL action better.

Getting ready

For this recipe, we will first create a new dashboard which has a map that shows state-level information. We will then embed a web page which will be a Wikipedia page and try to pass values from our Tableau view to show the relevant information on the web page. Let's get started.

How to do it...

1. Let us create a new dashboard and name it `Dashboard for URL action`. Make sure that you select the **Automatic** option as we did in one of the previous recipes to resize the dashboard and avoid scroll bars.

2. Then we will drag and drop the `Sales distribution by State` sheet. Refer to the following screenshot:

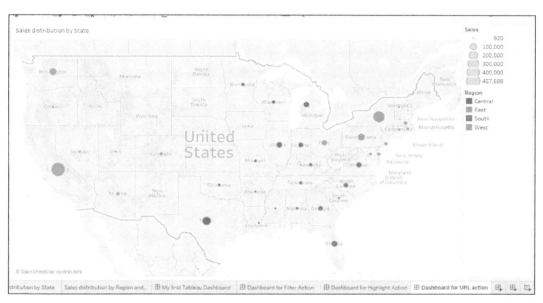

3. Before we embed a web page onto this dashboard, let us first remove the size and color legend by clicking on the cross which appears on the grey border of the legend when we select it. Then let us drag and drop the **Web Page** object from the left-hand side onto the dashboard. When we do that, we will get a small pop up box for typing the URL. Refer to the following screenshot:

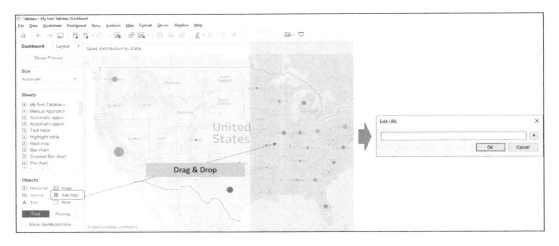

4. Enter the following as the URL: http://en.wikipedia.org/wiki/Wikipedia.

5. Click **OK** and return to the dashboard which will now be updated to show the following view:

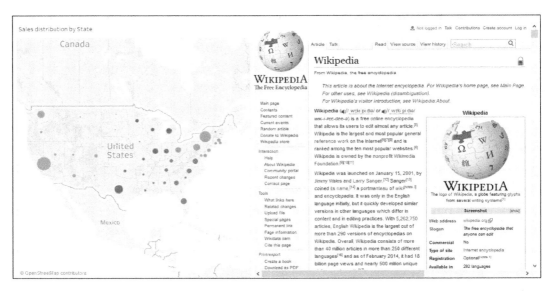

6. Now, what we want to do is that when we click on a particular **State** in the map, the adjacent Wikipedia page should give us information about the selected **State**. For this, we will first go to our web browser and see how the Wikipedia URL works. So, for example, if we look for California on a Wikipedia page, then our URL will update to `http://en.wikipedia.org/wiki/California`. For Texas, it will be `http://en.wikipedia.org/wiki/Texas`, and so on. The point is that, we need to make the last section of our URL dynamic and in order to do that, we will create a URL action from the **Map** to the web page.

7. In order to create a URL action, select **Dashboard | Actions...**.

8. From the **Add Action >** button, select the **URL...** option and once we do that, we will get the view shown in the following screenshot:

9. Name this action **State URL**. We will keep all the default selections the same except change the **Run action on:** from **Menu** to **Select**. We will also enter our Wikipedia URL in the **URL** section. The URL is as follows. `http://en.wikipedia.org/wiki/Wikipedia`.

10. Refer to the following screenshot to see the updated action:

11. Now, in order to dynamically pass the **State** names, we will have to replace the last section of the **URL** which reads Wikipedia with the **State** field which is available when we click on the arrow on the **URL** section. Refer to the following screenshot:

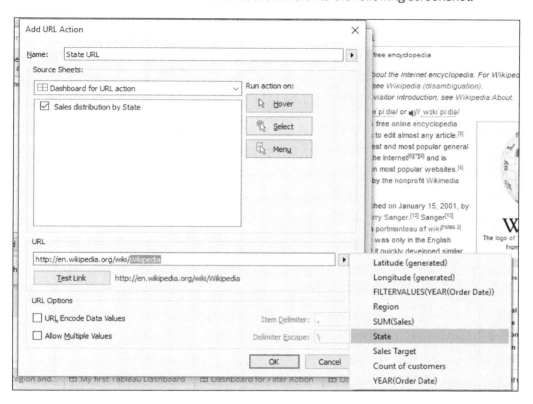

12. Our action will be updated as shown in the following screenshot:

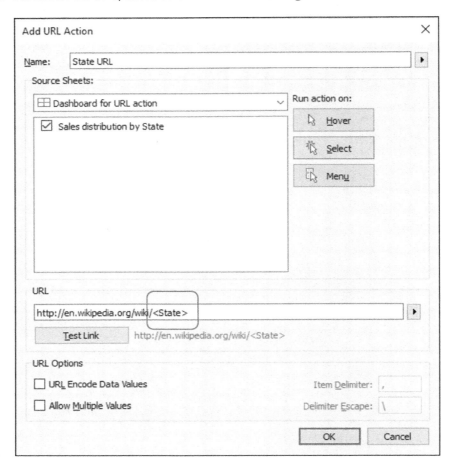

13. Click **OK** and test our action by selecting **California** in the **Map** to see the Wikipedia page update accordingly. Refer to the following screenshot:

How it works...

We have to be very careful when working with URLs as even a slight change in a spelling may not give us the desired output.

Also, since we are working with URLs, it is a good practice to make sure that the Internet connectivity is stable.

Now, when specifying the URL, there is a section which reads URL options. This section contains two options which are as follows:

- **URL Encode Data Values**: If our data contains values that use characters that are not usually allowed in a URL, then we need to make sure to select this option. For example, if one of our data values contains an ampersand, such as **Profit & Marketing**, then the ampersand will have to be translated into characters that our browsers will understand. In other words, if we want to include this value in the URL, then it needs to be URL encoded.

- **Allow Multiple Values**: If we are linking to a web page that can take lists of values, then we need to select this option. However, when we allow multiple values, we must also define the delimiter. A delimiter could be a comma or a tab and is basically a character that separates each item in a list. Once we have defined the delimiter, we will also have to define the delimiter escape.

Read more about URL actions by referring the following link:

```
http://onlinehelp.tableau.com/current/pro/desktop/en-us/actions_url.
html.
```

What we saw in the above recipes was how to create a dashboard and combine multiple visualizations on it and enable interactivity. One small but important point to remember about dashboards is that when we are done with our dashboards, as good practice, we should hide all the individual sheets that are part of the dashboard. This way, we minimize the number of tabs that will be visible to the end user. This could be the case when we may want to hide worksheets and just share the dashboard and not show the supporting worksheets. In order to do so, we need to right-click on the individual worksheet tab and select **Hide Sheet** or right-click on **Dashboard** and select the **Hide All Sheets** options. Refer to the following screenshots:

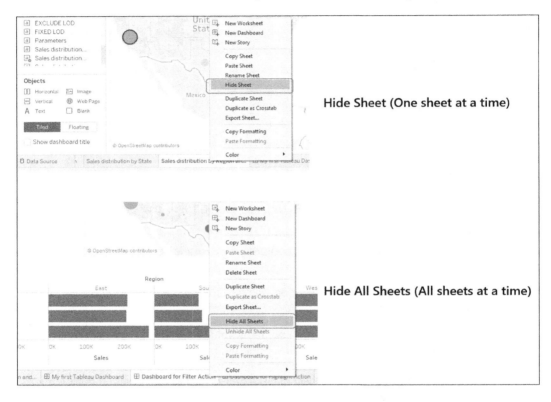

To show a hidden worksheet, we will have to right-click on the sheet name from the left-hand side panel on the dashboard and uncheck the **Hide Sheet** option. Refer to the following screenshot:

 In order to know more about all the three actions, refer to the following blog:

`https://public.tableau.com/s/blog/2015/06/chronicles-red-devils-highlight-filter-and-url-action.`

7
The Right MIX – Blending Multiple Data Sources

In this chapter, we will focus on various aspects of connecting to data and we will cover the following recipes:

- ▶ Understanding Multiple Table Join within a single database
- ▶ Understanding Multiple Table Join across databases
- ▶ Understanding Data Blending
- ▶ Understanding and using Unions
- ▶ Using Custom SQL Query to fetch data
- ▶ Working with Tableau Extracts

Introduction

So far, in all the previous chapters, we've created various visualizations. For each of these visualizations or sheets, we connected to a single data source at a time using the **Live** connect option in Tableau. However, there are going to be circumstances when data from a single database table or even for that matter a single database may not be sufficient from the point of view of our analysis. There may also be circumstances, where we may have to extract our data into the Tableau data engine and work offline to build our views in Tableau. In this chapter, we will focus on the various ways in which we can connect to data in Tableau.

Understanding Multiple Table Join within a single database

Often there will be instances where the data is stored in multiples tables of a database and for the sake of analysis, we are required to fetch the data from these tables.

For example, there may be a table called **Employee Master** which contains the employee details such as employee ID, their first name, last name, date of birth and so on. The salary/ compensation details could be stored in another table and the employment history could be stored in a separate table as well.

When conducting an analysis, we would want to consider all the information related to an employee and then proceed with our analysis. Thus, in this case, we are required to fetch the data from all the three tables, and while doing so we will also have to specify the Joins by defining a primary key. The primary key in this case could be Employee ID which is common across all the tables.

The functionality is called **Multiple Table Joins** and it is used when we want to connect to multiple tables/views of a single database. Let us understand this functionality by going through the following recipe.

Getting ready

For this recipe we will connect to the `Sample - Coffee Chain.mdb` file. This Access database consists of four tables namely **CoffeeChain Query**, **factTable**, **Location**, and **Product**. The **factTable** contains all our measures such as sales, profits, COGS, and so on.

The **Location** table consists the geographical information and the **Product** table consists of information about our products. Lastly, the **CoffeeChain Query** table is a table that consists of data from all the other three tables. So, instead of using the **CoffeeChain Query** table directly, we will fetch data from the **factTable**, **Location** and **Product** tables. Now, in order to get data from these raw tables, we need to have a common linking field. Between the **factTable** and **Location** table, **Area Code** is the common field and between **factTable** and **Product** table, **Product Id** is the common field. Thus **Area Code** will be used to link **factTable** and **Location** and **Product Id** will be used to link **factTable** and **Product**.

For our Mac users who can't connect to the Access database, we will use the `Sample - CoffeeChain (Use instead of MS Access).xlsx` Excel file which has exactly the same data.

We will continue using the same workbook `My first Tableau Workbook` and get started with the recipe.

How to do it...

1. Let us create a new sheet and rename it as `Multiple Table Join-single database`.

2. Click *Ctrl+D* to connect to the data and select the **Access** option, and then select the `Sample - Coffee Chain.mdb` file from `Documents\My Tableau Repository\Datasources\Tableau Cookbook data`. Our Mac user should select the **Excel** option and select the `Sample - CoffeeChain (Use instead of MS Access).xlsx` file from `Documents\My Tableau Repository\Datasources\Tableau Cookbook data`. Once we do that, we will get the following view:

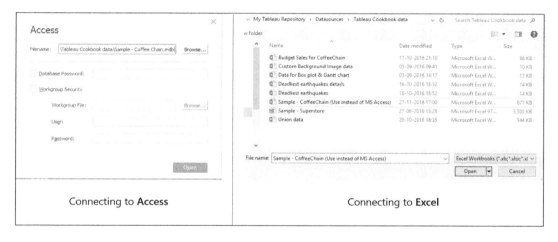

Connecting to **Access**   Connecting to **Excel**

3. Once we have browsed the relevant file, let's click on **Open** and we will get to see the following screenshot:

4. Drag **factTables** and drop it in the white space which says **Drag tables here**. Refer to the following screenshot:

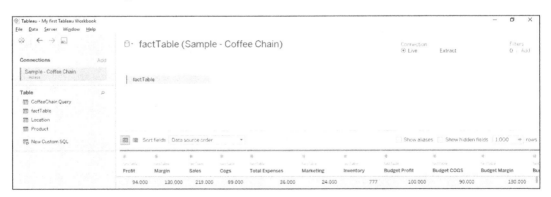

5. Instead of dragging and dropping, we can also double-click on the table name in the left-hand side section. Let's try double-clicking on the **Location** table followed by double-clicking on the **Product** table and our view will be updated as shown in the following screenshot:

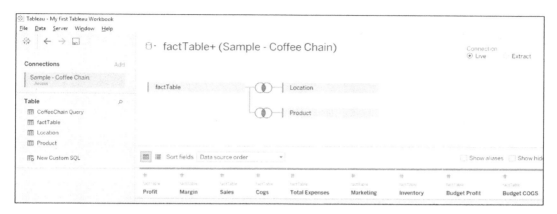

6. If we click on the **intersecting icon** between the **factTable** and the **Location** table and the **factTable** and the **Product** table, we will see that by default, Tableau has selected **Area Code** and **Product Id** as the linking keys between **factTable** and **Location** table and **factTable** and **Product** table respectively. Further, the default **Join** that is defined is an **Inner Join**. We will change this to a **Left Join** by clicking on the **Join** between the tables. Refer to the following screenshot:

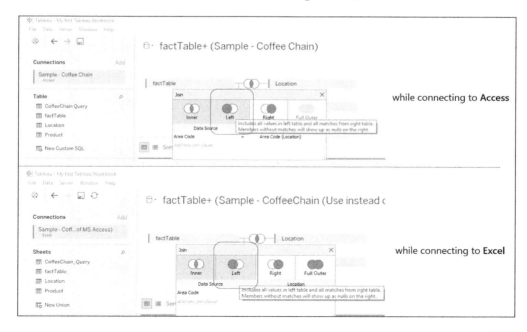

7. Let's do the same for the **Join** between **factTable** and **Product** table. Once we do that, our updated view will be as shown in the following screenshot:

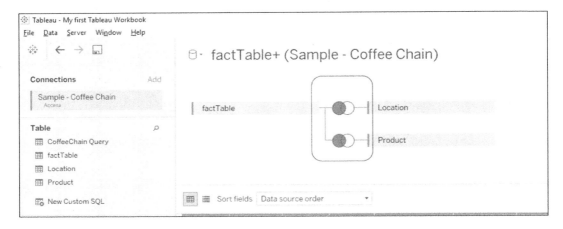

8. Now, we'll change the name of the data source from **factTable+ (Sample - Coffee Chain)** or for Mac user, from **factTable+ (Sample - CoffeeChain (Use instead of MS Access))** to **Multiple Table Join-single database** as shown in the following screenshot:

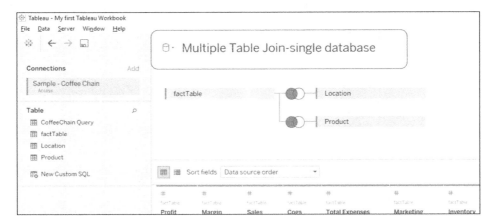

9. Next keeping the default **Live** option selected, click on the **Multiple Table Join-single database** sheet tab and once we do that, we will get the following view:

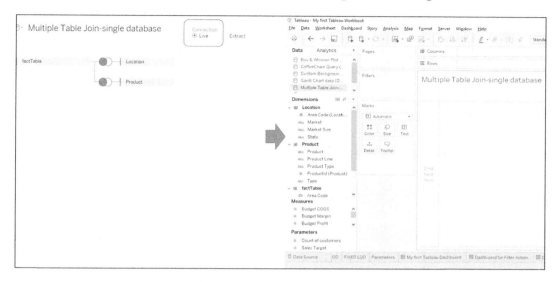

10. Notice the **Dimensions** and **Measures** section: You'll see all the **Dimensions** of **Location** table sheets grouped under **Location** table, the **Dimensions** of **Product** table and the **factTable** both grouped under **Product**. Since the **Location** and **Product** table does not have any measures, we do not see a similar grouping for **Measures**.

11. Next, let's double-click on **Area Code** which comes from the **factTable** table. This will create a map of the United States. However, if it doesn't, then we need to click on the **Edit Locations....** option in the **Map** section of the toolbar and make sure that the **Country/Region:** is selected as United States. We have already seen this functionality when we learnt about creating and using maps. Next, we will drag **Sales** from the **Measures** pane and drop it into the **Size** shelf, followed by dragging the **Market Size** field from the **Location** table and dropping it into the **Color** shelf. Lastly, we will right-click on the **Product Type** field in the **Product** table and select the **Show Filter** option. Once we do all of this, we will get the following view:

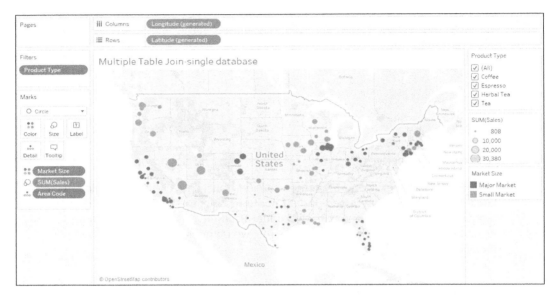

How it works...

As mentioned earlier, we will use the Multiple Table Join when we need to connect to data which is stored in separate tables in a single database. In the preceding recipe, the **factTable** contained the transactional data, the product details were stored in a separate table called **Product,** and the market details were stored in the **Location** table. When we want to analyze the sales of different products across different markets, we need to get data from all the three tables that belong to a single database named `Sample - Coffee Chain.mdb` or `Sample - CoffeeChain (Use instead of MS Access).xlsx`

Further, when we are linking *multiple tables*, there needs to be a common field which can be used as a linking field. If the tables have a field which is spelt exactly the same and has the same data type, then Tableau assumes that the field is our linking key. For example, in our recipe, **Area Code** and **Product Id** were already selected by Tableau as the linking fields. We can add additional links or even edit the existing link by clicking on the dropdown as shown in the following screenshot:

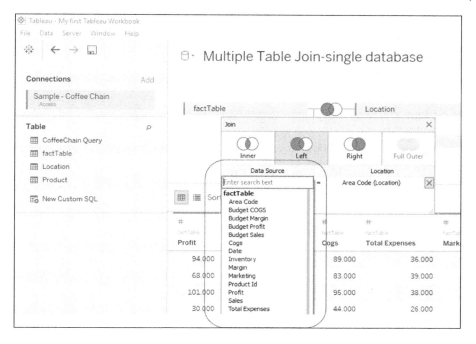

The following image shows the database mapping between three tables that we've used in our recipe:

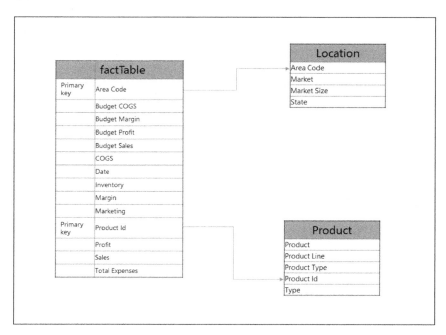

Further, we also need to specify the type of Join that needs to be used to link multiple tables. Depending on the database or the file that we are connected to, we will get the following types of Joins in Tableau:

- **Inner Join**: Will only fetch records that are common in both the tables. This is like an **Intersection** in Venn diagrams.

- **Left Join**: Will fetch all records from the *Left* table and only the matching records from the *Right* table.

- **Right Join**: Will fetch all the records from the *Right* table and only the matching records from the *Left* table.

- **Full Join**: Will fetch all the records from both the tables. This is like a **Union** in Venn diagrams.

Refer the following image to quickly understand the Joins:

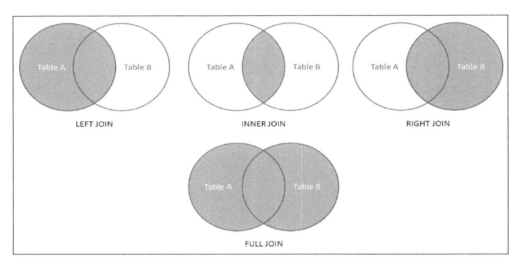

Understanding Multiple Table Join across databases

In the previous recipe, we saw how to connect to a single database which was an `Access` file named `Sample - Coffee Chain.mdb` or `Sample - CoffeeChain (Use instead of MS Access).xlsx` and join multiple tables within it. There could also be instances where the data resides in multiple data sources. For example, the transactional sales data could be getting captured in, let's say, a SQL database and the yearly/monthly budgets are defined in Excel. In this situation, Excel is one data source and SQL is another data source. In order to see whether the targets were met or not, we would be required to get data from both Excel as well as SQL.

Cross-database Joins help us make Joins across multiple databases across a single data source, or multiple databases across multiple data sources.

Let us take a look at how we can do a cross-database join in the following recipe.

Getting ready

For this recipe, we use two of the six datasets which have been uploaded on the following link:

`https://1drv.ms/f/s!Av5QCoyLTBpngh8QBp6ih44zjjbj.`

There are six files and we will download the Access database named `Modified CoffeeChain.accdb` and the Excel file named `Budget Sales for CoffeeChain.xlsx`.

Mac users can download the Excel file named `Modified CoffeeChain (Use instead of MS Access).xlsx` instead of the Access database.

Download and save these files in the `Documents\My Tableau Repository\Datasources\Tableau Cookbook data` folder.

The Access database contains measures such as **Sales, Profit,** and **Margin** for **Products** across various **States**. However, it doesn't have any information about **Budget Sales**. The Excel file which is the `Budget Sales for CoffeeChain.xlsx` file contains only the budget sales information which is missing in the Access database. We want to create one single view which pulls sales data from the `Access` file and the budget sales data from the Excel file. Let us see how this can be done.

Let us continue using the same workbook `My first Tableau Workbook`.

How to do it...

1. Let us create a new sheet and rename it `Multiple Table Join-cross database`.

2. Let us create *Ctrl+D* to connect to the data and select the **Access** option and then select the `Modified CoffeeChain` file from `Documents\My Tableau Repository\Datasources\Tableau Cookbook data`. Our Mac user should select the Excel option and then select the `Modified CoffeeChain (Use instead of MS Access).xlsx` file from `Documents\My Tableau Repository\Datasources\Tableau Cookbook data`. Once we have opened the `Modified CoffeeChain` file, we will get a view as shown in the following screenshot:

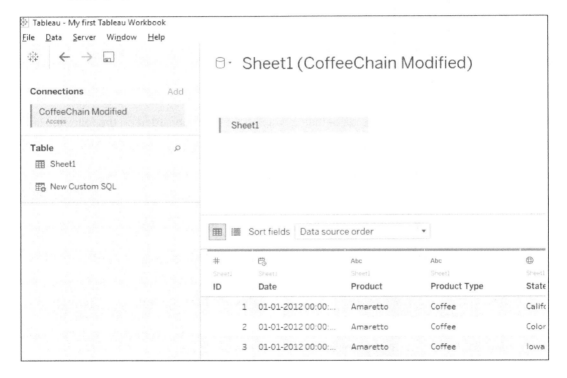

3. We will then connect to the `Budget Sales for CoffeeChain` file by clicking on the **Add** option in **Connections**. Refer to the following screenshot:

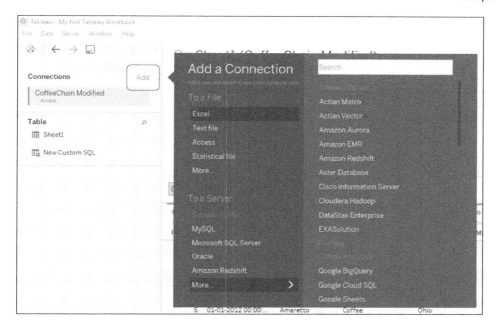

4. In the popup section, select the Excel option and browse the `Budget Sales for CoffeeChain` file from `Documents\My Tableau Repository\Datasources\Tableau Cookbook data`. Once we do that, we will see that the **CoffeeChain Modified** has a *blue bar* whereas **Budget Sales for CoffeeChain** has an *orange bar*, which indicates that **CoffeeChain Modified** is the primary data source and the **Budget Sales for CoffeeChain** is the secondary data source. Refer to the following screenshot:

5. Further, we will also see that the joining condition is not working and it has a red exclamation mark. If we hover over the exclamation mark, we will get a message saying that the **Date** field in the Access database is a **Date & Time** field, whereas in the Excel file, it is just a **Date** field. Refer to the following screenshot:

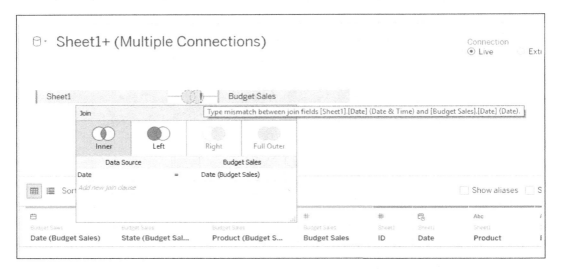

6. This is clearly a data type mismatch issue and, in order to rectify this, we will look for the **Date** field of the **Budget Sales for CoffeeChain** datasource in the data preview section and change the datatype to the **Date & Time** field. Refer to the following screenshot:

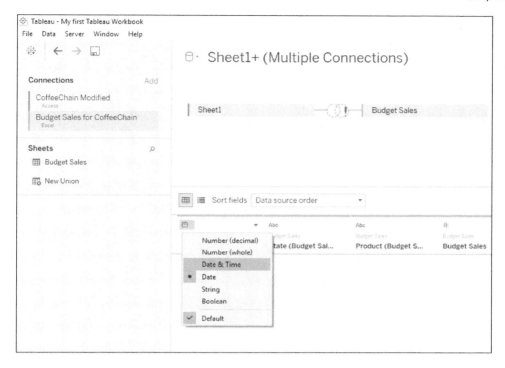

7. Once we change the datatype, our Join will be sorted as shown in the following screenshot:

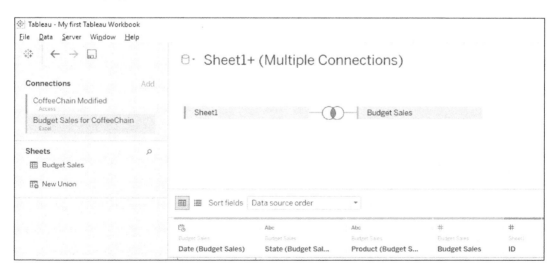

8. Now that the **Join** is sorted, let's add more linking fields on **Product** and **State** as well. Refer to the following screenshot:

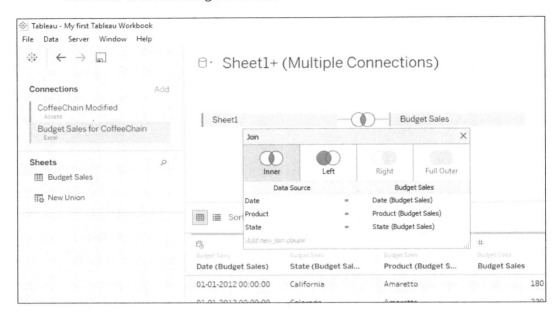

9. Now that we are sorted on the Joins, let us quickly change the name of the data source from **Sheet1+ (Multiple Connections)** to **Multiple Table Join-cross database** as shown in the following screenshot:

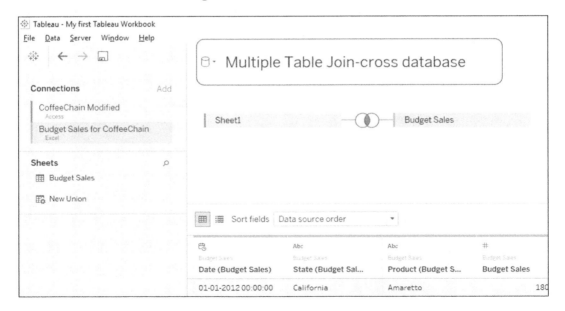

10. Let us click on the **Multiple Table Join-cross database** sheet tab in order to start building our visualization.

11. Next, we will create a **State** map by double-clicking on the **State** field from the **Sheet1** table in the **Dimensions** pane. In this case, the map doesn't show up, so let's make sure we select the country as **United States** from the **Edit Locations....** option in the **Map** section of the toolbar.

12. Let's then fetch **Sales** from the **Measures** pane and drop it into the **Size** shelf. Now we would want to compare the **Sales** and the **Budget Sales** and find out which states are below target and which states are above target. In order to do so, we will create a new calculated field and call it **Sales vs Budget Sales**: The formula could be as follows:

    SUM([Sales])<SUM([Budget Sales])

13. Refer to the following screenshot:

| Sales vs Budget Sales | ☐ Multiple Table Join-cross database | ✕ |

SUM([Sales])<SUM([Budget Sales])

▶

The calculation is valid.   [Apply]   [OK]

14. When we click **OK**, we will get a new measure which is of Boolean output. Let us the new field and drop it into the **Color** shelf as shown in the following screenshot:

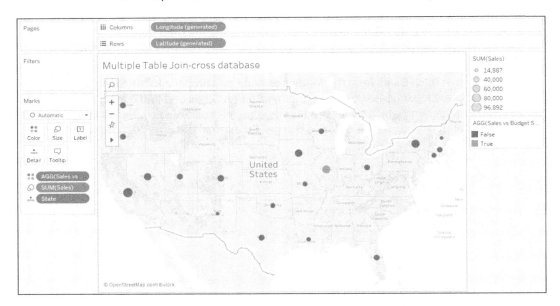

15. In the preceding screenshot, we can see that there is only one **State** which is below target. However, these targets are across all the products. If we wish to see the sales performance of all the states versus the budget values for a particular product, then let's make the provision for the user to select the desired product by creating a filter on **Product** from the **Sheet1** table by right-clicking on it and selecting the **Show Filter** option. Refer to the following screenshot:

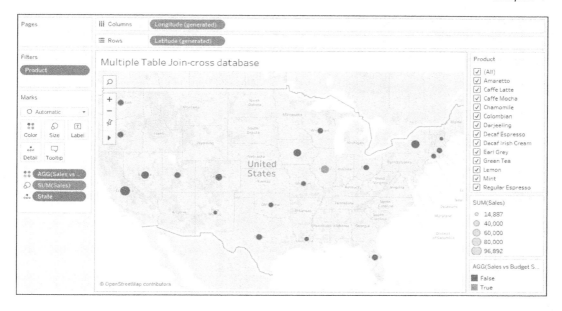

16. Next, let us make the filter a single select radio button option by clicking on the **Filter** dropdown and selecting the option of **Single Value (list)**. Refer to the following screenshot:

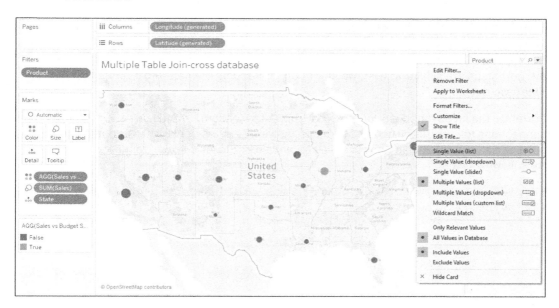

17. If we select **Colombian**, then our view will update as shown in the following screenshot:

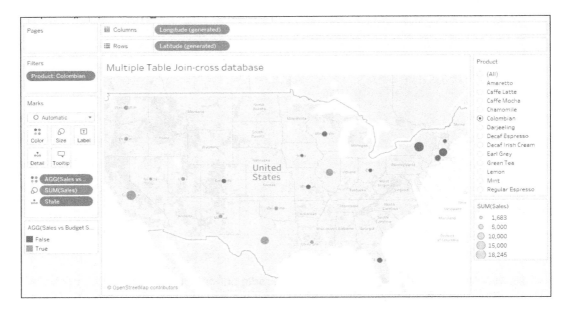

How it works...

In the earlier part of the recipe, we saw that for the link or the join condition to work, we need to make sure that the data types of the fields are the same. Once, we sort that issue, then the next steps are similar to what we saw in *Understanding Multiple Table Join within a single database* recipe.

Currently, the cross-database Joins are not supported for some sources. These include connections to cube data such as Microsoft Analysis Services or extract-only data sources such as Salesforce, Google Analytics, OData, and so on. To know more about Joins, refer to the following link:

```
http://onlinehelp.tableau.com/current/pro/desktop/en-us/joining_
tables.html#integration
```

Understanding Data Blending

In the earlier recipes, we saw how to join data from multiple data tables that are either within a single database or across multiple databases. The cross-database join functionality was introduced by Tableau in version 10.0 and, in versions prior to this, one could rely on the Data Blending functionality to get data from multiple data sources.

Even though the cross-database Join has made joining the data from disparate data sources fairly easy, the Data Blending functionality still exists and can be used where cross-database Joins won't work. For example, cross-database functionality can't be used with Salesforce or Google Analytics or even multi-dimensional cubes. One can also use Data Blending over cross-database Joins when the data is at a different granularity.

Let us explore this functionality in more details in the following recipe.

Getting ready

For this recipe, we will download the sample data that has been uploaded on the following link:

```
https://1drv.ms/f/s!Av5QCoyLTBpnhkx2T7tGF1MQ32MR
```

In this recipe, we will use the two datasets called `Deadliest earthquakes.xlsx` and `Deadliest earthquakes details.xlsx`. Let's continue working in the same Tableau file.

How to do it...

1. Click on the link to download these Excel files and let us save it in our `Documents\ My Tableau Repository\Datasources\Tableau Cookbook data` folder.

2. We will then create a new sheet in our existing Tableau workbook and rename it **Data Blending**.

3. Click *Ctrl+D* to connect to data, select the **Excel** option, select the `Deadliest earthquakes.xlsx` file and click on the **Data Blending** sheet tab.

4. Next we will again click *Ctrl+D* to make a new data connection and this time, we will connect to the `Deadliest earthquakes details.xlsx` file. We will see the two new data connections in our **Data** window. Refer to the following screenshot:

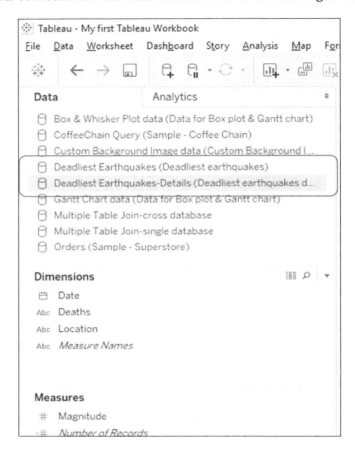

5. Next, let us click on the **Deadliest earthquakes** data source in the **Data** window to view its **Dimensions** and **Measures**. Drag the field called **Date** from the **Deadliest earthquakes** data source and drop it into the **Row** shelf. Next, drag the field called **Location** from the same data source and drop it right after the **Date** field in the **Rows** shelf. Refer to the following screenshot:

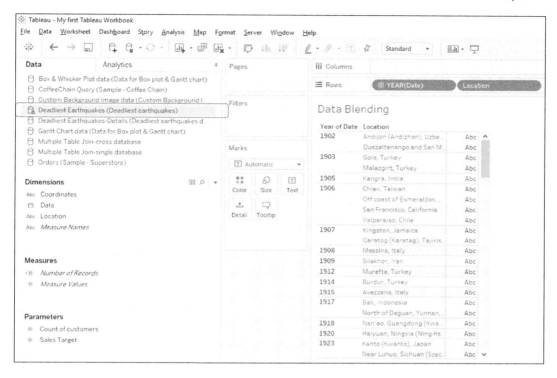

6. The preceding screenshot, shows a highlighted section. If you look carefully, we will see a small blue tick mark for the **Deadliest earthquakes** data source. This indicates, that the current worksheet, is referring to **Deadliest earthquakes** as the data source.

7. The **Deadliest earthquakes** data source, contains only the information in terms of **Coordinates**, **Location**, and **Date** of earthquakes. The magnitude of these earthquakes is captured in the **Deadliest earthquakes details** data source. Now, in order to use the **Magnitude** field, we will have to select the **Deadliest earthquakes details** data source in the **Data** window. When we do that, we will see two **link** icons, which are basically the common linking fields, highlighted in the following screenshot:

8. Next, we will select the **Magnitude** field from the **Measures** pane of the **Deadliest earthquakes details** data source and drop it into the **Columns** shelf of the **Data Blending** worksheet that we are currently working on. Refer to the following screenshot:

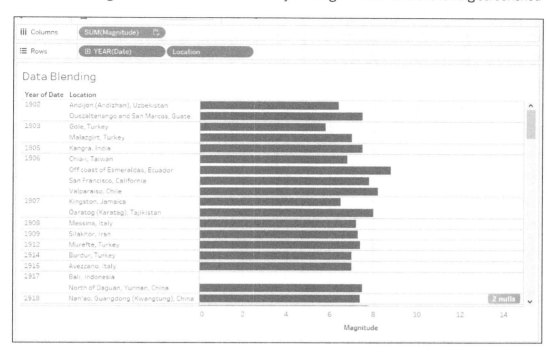

9. This is how we enable **Data Blending** in Tableau. However, as a final finishing touch, let's quickly put a magnitude filter by right-clicking on the **Magnitude** field and selecting the **Show Filter** option and only look at the earthquakes having a magnitude of **8** and above. Refer to the following screenshot:

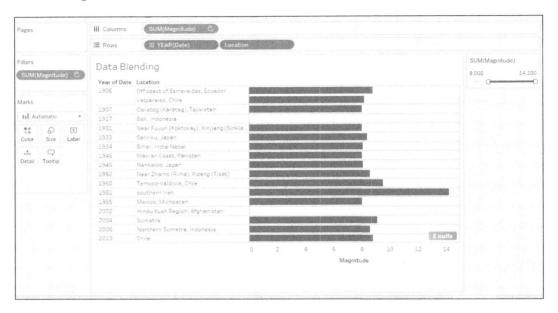

How it works...

As we saw in all the preceding three recipes, whether it is a Join or Data Blending, we will be required to use one or more common linking fields. When doing Data Blending, if the field names and the data types are exactly the same, then Tableau automatically selects these fields as the linking fields and marks them with an *orange* link.

Further, if we think the linking is not correct and that Tableau has just done the mapping only on the basis of the same name, then we can disable the link by clicking on it. When we disable the link, it will appear broken as shown in the following screenshot:

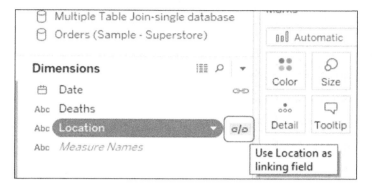

This disabled link can be enabled again by clicking on the gray broken link. At times, by default some fields are marked with the gray broken link icon indicating that they are potential linking fields. Further, in the **Data** window, the data sources that we are using will either have a *blue tick* mark or an *orange tick* mark. Refer to the following screenshot:

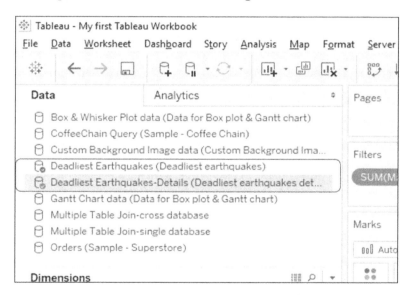

The *blue tick* mark indicates that the data source is being used as a *primary data source* and the *orange tick* mark indicates that the data source is being used as a *secondary data source*. Similarly, all the fields coming from the secondary data source will also have the *orange tick* mark to indicate that these fields are being fetched from the secondary data source. Refer to the following screenshot:

As mentioned earlier, Tableau will automatically recognize when a field from the primary data source also exists in a secondary data source and will use these fields for linking. However, this is only the case when the field names and their data types are exactly the same.

Imagine a situation where the field names aren't the same. For example, in one data source the field is referred to as Order ID and in the second data source, the same field is referred to as Transaction ID. In this case, Tableau will not define the linking fields automatically and we will have to define them ourselves. To do this, we'll have to click on the **Data | Edit Relationships...** in the toolbar. Refer to the following screenshot:

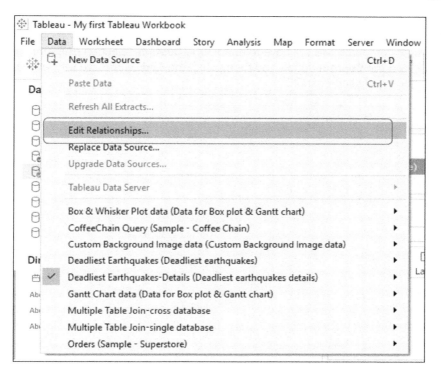

Once we do that, we will get the view as shown in the following screenshot:

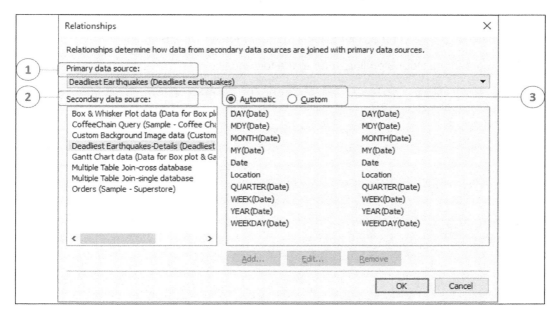

In the preceding option box, we can define our **Primary data source** *(ref. annotation 1)*. The **Secondary data source** can be defined in the following section *(ref. annotation 2)*. To define the linking fields manually, we will have to enable the **Custom** selection *(ref. annotation 3)*. Once we click on the **Custom** option and then select the **Add** button, we will get the view as shown in the following screenshot:

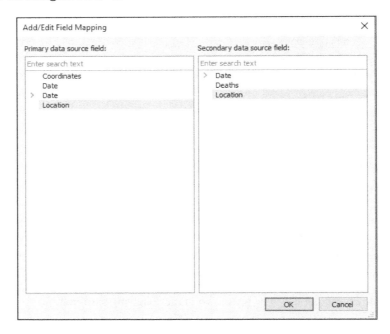

This is where we will select the linking fields manually for our Data Blending.

To know more about Data Blending, refer to the following link:

```
http://onlinehelp.tableau.com/current/pro/desktop/en-us/multiple_
connections.html
```

Data Blending in Tableau supports a Left Join and thus we need to select our primary data source carefully. Further, if we are working with multidimensional data sources (cubes), then we need to remember not to use them as the secondary data source. Multidimensional data sources can only be used as the primary data source when doing a Data Blending.

Understanding and using Unions

So far we have understood how Joins and Data Blending work. However, when we use Joins or blending, we end up appending columns from one table to another. Now imagine a situation where we need to append rows from one table to another. So, for example, imagine having separate tables for each quarter; each table contains the same information but only for the relevant quarter. Now if we wish to look at the performance of the entire year, then we will need the data from all these separate quarter tables. In this case, we will use the **Union** functionality. Let's see how we can do Unions in Tableau in the following recipe.

Getting ready

For this recipe, we will download the Excel file named `Union data.xlsx` that has been uploaded on the following link:

`https://1drv.ms/f/s!Av5QCoyLTBpnhkx2T7tGFlMQ32MR`

We will download this file and save it to the `Documents\My Tableau Repository\ Datasources\Tableau Cookbook data` folder. We will continue using the same workbook, `My first Tableau Workbook`. Let us get started with the recipe.

How to do it...

1. Let us create a new sheet and rename it as `Union`.

2. Click *Ctrl+D* to connect to the data and select the **Excel** option and then select the `Union data.xlsx` file from `Documents\My Tableau Repository\Datasources\Tableau Cookbook data`. Click on **Open** and we will get to see the data connection window. Refer to the following screenshot:

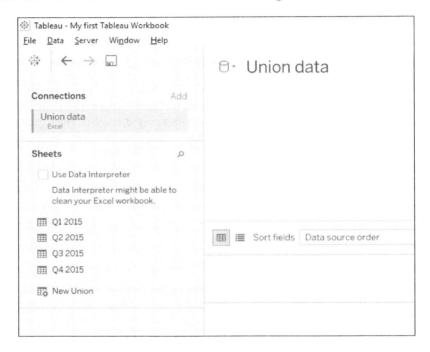

3. As we see in the preceding screenshot, once we establish a connection to the `Union data.xlsx` file, we will see that it contains four tables or worksheets named **Q1 2015**, **Q2 2015**, **Q3 2015**, and **Q4 2015**. Now we would like the data from all these tables or worksheets to be appended one below the other in one view so we can take a look at the total yearly values. In order to do so, let's start by double-clicking on the **New Union** option as shown in the following screenshot:

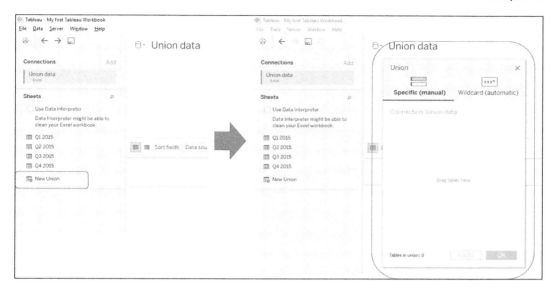

4. Next, let us drag **Q1 2015** into the new box which says **Union**. Refer to the following screenshot:

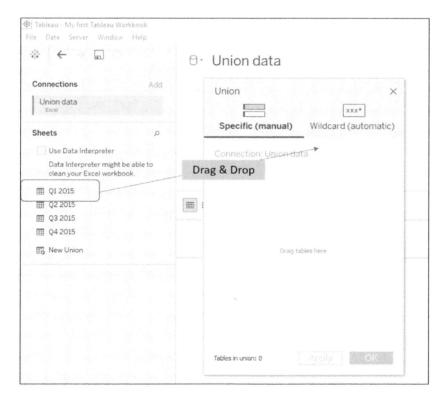

5. We'll do the same for the rest of the tables and then our view will update as shown in the following screenshot:

6. Now, click **OK**. Our view will be updated as shown in the following screenshot:

7. Click on the **Union** sheet tab to view the **Dimensions** and **Measures** of this Union operation.

8. Right-click and drag the **Date** field from the **Dimensions** pane and drop it into the **Columns** shelf. Select the **DAY(Date)** option as shown in the following screenshot:

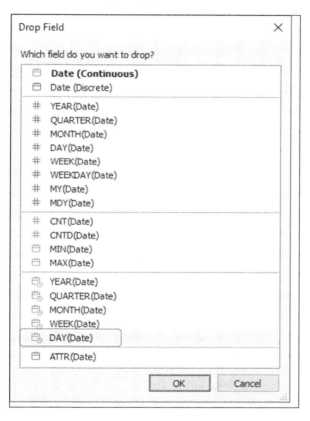

9. Next, let us drag **Sales** and drop it into the **Rows** shelf followed by dragging the **Quarter** field and dropping it into the **Color** shelf. Refer to the following screenshot:

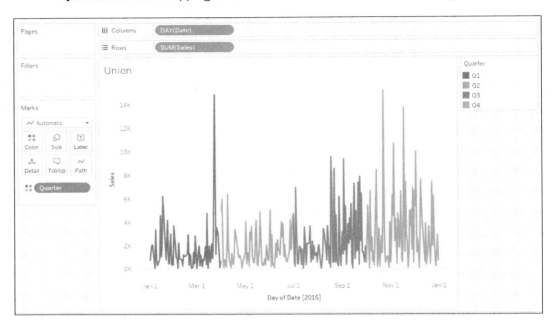

How it works...

As we saw in the earlier recipe, when we do a Union of all the four tables or worksheets, we get a single datasource with all the data appended row-wise. Further, if we take a look at the data file, the first three quarters had only the **Sales** and **Profit** fields, whereas the fourth quarter has a new measure called **Quantity**. However, when we are doing a Union, we get a new column for **Quantity** and this column shows **null** for the first three quarters and data only for the fourth quarter.

Further, there could be a situation where the field names across the tables do not have the same column header names. For example, one table could have a field called **Product** and the other could have a field called **Product Name**; however, these two fields are essentially the same. When doing a Union, this will give us two separate fields. To avoid this, we can use the **Merge mismatched fields** option. Refer to the following screenshot:

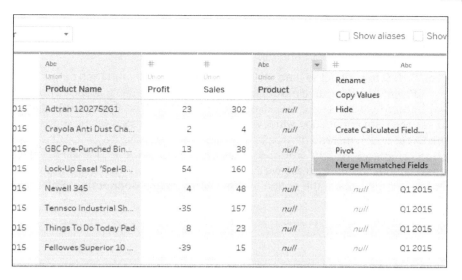

Further, when we do a Union across tables, there is some metadata information such as `Sheet` and `Table name` that is created in addition to the actual data. These fields help us get information about where our values are coming from.

Using Custom SQL Query to fetch data

When connecting to the data, there may be instances where we would want to connect only to a specific query rather than the entire data source, or use some specific filters before getting the data into Tableau. There could also be instances where we may want some calculation to be pre-computed before fetching it into Tableau. In all these situations, we can write a **Custom SQL** to fetch the data in Tableau. For using **Custom SQL Query** option in Tableau, we need to be familiar with writing SQL queries. Let's see how to use the **Custom SQL** option in Tableau.

Getting ready

We will use the `Sample - Coffee Chain.mdb` data or `Sample - CoffeeChain (Use instead of MS Access).xlsx` and we will continue working in the same workbook. We have already established a connection to the `Sample - Coffee Chain.mdb` Access file, or `Sample - CoffeeChain (Use instead of MS Access).xlsx` Excel file for our Mac users, for some of our previous recipes. However, for this recipe, we will make an altogether new connection by using the **Custom SQL** option. Let us see how that can be done.

How to do it...

1. Let us create a new sheet and rename it `Custom SQL`.

2. Click *Ctrl+D* to connect to data, select the **Access** option and then select the `Sample - Coffee Chain.mdb` file from `Documents\My Tableau Repository\Datasources\Tableau Cookbook data`. Click on the **Open** button and we'll get to see the data connection window. For Mac users, this step will be modified to select the **Excel** option instead of Access. We will select the `Sample - CoffeeChain (Use instead of MS Access).xlsx` Excel file. However, we will not click on the **Open** option directly. Instead, we'll click on the dropdown from the button which reads **Open**, and then select the option of **Open with Legacy Connection**. Refer to the following screenshot:

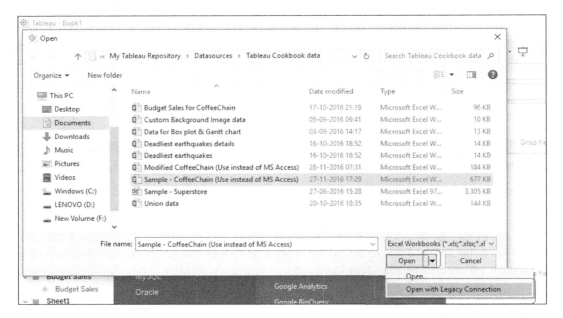

3. Once we have connected to the relevant data source, double-click on the **New Custom SQL** option. Refer to the following screenshot:

4. When we double-click on the **New Custom SQL** option, we will get the following view:

5. The text box is where we will type our Custom SQL Query. Let's type a very simple SQL query which will fetch data only for **Central** region. Refer the following SQL query:

```
SELECT * FROM [CoffeeChain Query] where Market='Central'
```

6. For Mac users, using Excel as a datasource, the preceding query will be updated as follows:

```
SELECT * FROM [CoffeeChain_Query$] where [Market]='Central'
```

7. Let us **OK** to proceed and then click on the **Custom SQL** sheet tab. Now drag **Market** and drop it into the **Rows** shelf. Next, drag **State** and drop it after **Market** in the **Rows** shelf. Lastly, let us drag and drop **Sales** in the **Columns** shelf and our view will be as shown in the following screenshot:

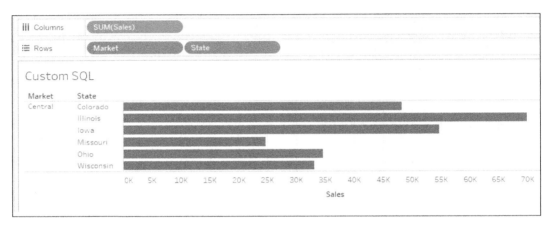

8. As a last step, let's convert this bar chart into a packed bubbles chart by selecting the **packed bubbles** option from the **Show Me!** option. After we get the packed bubbles chart, we'll quickly replace **Market** from the **Color** shelf with **State** field by dragging the **Sales** fields from the **Dimensions** pane. After we do that, we'll get the following view:

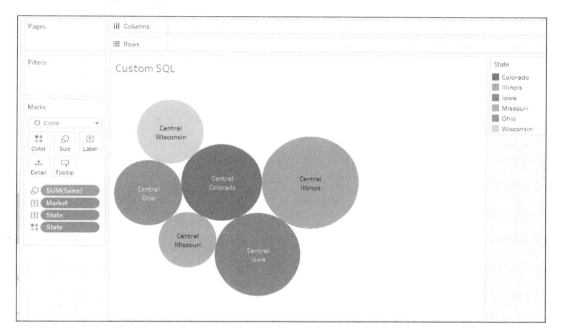

How it works...

When working with Custom SQL, we need to remember that every database has slightly different SQL syntax and hence the Custom SQL written for one data source may not work with another. Further, for Excel and text file data sources, Custom SQL is available only when using the legacy connection or in workbooks that were created before Tableau Desktop 8.2. In order to use the Custom SQL for Excel in Tableau Desktop 8.3 and beyond we simply need to select the **Microsoft Excel** option under data sources and then open the desired Excel file using the legacy connection. Refer to the following screenshot:

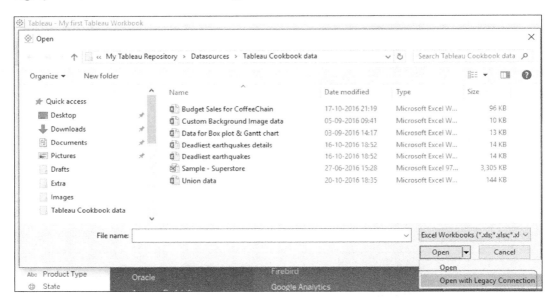

Further, when working with Custom SQL, there's an option called **Insert Parameter**. This feature essentially helps us replace a constant value with a dynamic value in our **Custom SQL Query**. This can then be used to modify the connection on-the-fly by changing the values in the Parameter. For example, in our preceding recipe, we had hard coded the Custom SQL to fetch records only for the **Central** region. However, we can make this connection dynamic by replacing it with the following part which says Market = 'Central' to Market = [Region Parameter].

[Region Parameter] could be a parameter which is already part of the workbook or we can create it from scratch in the **Custom SQL Query** box itself. Refer to the following screenshot:

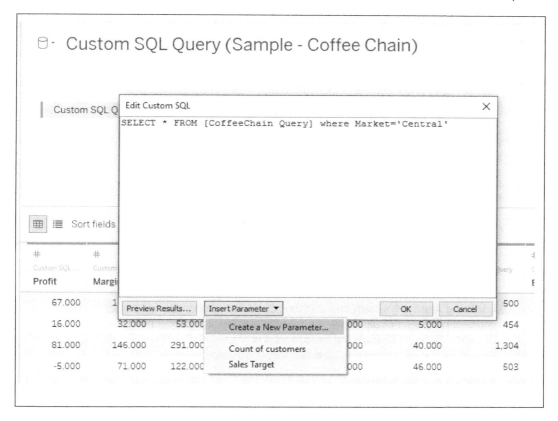

We can then use this parameter control to switch the `Market` and pull in the data for each `Market` of interest without having to edit or duplicate the connection. However, we need to remember that parameters can only replace literal values and not replace the expressions or identifiers such as table names.

Refer to the following link to learn more about **Custom SQLQuery** in Tableau:

`http://onlinehelp.tableau.com/current/pro/desktop/en-us/customsql.html`

Further, apart from giving us the flexibility to define our own input data by writing a **Custom SQL Query**, Tableau also allows us to use the **Stored Procedures** to define our data connection for certain databases such as **SAP Sybase ASE**, **Microsoft SQL Server**, or **Teradata**.

Working with Tableau Extracts

As discussed in our first chapter, there are two options of connecting to our data, namely, **Live** and **Extract**. With the **Live** option, Tableau connects directly to our data and maintains a **Live'** connection with the data source. In **Live** connection, Tableau leverages the capabilities of our data source and hence the speed of our data source will determine the performance of our analysis. Whereas, the **Extract** option helps us import the entire data or subset of our data into Tableau's fast data engine as an Extract. This basically creates a .tde file which stands for **Tableau Data Extract**.

So far we have used the **Live** connect option for connecting to our data sources. However, in this section, we will focus on the **Extract** option.

Typically, Extracts are used for the following reasons:

▸ **Improving performance**: If the data source speed is hampering the performance of our analysis, then we can use an **Extract**. This could be the case when connecting to flat files such as Excel, text files, Access, and so on.

▸ **Enabling more advanced capabilities**: Connecting **Live** to Excel using the legacy connection does not allow certain functions to be used; for example, **Count Distinct**, **Creating Sets**, or **Combining Sets**, and so on. Creating an **Extract** helps overcome this limitation of connecting **Live** to Excel using legacy connection.

▸ **Doing an offline analysis**: An **Extract** helps provide offline access to our data.

We can create Extracts at two levels. The first is when we are connecting to the data, and the second is after we have already connected to the data using the **Live** connection. The first approach is fairly simple as we get the **Live** or **Extract** option right at the stage where we define the data sources. Refer to the following screenshot:

As mentioned earlier, when we create an **Extract**, we create a `.tde` file. This `.tde` file is a compressed version of our data, stored in a **columnar** fashion which is stored on our computers. Further, because of its **architecture-aware** nature, the **Extract** file allows us to fully exploit all our machine memory without really having to limit our data size to the capacity of our hardware. Unlike some other tools, the in-memory concept of Tableau is slightly different. Rather than getting all the data onto our machine memory all at once, Tableau will store the data on our disk and load it into the memory as and when required for our visualization. This makes sure that the `.tde` has the speed benefits of the traditional in-memory solutions without the limitations of having to fit our data into the memory all at once.

Creating the **Extract** from the data connection window is simple as we just need to select the radio button which reads as **Extract**. However, in this recipe, we will take a look at how to create an **Extract** after we have already gone ahead with the default **Live** connection. A point to remember is that no matter which approach we take, it still gives us the same window for doing the necessary selections for creating our Extracts. Let's get started with the recipe to create an **Extract**.

Getting ready

We will create an Extract on the already connected data source called **Orders (Sample - Superstore Subset (Excel))** in Tableau. In the previous recipes, we had connected **Live** to the **Orders** sheets of the `Sample - Superstore Subset (Excel).xlsx` file.

Since, we have already made a **Live** connection to this data source, we will see how to create an **Extract** after the data source had been connected.

How to do it...

1. Let us create a new sheet and rename it `Extract`.

2. In the **Data** window, right-click on the **Orders (Sample - Superstore Subset (Excel))** data connection and select the option of **Extract Data.....**. Refer to the following screenshot:

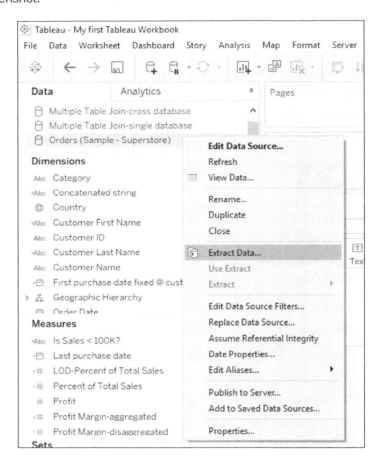

3. When we do that, we get a dialog box as shown in the following screenshot:

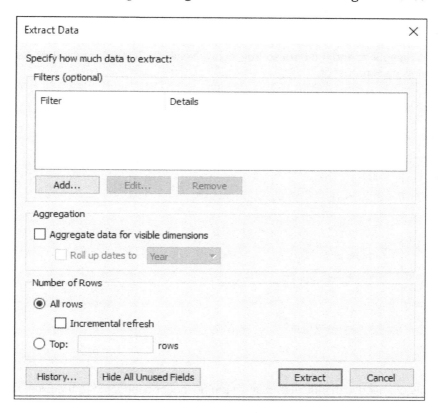

4. We will click on the **Extract** button at the bottom of the dialog box and when we do that, we will be asked to save the .tde file. Save this .tde file as Orders (Sample - Superstore).tde to Documents\My Tableau Repository\ Datasources\Tableau Cookbook data.

5. Once we save the `.tde` file to our desired location, we may get a message box saying **Processing Request** which essentially gives us an update on how many rows of data are being retrieved into the `.tde` file. However, if the dataset is small, then we may not even get this message. In either case, once the import is done, the message box will disappear and the data source icon will change in the **Data** window. Refer to the following screenshot:

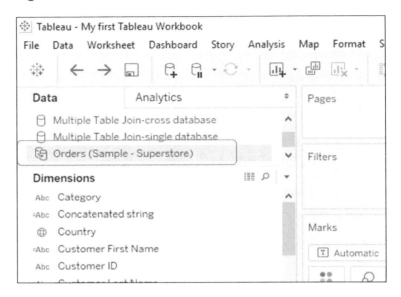

6. This changed icon indicates that we are no longer connected to the Excel file using a **Live** connection, and instead we are working with an **Extract** of the data. Now, in order to use this data, we will create a view for our sheet by creating a bar chart of **Profit** by **Ship Mode**. Refer to the following screenshot:

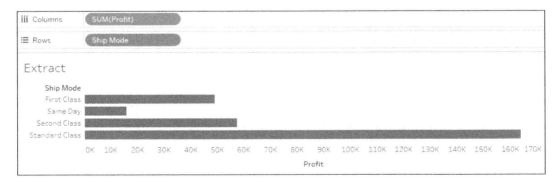

How it works...

When we create an **Extract** either at the stage of establishing the data connection for the first time or after we have already connected to the data using the default **Live** connection, we get the dialog box as shown in the following screenshot:

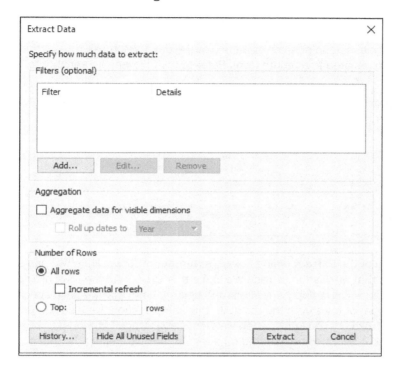

The first section which says **Filters (optional)** is the section where we define the filters to fetch the subset of the entire data. In order to do so, we will have to click on the **Add...** button and we will get the list all the **Dimensions** and **Measures** that are available in the dataset.

Please note that, if we are using the **Filter** option for extracting data at the point of making the connection for the first time, then we will get only the fields that are coming from the data, whereas when we use this option at the point where we have already created a **Live** connection and then wish to create an **Extract**, then we will also get the list of calculated fields (if any) that we may have created while being connected **Live** to the data.

Further, the next section of the **Extract** dialog box says **Aggregation**. Here we can specify whether to aggregate the data for visible dimensions by selecting the option of **Aggregate data for visible dimensions**. When we select this option, then the measures are aggregated using their default aggregation and this in turn reduces the size of the Extract file and also helps in improving the performance. Further, when we select this option, there is another selection which gets enabled called **Roll up dates to**. This option helps us to aggregate the data at a specified date level such as Year, Quarter, Month, and so on. So if we have day level transactional data, and we select the option of aggregating data by rolling up dates at a month level, then instead of showing values at the day level, these transactional day level values will be aggregated to a month level. Refer to the following screenshot for more clarity:

Original Data			Aggregated Data (no roll up)			Aggregated Data (rolled up to months)		
Date	Category	Sales	Date	Category	Sales	Date	Category	Sales
01 March 2015	Furniture	$100	01 March 2015	Furniture	$100			
01 March 2015	Office Supplies	$500	01 March 2015	Office Supplies	$1300	Mar-15	Furniture	$800
01 March 2015	Office Supplies	$800	01 March 2015	Technology	$350	Mar-15	Office Supplies	$1300
01 March 2015	Technology	$350	02 March 2015	Technology	$850			
02 March 2015	Furniture	$550	02 March 2015	Furniture	$700	Mar-15	Technology	$1200
02 March 2015	Furniture	$150						
02 March 2015	Technology	$850						
Each record is shown as a separate row.			Records with the same date and category have been aggregated into a single row.			Dates have been rolled up to the Month level and records with the same category have been aggregated into a single row.		

The next section of the **Extract** dialog box says **Number of Rows**. Here, we can select the number of rows that we wish to extract. We can either extract **All** the rows or **Top N** rows. In this case, Tableau will first apply any filters and aggregations that we have specified and then extract the number of rows from the result. In this same section, we also see an option of **Incremental refresh**. As you know, when we create an Extract it stores data at a particular point in time and it needs to be updated on a regular basis to reflect the latest data, while in order to refresh the Extract, we can select the **Incremental refresh** option. This option will append only those records that are newly added in the data source into our Extract. It will not hamper the existing records. This will reduce the refresh time of the Extract. However, if we don't select this option, then by default Tableau does a full refresh and the whole Extract is regenerated right from the first record. This ensures that we have an exact copy of the underlying data source. However, a full refresh will typically take more time as compared to the Incremental refresh depending on how big the extract is.

In order to refresh the Extract in Tableau Desktop, we will have to right-click on the extracted data source in the **Data** window and select the **Extract | Refresh** option. Refer to the following screenshot:

Further, just after the **Number of Rows** section in the **Extract** dialog box, there is a button called **History...** which shows us the history of when the Extract was refreshed. The **Extract History** dialog box shows the date and time for each refresh, whether it was full or incremental, the number of rows that were added, and the name of the source file if the refresh was from a file. Just adjacent to the **History** button, there is also another button called **Hide All Unused Fields.**This basically excludes all the unused fields or hidden fields from the **Extract** that is being generated.

Now, once we have created an Extract and we wish to toggle between the **Live** connection and the **Extract**, then we can do so by unchecking the **Use Extract** option that is available when we right-click on the extracted data source in the **Data** window. Refer to the following screenshot:

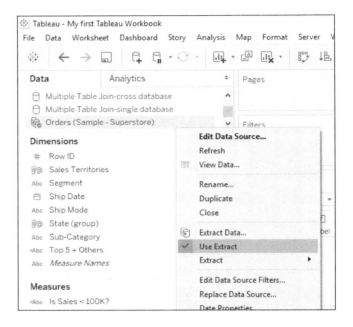

 In order to know more about Extracts, refer the following link: http://onlinehelp.tableau.com/current/pro/desktop/en-us/extracting_data.html

8

Garnish with Reference Lines, Trends, Forecasting, and Clustering

In this chapter, we will cover:

- ▶ Understanding how to create and use trend lines
- ▶ Understanding and using the forecasting functionality
- ▶ Understanding and using reference lines - bullet chart
- ▶ Understanding how to perform clustering

Introduction

There are often circumstances when we need to show some benchmarks and then compare actual performance against those benchmarks. We may also be required to find out the trend of our business to understand whether the underlying market conditions are working in our favor or not. Further, looking at the historic performance, we may also be required to do some forecasting in order to decide on future targets. Keeping these points in minds, we will focus on some specific analytics in terms of computing and understanding the trends in our data; using the built-in forecasting model to compute a forecast from our data; and, lastly, understanding how we can benchmark our data against thresholds using reference lines.

Understanding how to create and use trend lines

Trend lines are typically used to observe the relationship or correlation between two variables, where the shape of the trend line indicates the type of the relationship between the variables; for example, how is our profit value related to our marketing expenses, or how is our profit value related to the discounts that we are offering?

Further, trend lines can also be used to indicate the general pattern or direction of time series data; for example, to plot the change in variables such as sales, profit or cost over a period of time. While line charts, when used to show such changes, may show fluctuations in values over a period of time, a trend line plotted in addition to this line chart would also help us understand the general direction of the change.

At times, trend lines can also be used for basic forecasting, based on an extrapolation of the trend line.

Let us go through the following recipe to see how to generate a trend line.

Getting ready

For this recipe, we will use the fields from the already connected **CoffeeChain Query** table in the `Sample-Coffee Chain.mdb` file or the `Sample-CoffeeChain` (Use instead of MS Access) `.xlsx` file for our Mac users. We will begin by creating a **line chart** by using the **Date** field and the **Profit** field. We will continue working in the same workbook: `My first Tableau Workbook`. Let us get started with the recipe.

How to do it...

1. Let us create a new sheet and rename it as `Trend line`.

2. Select the **CoffeeChain Query (Sample - Coffee Chain)** data source from the **Data** pane to see the **Dimensions** and **Measures** of that data source. Refer to the following screenshot:

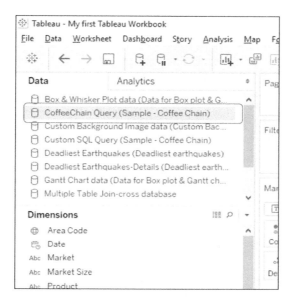

3. Next, let us right-click and drag the **Date** field from the **Dimensions** pane and drop it into the **Columns** shelf, and select the **DAY(Date)** option as shown in the following screenshot:

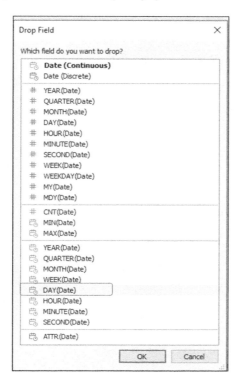

4. We will then drag **Profit** from the **Measures** pane and drop it into the **Rows** shelf; our view will update to the following:

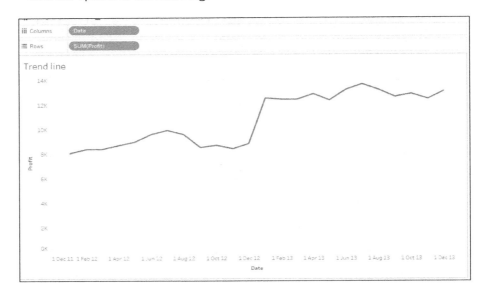

5. Now that we have our line chart, let's enable our **Trend Line**. In order to do so, click on the **Analytics** pane, which is next to the **Data** pane. Refer to the following screenshot:

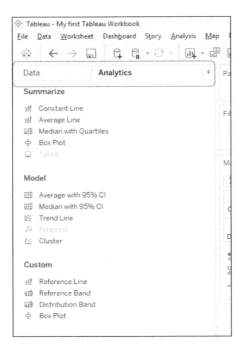

6. Once we do that, we will get to see the **Summarize** pane, **Model** pane, and **Custom** pane. Drag the **Trend Line** option from the **Model** pane over to the chart. Refer to the following screenshot:

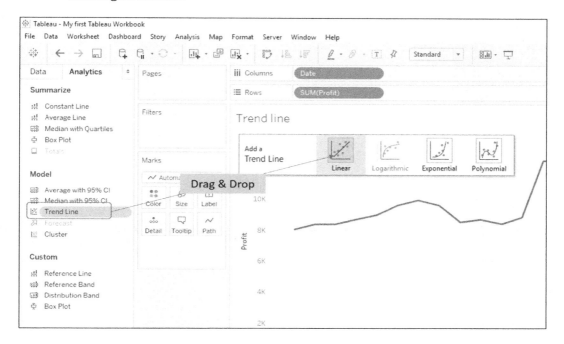

7. Select the box which says **Add a Trend Line** and we get these options: **Linear**, **Logarithmic**, **Exponential**, and **Polynomial**. We will select the **Linear** option and our view will update to the following:

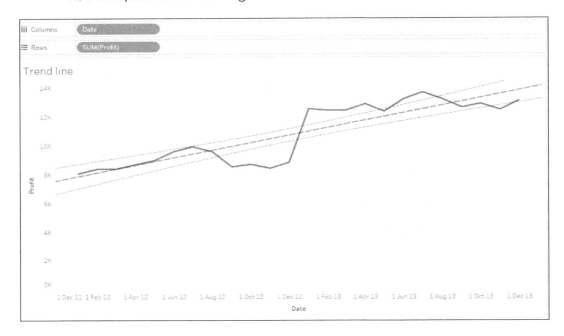

8. The thick gray dashed line is our **Trend line** and lines before and after our **Trend line** are called confidence bands. If we don't want them, they can be removed by selecting the **Edit Trend Line...** option from **Analysis | Trend Lines** option in the toolbar. Refer to the following screenshot:

9. Once we do that, we will get a new dialog box as shown in the following screenshot:

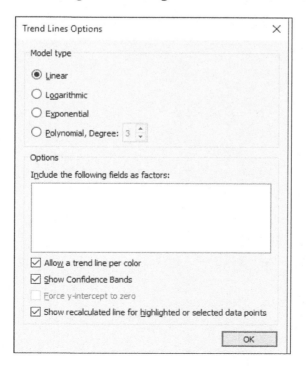

10. We will then uncheck all the options from the bottom section of the dialog box as shown in the following screenshot:

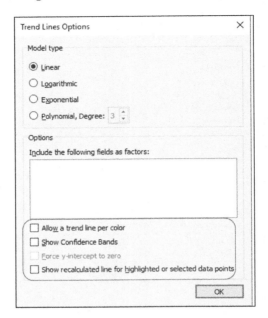

11. Once we do that, our view will update as shown in the following screenshot:

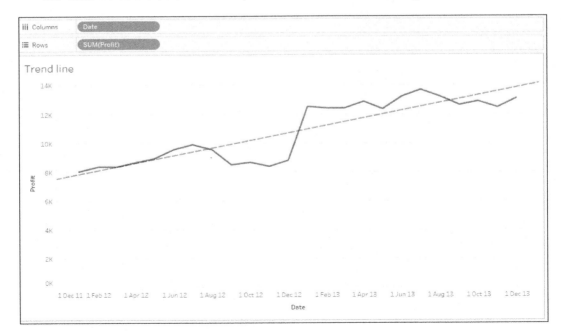

How it works...

In the previous screenshot, the gray line is the **Trend line**. We created this **Trend line** to find the overall trend of our **Profit**. As we see in the previous screenshot, the **Trend line** has an upward direction, thus indicating an upward trend. However, in order to understand the significance of this **Trend line**, we will have to enable the **Describe Trend Model...** option via the **Analysis | Trend Lines** option in the toolbar. Refer to the following screenshot:

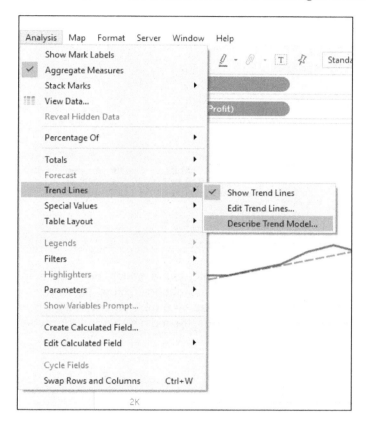

Once we enable the **Describe Trend Model...** option, we will get a dialog box as shown in the following screenshot:

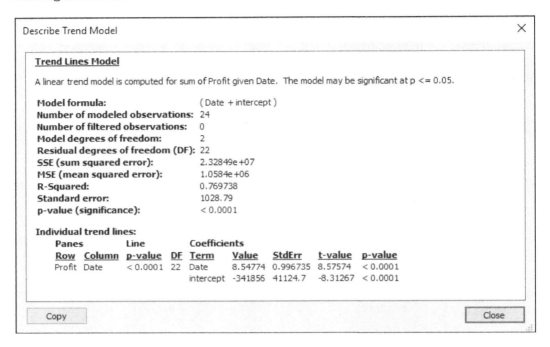

This dialog box helps us understand the quality of the model's predictions and also helps us test the significance of the model or the contributing factors. Significance testing is determined by the **p-value**. Typically, a **p-value <= 0.05** is considered good when using the 95% confidence rule. The smaller the **p-value**, the more significant the model or factor is.

The **p-value** can also be quickly checked by simply hovering over the trend line. Refer to the following screenshot:

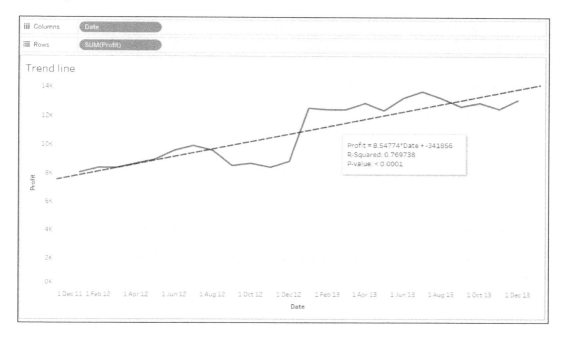

Further, there are four models to choose from when it comes to generating trend lines. We can select any of the four models by selecting the option of **Trend Lines | Edit Trend Lines...**. As we saw earlier, they are **Linear**, **Logarithmic**, **Polynomial**, and **Exponential**.

To know more about these models, refer to the following link:

```
https://onlinehelp.tableau.com/current/pro/desktop/en-us/trendlines_
model.html
```

Further, an important point to remember about trend lines is that, in order to enable them, both our *x* and *y* axes should contain a numeric field or a field that can be interpreted as a number. Refer to the following screenshot:

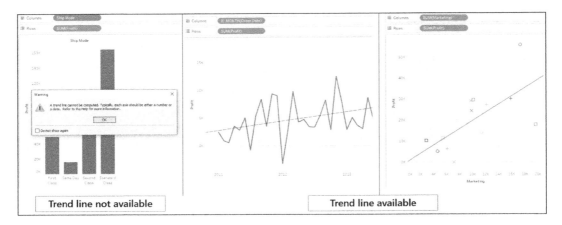

When a trend line cannot be computed, then Tableau will give us a warning as shown in the following screenshot:

Understanding and using the forecasting functionality

There may be several circumstances where we need to read historical data and to extrapolate this historical data to get an approximate idea of what to expect in the future. These forecasted values can help us in, say, budget planning or even redefining our current strategies.

The forecasting functionality in Tableau uses an built-in statistical model that enables us to estimate future values by extrapolating historical data while also taking trend and seasonality into consideration. Among the various models that are available for forecasting, Tableau uses the exponential smoothing model.

An important point to remember is that there are plenty of external factors that govern the actual data and hence the forecast will give us an approximate idea of what to expect in future. The accuracy of this forecast however will depend on the quality of the historical data.

Getting ready

In order to enable the forecasting functionality in Tableau, let's continue working in our existing workbook and use the **Order Date** and **Profit** fields from the **Orders** data from `Sample - Superstore Subset.xlsx`.

How to do it...

Let's see how to do forecasting in Tableau:

1. Let us create a new sheet and rename it `Forecasting`.

2. Select the **Orders (Sample - Superstore)** data source from the **Data** pane to see the **Dimensions** and **Measures** for that data source. Refer to the following screenshot:

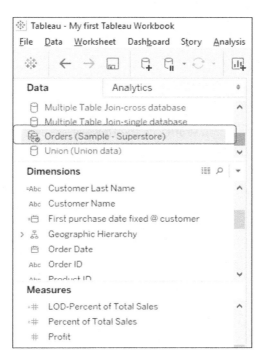

3. Next, let us right-click and drag **Order Date** from the **Dimensions** pane, drop it into the **Columns** shelf, and select the **MONTH(Order Date)** option as shown in the following screenshot:

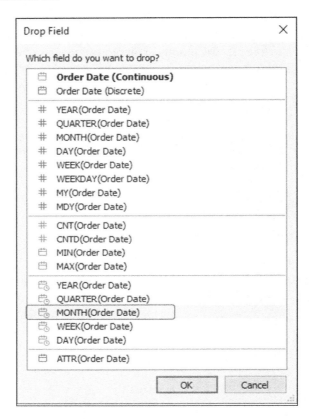

4. Let us then drag and drop **Profit** into the **Rows** shelf and our view will update as shown in the following screenshot:

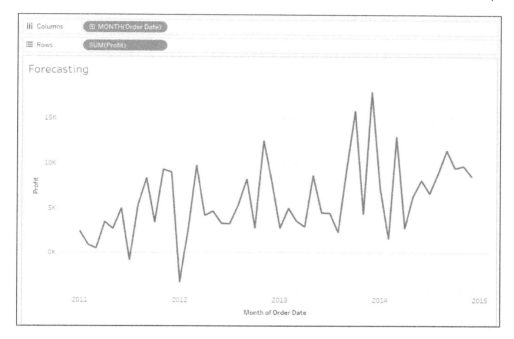

5. We will the click on the **Analytics** pane, which is next to the **Data** pane, and then drag the **Forecast** option from the **Model** pane over to the chart. Refer the following screenshot:

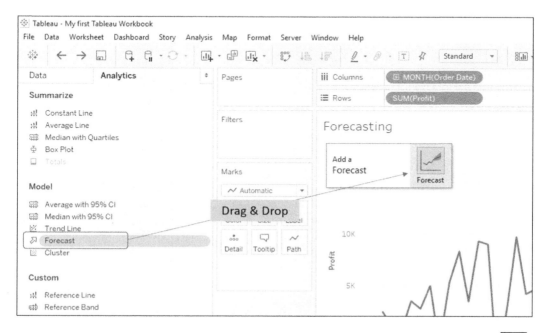

6.   Our view will now update to the following:

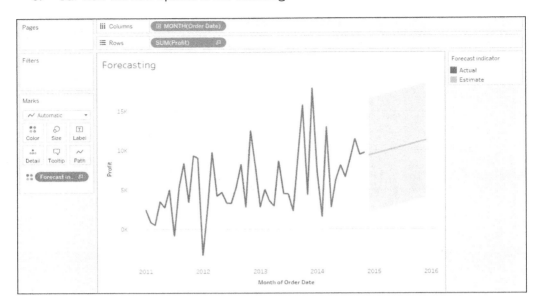

7.   Now, in the preceding screenshot, we can see that the dark blue color is our actual **Profit** whereas the light blue color is the estimated or forecasted **Profit**. However, the estimated **Profit** is a straight line and it may not be giving us an accurate picture, so let's see if we can change that. We will select **Forecast Options...** via the **Analysis | Forecast** option in the toolbar. Refer to the following screenshot:

8. Once we do that, we will get a new dialog box, where we will keep most of the default selections as-is; we will only make changes in the **Forecast Model** section as shown in the following screenshot:

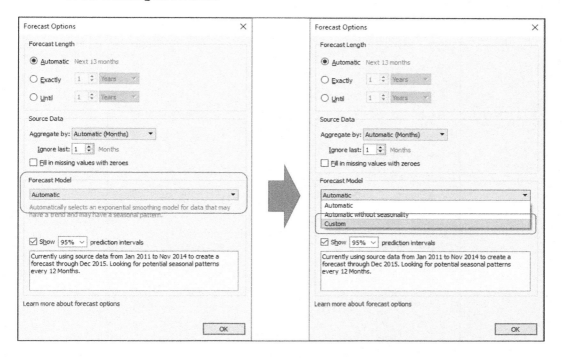

9. After we change the **Forecast Model** from **Automatic** to **Custom**, our dialog box will update as shown in the following screenshot:

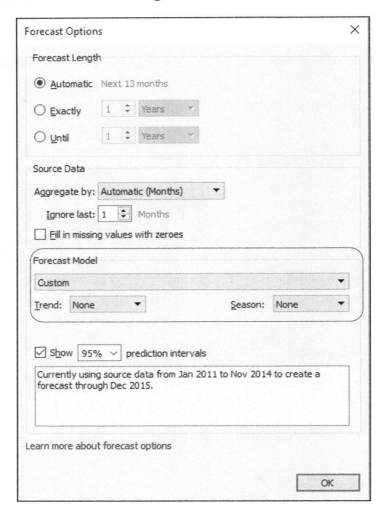

10. Next, we will click on the **Trend** and **Season** drop-downs and select the **Additive** option in both. Refer to the following screenshot:

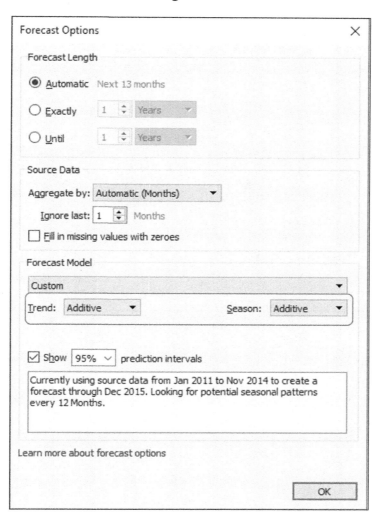

11. When we select **OK** after selecting the **Additive** option from both the **Trend** and **Season** drop-down, our view will update as shown in the following screenshot:

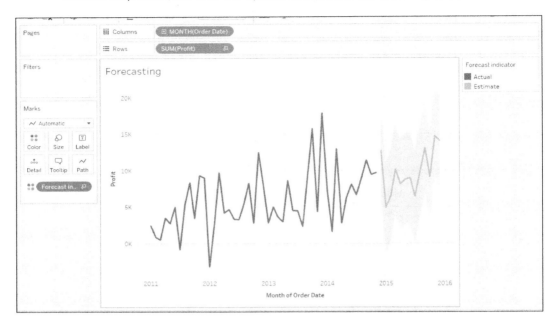

How it works...

In the previous screenshot, the dark blue line is the actual **Profit** whereas the light blue line is the estimated **Profit**. Further, the light blue band is the **95% prediction interval**, which can be changed to either **90%** or **99%**. Refer to the following screenshot:

In the previous example, Tableau is reading our historic data from January **2011** to November **2014** and creating a forecast through December **2015** while looking for **potential seasonal patterns every 12 months**. In the previous recipe, when we selected the **Additive** option for **Trend** and **Season**, we indicated to Tableau that our business is subject to seasonality. However, if we wish to look for more information, we can select the **Describe Forecast...** option via **Analysis | Forecast** in the toolbar. Refer to the following screenshot:

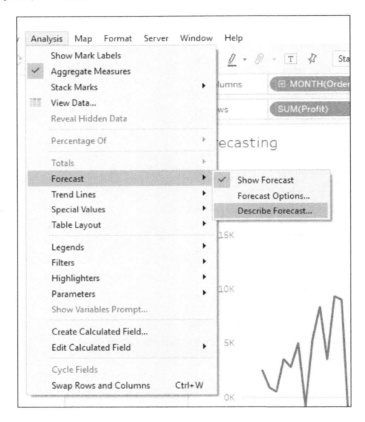

Once we do that, we will get a new dialog box as shown in the following screenshot:

In the previous recipe, we saw how to do a quick forecast. To learn more about the forecasting functionality in Tableau, refer to the following link:

```
http://onlinehelp.tableau.com/current/pro/desktop/en-us/forecasting.
html
```

Understanding and using reference lines – the bullet chart

Reference lines are typically used for providing a visual comparison against benchmark values. Imagine having a vertical bar chart showing product sales. Further, imagine that these products have a budget value that they are supposed to achieve. Now, if we are able to show a small line which represents the budget thresholds for each of the products, then we can provide a quick visual display to see which products are not exceeding target and which products are exceeding the target. The chart type which is typically used to do a target versus actual comparison is called a bullet chart.

Bullet charts were developed by Stephen Few. A bullet chart is an extension of the regular bar chart, where the length or height of the bar represents the actual values and the horizontal or vertical reference line represents the target.

Getting ready

Let us take a look at bullet charts in detail in the following recipe:

For this recipe we will use the fields from the already connected **CoffeeChain Query** table of `Sample-Coffee Chain.mdb` file or the `Sample-CoffeeChain` (Use instead of MS Access) `.xlsx` file for our Mac users and continue working in our **My first Tableau Workbook**. We will begin by creating a bar chart by using the **Product Type** field, **Product** field and the **Sales** field. We will also use the **Budget Sales** field for our reference line. Let us get started with the recipe.

How to do it...

1. Let us create a new sheet and rename it as `Reference Line-Bullet chart`.

2. Next, let us make sure that we select the **CoffeeChain Query (Sample - Coffee Chain)** data source from the **Data** pane. Following this, we will create a bar chart by dragging **Sales** field from the **Measures** pane and dropping it into the **Rows** shelf and then dragging the **Product Type** field from the **Dimensions** pane and dropping it into the **Columns** shelf, followed by dragging the **Product** field from the **Dimensions** pane and dropping it into the **Columns** shelf, right after the **Product Type** field. This will create a bar chart as shown in the following screenshot:

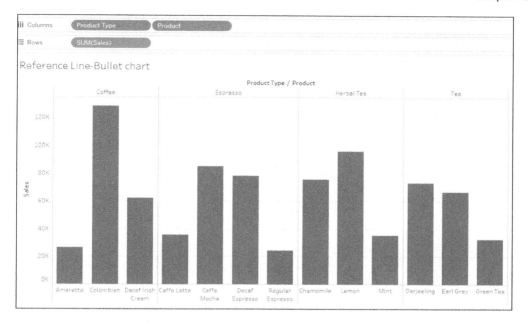

3. Now, we need small horizontal lines for each **Product** to show their **Budget Sales**. For doing this, we will drag the **Budget Sales** from the **Measures** pane and drop it into the **Detail** shelf. Refer to the following screenshot:

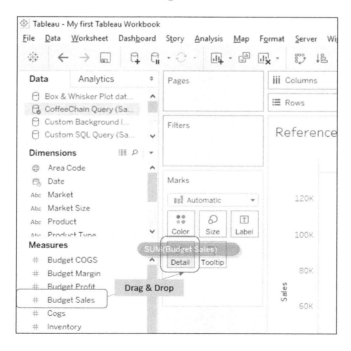

4. Let us right-click on **Sales** axis in the view and select the **Add Reference Line** option. Refer to the following screenshot:

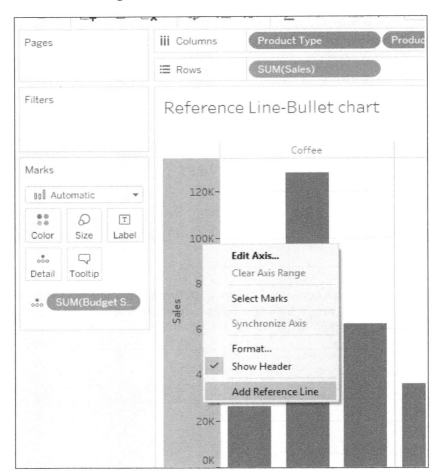

5. Once we do that, we will get the dialog box shown in the following screenshot:

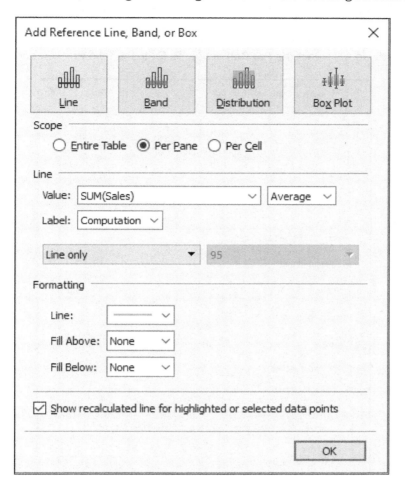

6. The dialog box gives us a choice to select from either a reference **Line** or a **Band** or **Distribution**, or **Box Plot**. We will keep the default **Line** option and then move to the next section which says **Scope**. In this section, we are presented with three choices: **Entire Table**, **Per Pane** and **Per Cell**. Now, since we want a reference line for each product, we will select the **Per Cell** option. Refer to the following screenshot:

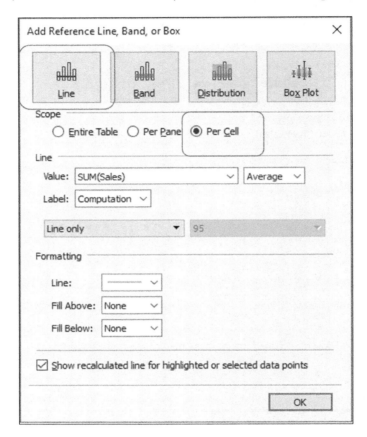

7. The section which is called **Line** is where we will select the field that we want as a reference. The current selection is **Value: | SUM(Sales)**. We will change that to **SUM(Budget Sales)**. Refer to the following screenshot:

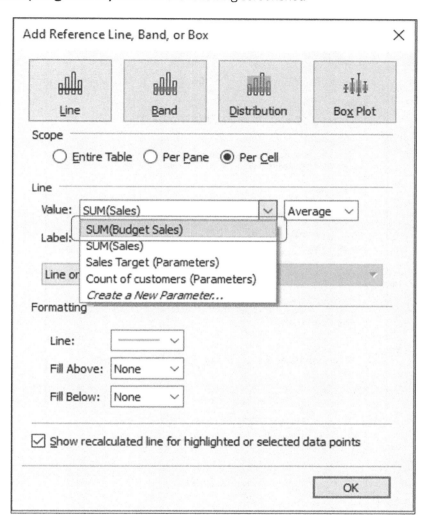

8. We will keep the default aggregation as **Average**. We will then move to the **Label:** section where we will select the **None** option. Refer to the following screenshot:

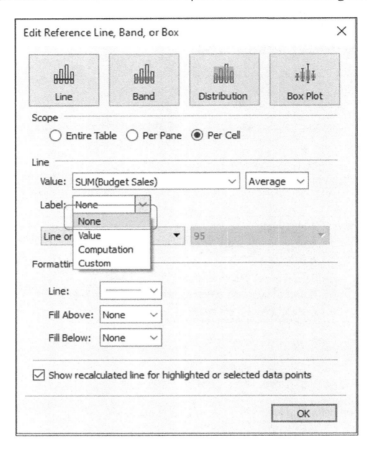

9. Keeping the rest of the selections as it is, click **OK** and our view will update as shown in the following screenshot:

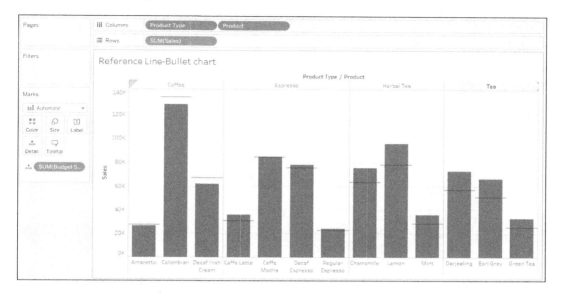

How it works...

In the previous chart, the height of the bar indicates the actual **Sales** value whereas the gray horizontal line over each product indicates the **Budget Sales** value. The products where the bar crosses the line have exceeded their targets, whereas the products where the bar does not cross the line have failed to achieve it. Thus, we can see that **Columbian** coffee is below-target whereas **Lemon** herbal tea is over-target.

Previously in the recipe we selected the **Per Cell** option. This was because we wanted **Budget Sales** to be shown for all the products individually. However, if we had wanted to look at the **Budget Sales** for each **Product Type**, then we would have selected the **Per Pane** option. The **Entire Table** option would have given us the **Budget Sales** for the all the products combined. Refer to the following screenshot:

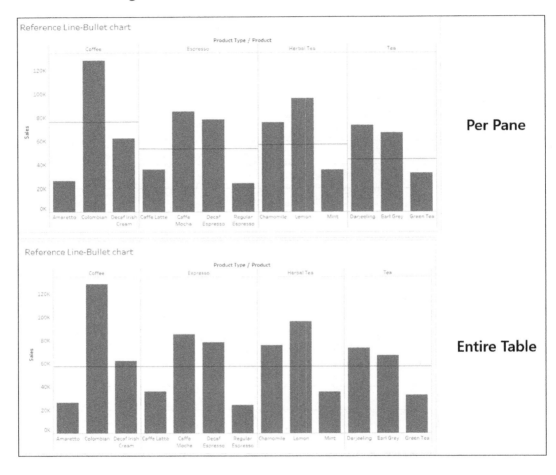

Further, if we had selected the **Band** option instead of **Line**, our dialog box would then update as shown in the following screenshot:

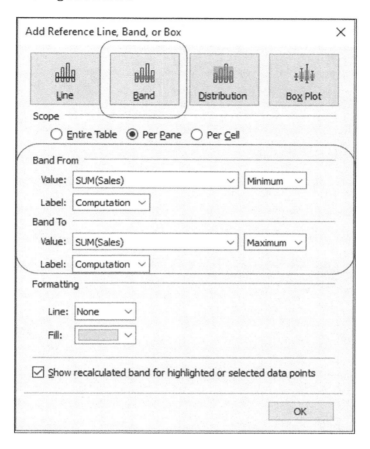

Previously we created the bullet chart from scratch by dragging and dropping fields. However, a quick and easy way of creating a bullet chart is from the **Show Me!**. To do this, let us select **Product Type**, *Ctrl* + select **Product**, *Ctrl* + select **Sales**, and *Ctrl* + select **Budget Sales**. Then select the **Bullet chart** option via **Show Me!**. Refer to the following screenshot:

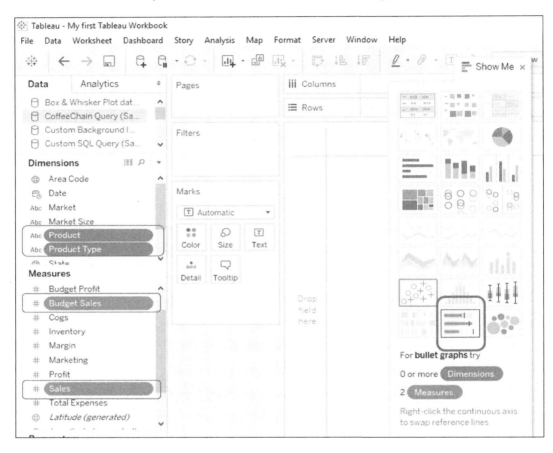

We will now get the view shown in the following screenshot:

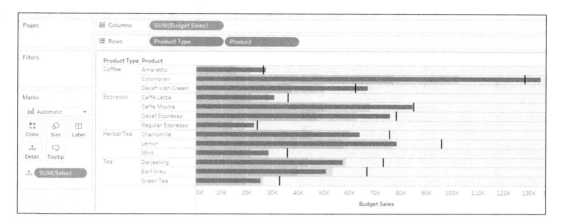

If we convert the previous horizontal chart to a vertical chart using the **Swap** button in the toolbar, then our view will update as shown in the following screenshot:

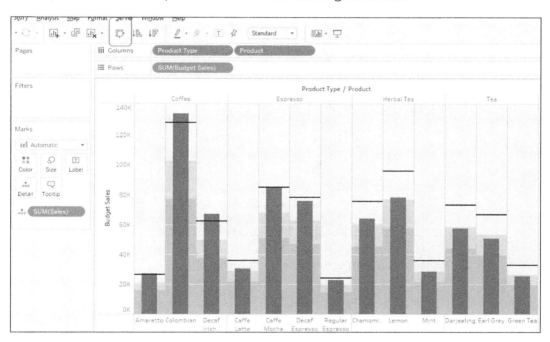

If we look carefully, we will notice that the **Sales** field and the **Budget Sales** field have interchanged. So, instead of having **Budget Sales** in the **Detail** shelf, we have **Budget Sales** on the axis, and instead of having **SUM(Sales)** on the axis, we have it in the **Detail** shelf. Because of this, the chart is giving a misleading picture where it is showing that **Columbian** coffee has exceeded target whereas **Lemon** herbal tea is below target. In order to fix this, we will right-click on the axis which says **Budget Sales** and select the option of **Swap reference line fields**. Refer to the following screenshot:

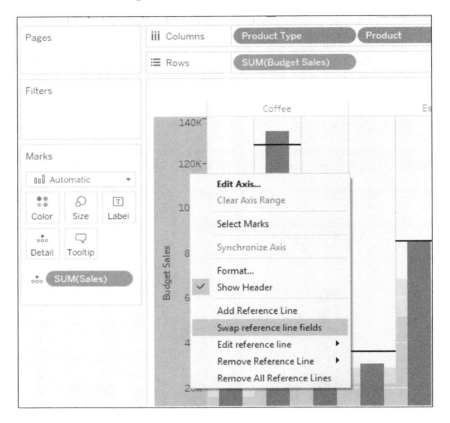

This will update our view as shown in the following screenshot:

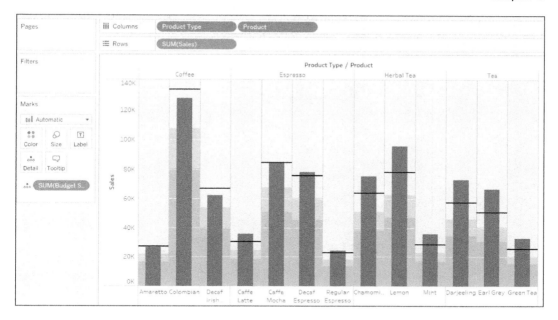

Now, in the previous screenshot, we will see the reference line as well as some gray bands. This is the **Distribution** of **Budget Sales**. So if we hover over the band, we will see what it is representing. In the previous screenshot, the gray bands indicate 60% of Budget and 80% of Budget. Refer to the following screenshot:

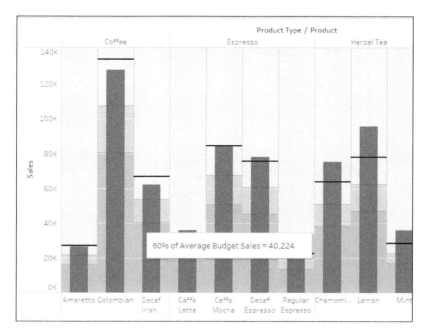

We can edit these distribution bands by right-clicking on the axis and selecting **Edit reference line | 60%, 80% of Average Budget Sales**. Refer to the following screenshot:

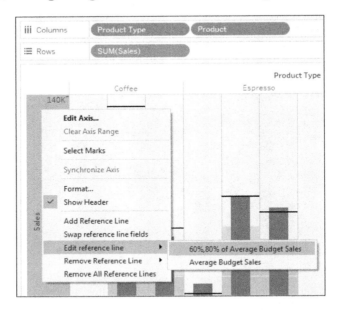

Once we select this option, we will get a view as shown in the following screenshot:

If we change **Percentages:**, then our view will update to show the gray bands as per our selection.

As we can see in the preceding screenshot, when we select the **Distribution** option, we can look at **Percentages**, **Percentiles**, **Quantiles** and **Standard Deviation**.

Further, reference lines can be made dynamic by taking inputs from the end user through parameters. Refer to the following screenshot:

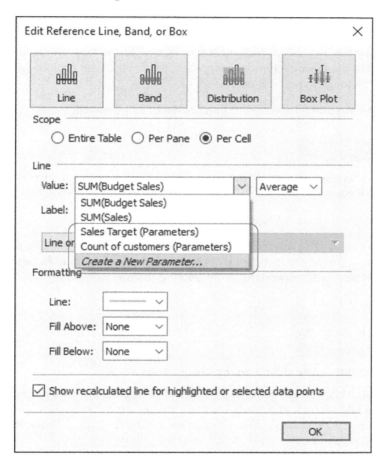

Understanding how to perform clustering

Often we are required to quickly locate distinct and well separated groups in our data, for example, grouping customers who have the same buying patterns, or patients with similar symptoms, and so on. More often than not, this can be done using the grouping functionality that we saw in previous chapters.

However, this can be challenging, as finding patterns via manual inspection for complex and distributed datasets with no obvious patterns can be very tough.

The new clustering functionality in Tableau automatically groups together similar data points by finds patterns in data using a K-means algorithm to help the user explore patterns in the data that would be tough to pick out otherwise.

Let us explore the clustering functionality in more detail in the recipe.

Getting ready

We will use a new dataset for the following recipe. The dataset is a .tde, file which has been uploaded on the following link:

https://1drv.ms/u/s!Av5QCoyLTBpnhks3n2mxItiI7-tb.

The file is called World Indicators.tde. We will download this extract file and save it to the Tableau Cookbook data folder in **Documents** | **My Tableau Repository** | **Datasources**. We will continue working in our existing Tableau workbook.

Let's get started.

How to do it...

1. We will create a new sheet and rename it Clustering.
2. Let us then click on *Ctrl+D* to connect to the data, select the **More...** option from the **To a File** section, and browse to the .tde file from Documents | My Tableau Repository | Datasources | Tableau Cookbook data folder. Refer to the following screenshot:

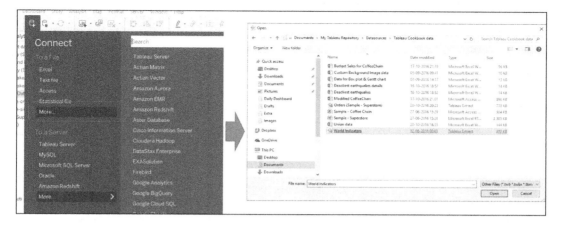

3. Once we do that, our view will update as shown in the following screenshot:

4. We will go ahead with the default **Live** option and click on the **Clustering** sheet to view the **Dimensions** and **Measures** for this new data source. Refer to the following screenshot:

5. Next, let us drag the **Country** field from the **Dimensions** pane and drop it into the **Rows** shelf, followed by dragging the **Internet Usage** field from the **Measures** pane and dropping it into the **Columns** shelf. This will create a bar chart as shown in the following screenshot:

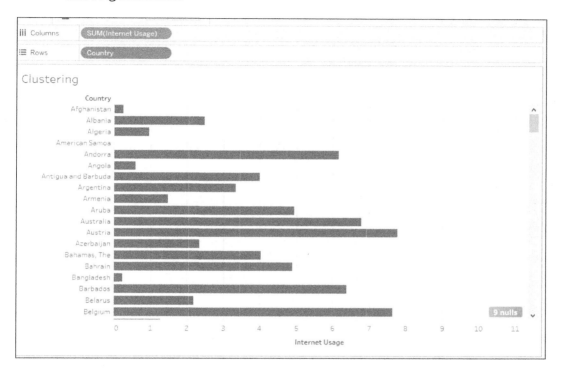

6. We will then drag **Internet Usage** field again from the **Measures** pane and drop it into the **Label** shelf. We will then sort the bar chart in descending order of **Internet Usage** using the **Sort** option on the toolbar. Refer to the following screenshot:

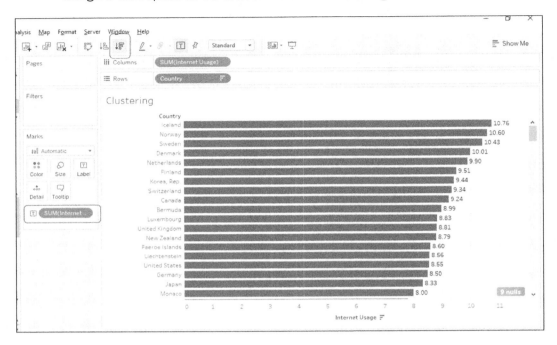

7. Next, we will click on the **Analytics** tab and simply double-click on the **Cluster** option from the **Model** pane. This will update our view as shown in the following screenshot:

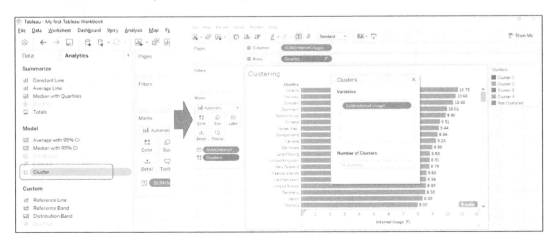

8. Our view will now update as shown in the following screenshot:

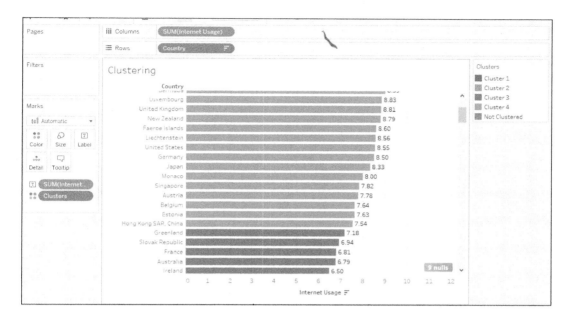

9. Next, let us quickly convert this into a map by selecting the **symbol maps** option from **Show Me!**. This will update our view as shown in the following screenshot:

10. Finally, drag the **Clusters** field from the **Rows** shelf and drop it into the **Color** shelf. This will update our view as shown in the following screenshot:

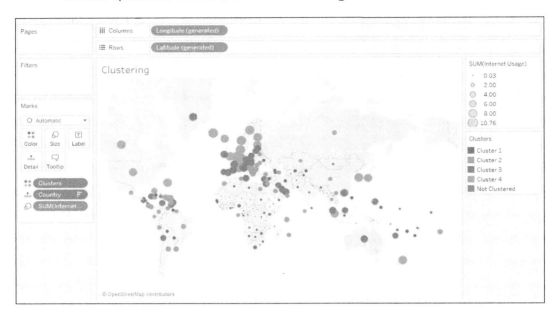

How it works...

If we now take a look at the bar chart we created earlier, we will see the light blue color, which represents Cluster 4 and indicates that Internet usage is very high; the red color, which represents Cluster 3, indicates that Internet usage is high; the orange color, which represents Cluster 2, indicates Internet usage is moderate; the dark blue color, which represents Cluster 1, indicates that Internet usage is low; and the green color, which represents Not Clustered, indicates a complete lack of any Internet usage data.

As mentioned earlier, Tableau uses the K-means clustering algorithm; to understand this in a little more detail, we can right-click on the **Clusters** field, which is currently placed in the **Color** shelf, and select **Describe clusters...**. Refer to the following screenshot:

We will now get the following view:

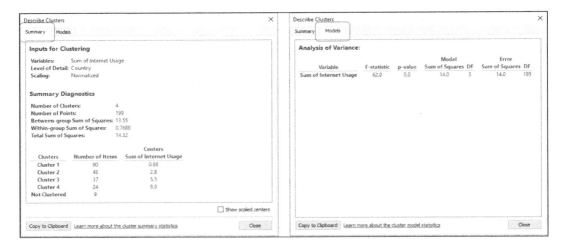

 To learn more about clustering in Tableau, refer to the following link:
https://onlinehelp.tableau.com/current/pro/desktop/
en-us/clustering.html

9
Bon Appétit! Tell a Story and Share It with others

In this chapter, we'll cover following recipes:

- ▸ Understanding and using story points
- ▸ Saving our work as a packaged workbook
- ▸ Publishing our work to Tableau Server or Tableau Online

Introduction

In the earlier chapters, we saw how to analyze our data by building visualizations and dashboards. Now, it is time for us to also focus on how to share our findings with others. This chapter focuses on how we can present our work to our end users. We will look at how to share ready insights with end users by creating storyboards and the different ways of saving and sharing our work with others.

Understanding and using story points

When we build dashboards, we give our end users a holistic view of the data. However, to see what is really happening with the data, the users need to interact with the dashboard and uncover insights all by themselves. We can make this process a little easier for the end users by guiding them via some instructions on the dashboard; however, it is still an investigative approach. It can be time-consuming for the end users to first find the insights and then take action, so rather than making our users dig out the findings, it would be great if we could give them some readily consumable insights by placing data in an easy-to-understand manner.

Story points in Tableau help us achieve this objective by giving us a framework for walking the end users through series of data points that require attention. Very simply put, story points in Tableau helps us tell stories about our data while still being connected to the data, so when the data changes, our story updates accordingly.

Getting ready

For this recipe, we will use the fields from the already connected `World Indicators.tde` dataset that we downloaded for our earlier chapter from the following link: `https://1drv.ms/u/s!Av5QCoyLTBpnhks3n2mxItiI7-tb`.

We downloaded this extract file earlier and saved it to our `Tableau Cookbook data` folder in `Documents/My Tableau Repository/Datasources`. We will continue working in the same workbook `My first Tableau Workbook`. Since we have already made a connection to this `.tde` file, it should be available for us to use in the **Data** window of the Tableau workbook. Let us get started with the recipe.

How to do it...

1. Let us create a new sheet and rename it to `Global Energy Usage`.

2. Select the `World Indicators.tde` data source from the **Data** pane to see the **Dimensions** and **Measures** of that data source. Refer to the following screenshot:

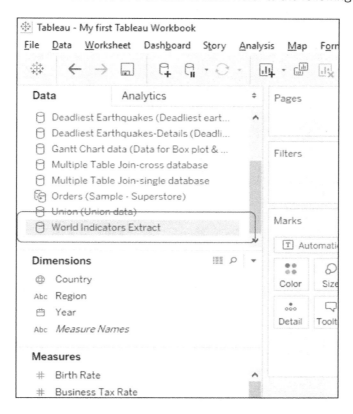

3. Next, we will drag the **Country** field from the **Dimensions** pane and do a *Ctrl* + select on the **Energy Usage** field in the **Measures** pane and then select the **filled maps** option from **Show Me**. Refer to the following screenshot:

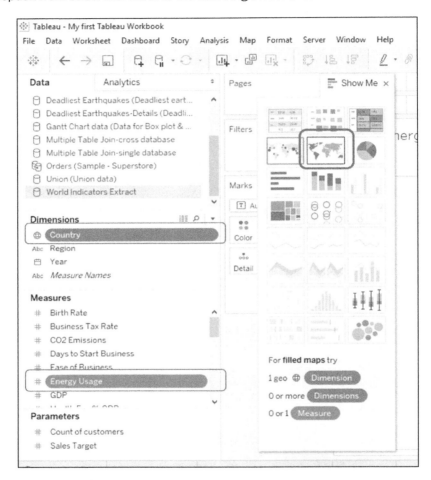

4. Once we do that, we will get the following view:

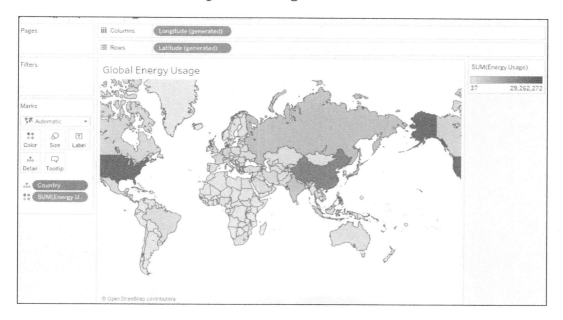

5. In the preceding chart, we can clearly see that the US and China are highest in terms of overall energy usage. Now that we have found this information, the next question that comes to mind is how has the energy usage trend been for both the US and China? Have they been the highest energy consumers all throughout the timespan? And so on. To find this information, we will create a new sheet and rename it `Energy Usage Trend for US & China`.

6. Let us drag **Year** from the **Dimensions** pane and drop it into the **Columns** shelf. Then, drag the **Energy Usage** field from the **Measures** pane and drop it into the **Rows** shelf. Refer to the following screenshot:

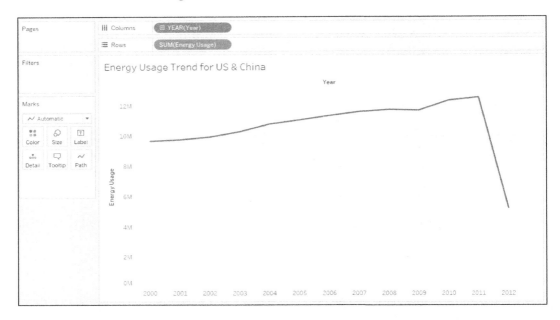

7. Once we do that, we will get to see the overall energy usage trend. However, we need to focus only on the US and China. So, let us drag the **Country** field from the **Dimensions** pane into the **Filter** shelf and select only **United States** and **China**. Refer to the following screenshot:

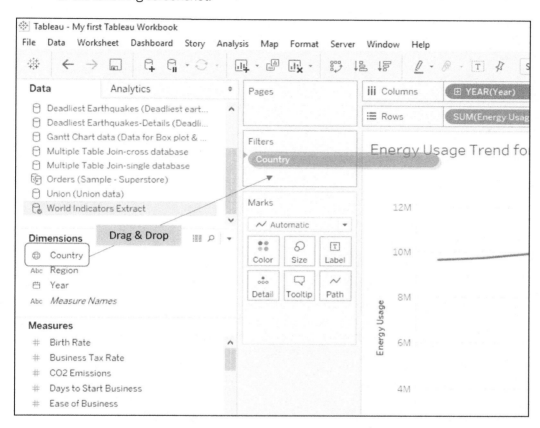

8. Once we do that, once again, drag **Country** from the **Dimensions** pane and drop it into the **Color** shelf. This will update to the following view:

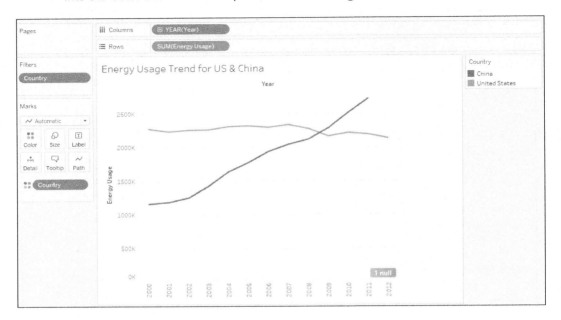

9. This view throws out an interesting finding. As we can see, the United States, which is the orange line, has been consuming energy in a steady manner, whereas China, which is the blue line, had a recent exponential growth in energy consumption to the point where it has surpassed the energy consumption of the United States.

10. Lastly, let's see whether the increase in energy usage for China has led to an increase in the CO2 emissions as well. In order to find this, let's duplicate the earlier sheet named `Energy Usage Trend for US & China` and rename it as `Energy Usage vs CO2 Emissions`. We'll then make some quick modifications to this sheet. To begin with, remove **Country** field from **Color** shelf and place it in the **Rows** shelf. Refer to the following screenshot:

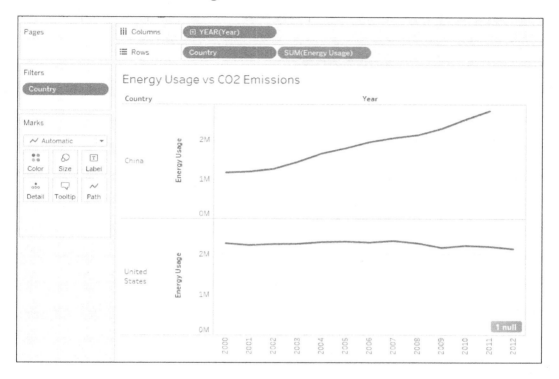

11. Next, drag the CO2 Emissions field from the **Measures** pane and drop it onto the **Energy Usage** axis. Refer to the following screenshot:

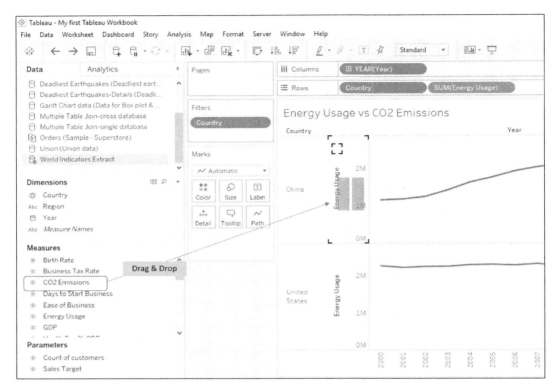

12. Once we do that, our view will update, as shown in the following screenshot:

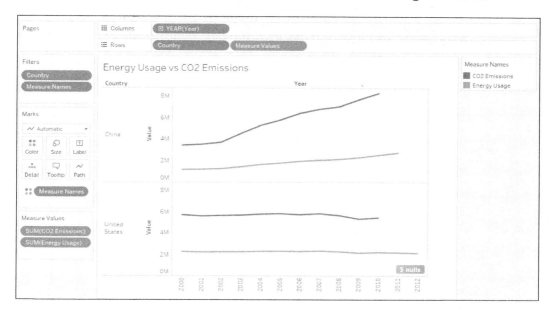

13. In the preceding chart, we can clearly see that Energy usage vs CO2 Emissions trend has been steady for United States whereas for China the CO2 Emissions have increased multiple times with the increase in Energy Usage. Further more, in this chart, the line color indicates the **Measures** and not the **Country**, as shown in the previous sheet. This can be confusing for our end users. Therefore, let's quickly make sure to change the color in the preceding chart and to do so, we will right-click on the **Color** legend and select the **Edit Colors...** option. Select the new colors and our view will update as shown in the following screenshot:

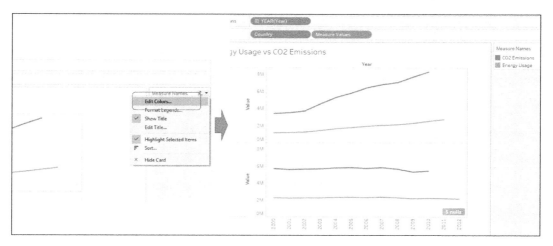

14. Now that we have our sheets ready, let's proceed to create the storyboard. We will begin by selecting the **New Story** option from either the **Story | New Story** from the toolbar or from the tab that looks like an open book, next to the **New Worksheet** and **New Dashboard** tab at the bottom. Refer to the following screenshot:

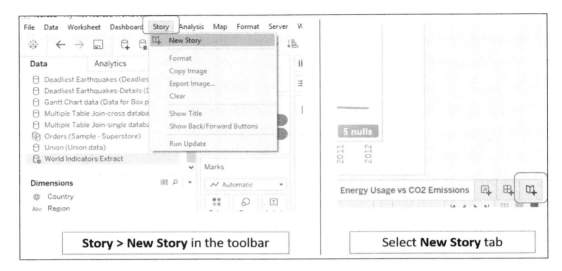

Story > New Story in the toolbar   Select **New Story** tab

15. Once we do that, we will get the following view:

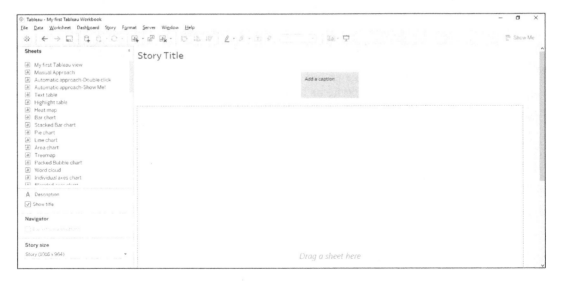

16. Rename it to `My sample storyboard` instead of `Story 1`. Now, just like we dragged the sheets on our dashboard earlier, we will drag the sheets on the **Story**. Refer to the following screenshot:

17. This action will update our following view:

18. In the preceding image, we see that there is a vertical scroll on the right-hand side. This is because the **Story** size on the left-hand side bottom section is currently set to **1016** x **964**. Let's change that to **Automatic**. Refer to the following screenshot:

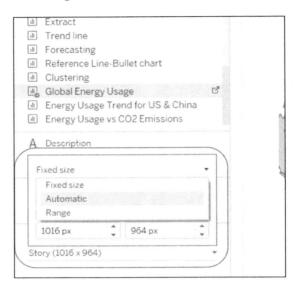

19. Once we do that, we will get rid of the scroll bar and our view will update as shown in the following screenshot:

20. Next, let's get the `Energy Usage Trend for US & China` sheet on the story. We will drag the sheet from our **Sheets** section on the left-hand side and drop it over the button which reads **New Blank Point**. Refer to the following screenshot:

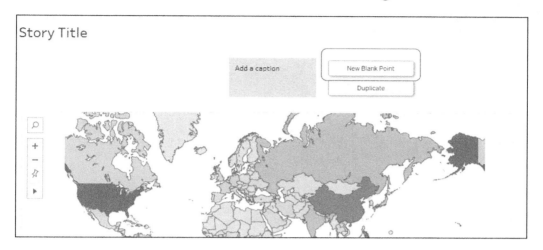

21. However, when we are in the process of dragging and dropping, the **New Blank Point** tab changes and reads as **Add New Point**. Refer to the following screenshot:

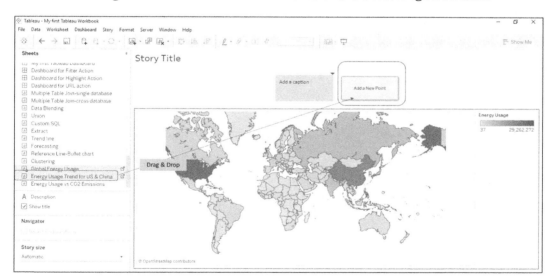

22. Once we drop the sheet, our view will update, as shown in the following screenshot:

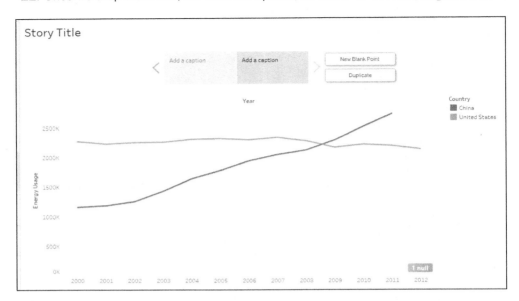

23. After we are done with getting the `Energy Usage Trend for US & China` sheet, let's also get the `Energy Usage vs CO2 Emissions` sheet by dragging and dropping it into the next **Add New Point** tab. Once we do that, our view will be as shown in the following screenshot:

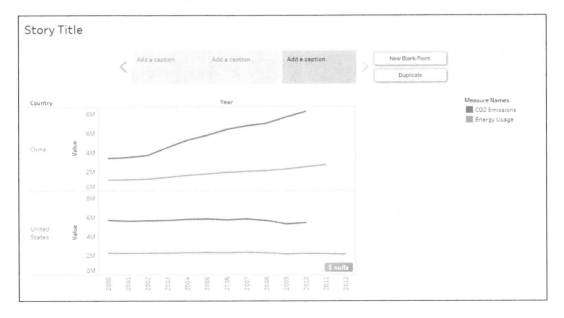

24. Now that we have all three sheets on the Storyboard, let's quickly add some finishing touches. There are three tabs which read as **Add a caption**, so let's begin by clicking on the **Add a caption** tab which is first from the left. This will show the **Global Energy Usage** map. Double-click on the tab to start typing. Since this tab gives us the overall energy usage across various countries, we will type Energy usage across the Globe; on the next **Add a caption** tab, type Energy usage trend across years for US & China, and finally, on the third **Add a caption** tab, type Energy usage vs CO2 emission trend across years for US & China. This will update our view to that shown in the following screenshot:

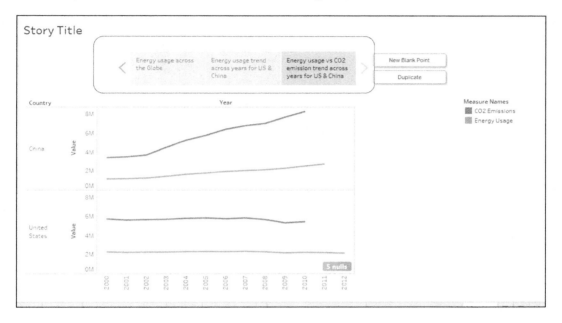

25. This is how we create a Story. Now, to run through our Story, we can either click on each of the tabs on top in a sequential manner or use the forward or backward arrows. Next, let's make sure we change the title of our Story to something meaningful: double-click on the text which reads **Story Title** and change it to `Energy Usage Story`. Refer to the following screenshot:

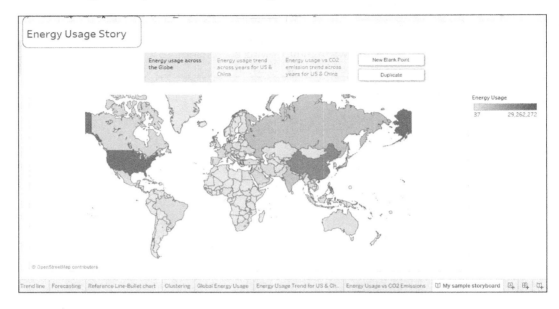

26. Lastly, we need to make sure we hide all the extra sheets that are already part of the Story. To do so, right-click on the **Story** tab which reads as `My sample storyboard` and select the **Hide All Sheets** option. Refer to the following screenshot:

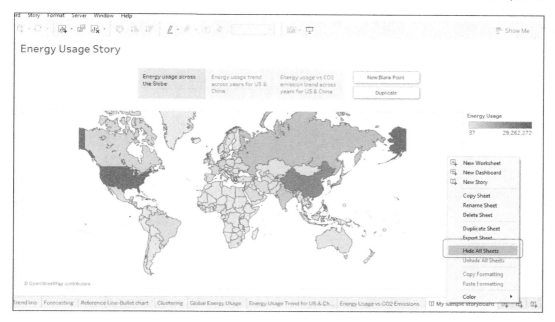

How it works...

In the preceding recipe, we saw how to create a story. Now, when we click on each tab, it gives us one Story point from the entire Story we are trying to convey to the end user.

In the earlier recipe, we pulled individual sheets on to our storyboard. However, in case we wish to use our dashboards as story points, we can do that as well. When we look at the Sheets section on the left-hand side, we will see the list of all the worksheets, as well as the dashboards we have created so far. Refer to the following screenshot:

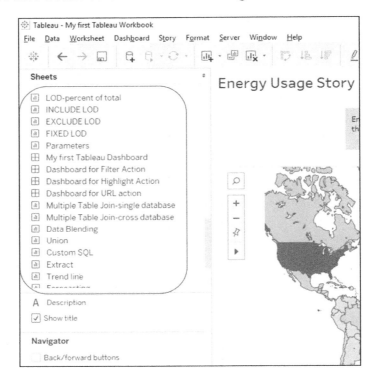

Further more, in the preceding recipe, if we want to give more details to our end user or perhaps explain why we are narrowing our focus only to the US and China, we can do so by adding descriptions to our story points. For this, we can select our desired Story point and then double-click on **Description** in the left-hand section. Refer to the following screenshot:

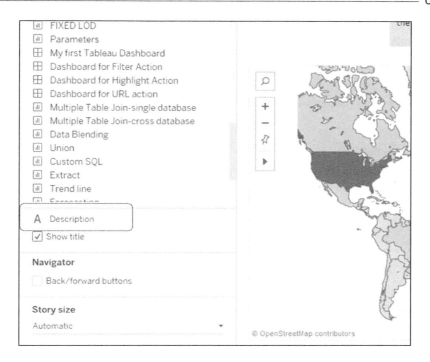

To learn more about Story, refer the following link: `http://onlinehelp.tableau.com/current/pro/desktop/en-us/stories.html`.

Saving our work as a packaged workbook

In the first chapter, we briefly saw how to save our work in Tableau by saving `My first Tableau Workbook` with the `.twb` extension. This `.twb` file is a proprietary file format in Tableau, and the file saved with the `.twb` extension is referred to as a Tableau workbook.

This `.twb` file is an XML document that contains information regarding the sheets, dashboards, and so on that we have created in Tableau. The `.twb` file is an interactive file that contains only the metadata information about our data and not the actual data, because of which it is constantly referencing a datasource. What this means is that, if we wish to share our work with our end users in a `.twb` format, then we need to make sure that they have the access to the data that the `.twb` file is referencing. If they don't they will not be able to use the workbook and this process will require our end users to have a Tableau Desktop installed on their machines to access our workbook. Because of these reasons, the approach of saving our file as a `.twb` can often be restrictive and we will need to find an alternative approach to saving our work in a manner that removes the dependency on whether our end users have the necessary access or permissions to connect to our data.

The other file format that can be used to share the interactive version of our work is the Tableau packaged workbook. The extension of these files is .twbx. When we save the file as a .twbx, Tableau packages the data along with our visualizations into a single file and saves it. This way, even if the end user doesn't have any access to the live data sources, he/she can still view and interact with our visualizations. Since we have already seen how to save as a .twb, let us now see how to save the file as a .twbx.

Getting ready

We will use our existing workbook and save it as a Tableau packaged workbook. Before we begin, let us make sure to keep the My first Tableau Workbook.twb open. Let us see how to save a tableau packaged workbook.

How to do it...

1. Let us click on the file option in the toolbar. Refer to the following screenshot:

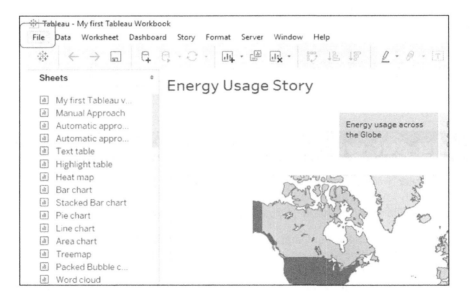

2. We will then select the **Export Packaged Workbook...** option. Refer to the following screenshot:

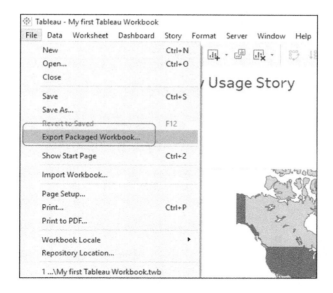

3. Once we do that, we will be asked to save the file. By default, we will be asked to save the file in `Documents\My Tableau Repository\Workbooks`. Let's just make sure to save it in the `Documents\My Tableau Repository\Workbooks` folder. Refer to the following screenshot:

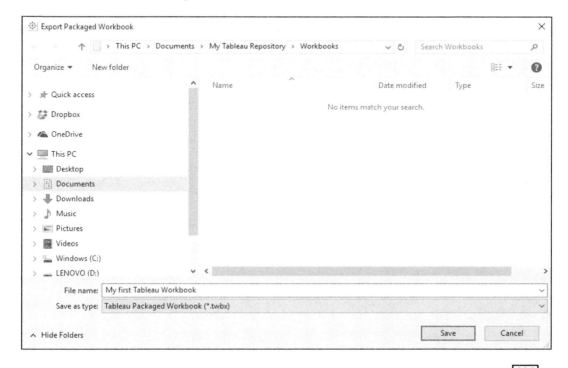

4. Now, change the **File name:** from My first Tableau Workbook to My first Tableau Packaged Workbook. Refer to the following screenshot:

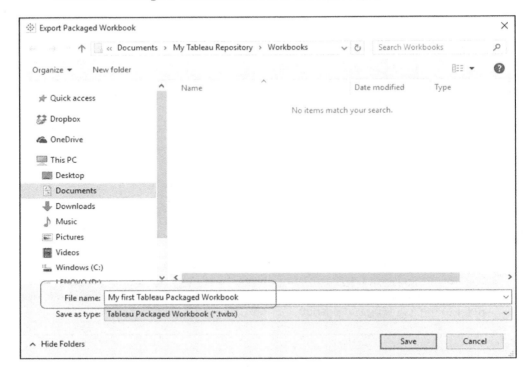

5. Let us keep the rest of the selections as they are and click on **Save**.

How it works...

The preceding recipe explains how we can save our workbook as a packaged workbook.

Once we click save, we will get a new file in our in Documents\My Tableau Repository\ Workbooks folder. Refer to the following screenshot:

We now have two files in the `Documents\My Tableau Repository\Workbooks` folder. As we can see in the preceding screenshot, the `My first Tableau Workbook`, which is the `.twb` file, and the `My first Tableau Packaged Workbook`, which is the `.twbx` file, have different sizes. The file size of `My first Tableau Packaged Workbook.twbx` is more than the file size of `My first Tableau Workbook.twb`, as the `My first Tableau Packaged Workbook.twbx` also contains the copy of our data; whereas, as mentioned earlier, the `My first Tableau Workbook.twb` does not contain the data but only the information related to our data.

In the previous recipe, we saw the **File | Export Packaged Workbook...** option. However, we can also save a file as a packaged workbook by using the **File | Save As...** option from the toolbar. Refer to the following screenshot:

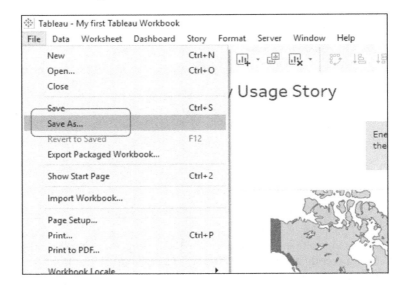

This packaged workbook can either be accessed via Tableau Reader, where the user simply interacts with our visualizations by using the functionality that we have designed using the Tableau Desktop, or it can also be accessed via the Tableau Desktop where the file becomes editable and the user can either use the existing functionality that we have designed or create new views and functionalities altogether.

The point of saving our work as either the `.twb` or the `.twbx`, is to provide interactivity to our end users. However, there can be instances where the user wants simple static snapshots of our dashboards for quick consumption without any interactivity. In this case, we can do the following:

▶ Export as an image

▶ Print to PDF

Further more, if we're working with worksheets instead of dashboards, we can also do the following in addition to the previously mentioned options:

▶ Export as data

▶ Export as a crosstab to Excel

To export from the worksheet, we need to click on the **Worksheet | Export** option from the toolbar. Refer to the following screenshot:

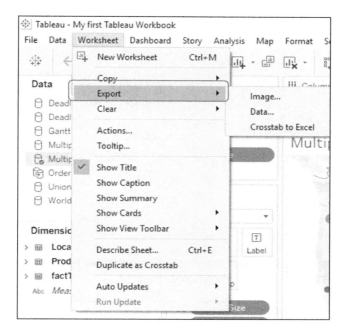

To export from the dashboard, we need to click on the **Dashboard | Export Image...** option or **Dashboard | Copy Image** from the toolbar. Refer to the following image:

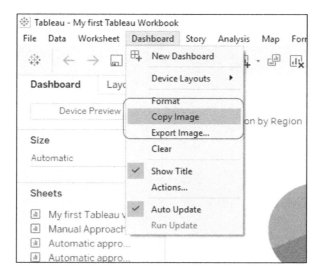

To export from the dashboard, we need to click on the **Story | Export Image...** option or **Story | Copy Image** from the toolbar. Refer to the following screenshot:

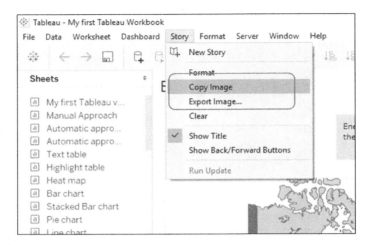

Further more, to print our work to PDF, we must select the **Print to PDF...** option from the **File** menu in the toolbar. Refer to the following screenshot:

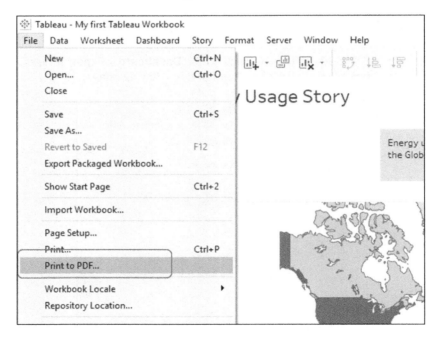

To learn more about these options, refer to the following link: `https://onlinehelp.tableau.com/current/pro/desktop/en-us/save.html`.

Publishing our work to Tableau Server or Tableau Online

When we share a packaged workbook with our end users, they will need to have the Tableau Reader to use and interact with it. Just as we need a PDF reader to open a PDF file, similarly, we will need a Tableau Reader to open a Tableau packaged workbook. In the previous recipe, we learned that when we save the file as a packaged workbook, it also packages a copy of the data. This copy of the data is actually a static snapshot of the data at a particular point in time. So, every time our end users need the dashboards with the updated data, we will have to open the file in Tableau Desktop, refresh the data and re-save the file as a packaged workbook, and then share it via e-mail, shared drives, and so on. This solution becomes cumbersome, but it's fine for one of, ad-hoc analysis. However, imagine doing this for workbooks that are going to be used every day or every hour. In these situations, this kind of manual intervention to update our data is not the best way forward and we can save a lot of time and effort by simply publishing our work on either a Tableau Server or Tableau Online.

Publishing our work on a Tableau Server or Tableau Online, not only helps us maintain and control our data refresh frequencies and schedules but also have better control on the collaboration and distribution of our work with others, while also supporting access management and permission-based interactivity.

Tableau Server is an online and mobile solution for sharing and consuming our Tableau projects. Tableau Online is a hosted version of Tableau Server with no requirement for an in-house setup.

Let's quickly look at how we can publish our work to Tableau Server or Tableau Online in the following recipe.

Getting ready

We will use our existing `My first Tableau Workbook.twb` workbook and try to publish it to Tableau Server. The important part of this recipe is to make sure that we have access to either the Tableau Server or the Tableau Online and that we can publish to the same. Let us look at the steps to publish to publish to Tableau Server.

How to do it...

1. To publish to Tableau Server, we will have to click on the **Server | Publish Workbook...** option in the toolbar. Refer to the following screenshot:

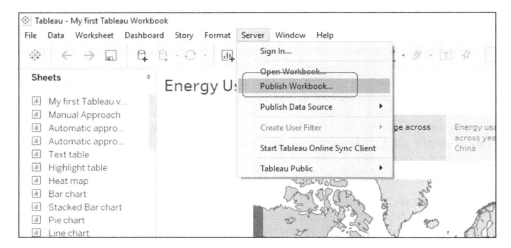

2. Once we select the relevant option, we will get a dialog box as shown in the following screenshot:

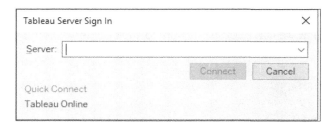

3. We will enter the details of the server that we wish to connect to in the type-in box that reads as **Server:** and then click on the **Connect** button. Once we do that, we will get another dialog box that requires us to enter our **Username** and **Password**. Refer to the following screenshot:

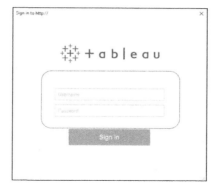

4. Once our access rights are validated, we will get the options to publish as shown in the following screenshot:

5. We can click on the **Publish** button, once we have selected/entered the relevant details.

How it works...

The preceding recipe explains how we can publish our workbook to Tableau Server. Once the workbook is published on Tableau, our end users must login to the Tableau Server via either a web browser or via the Tableau app on their iPads/tablets or mobile phones. After they are authenticated, the end users will only see the views that they have been given access to on the Tableau Server.

The preceding recipe only explains the broad steps to publish our workbook to Tableau Server. However, there are a lot of small things to keep in mind while publishing our workbook to Tableau Server, and to learn more about the same, refer to the following link:

`https://onlinehelp.tableau.com/current/pro/desktop/en-us/publish_workbooks_howto.html`.

Now, just like we can publish our workbook to Tableau Server, we can also publish our data source to Tableau Server. To know more about this, refer to the following link: `https://onlinehelp.tableau.com/current/pro/desktop/en-us/publish_datasources.html`.

To learn more about publishing to Tableau Server in general, refer to the following link: `https://onlinehelp.tableau.com/current/pro/desktop/en-us/publish_overview.html`.

If we don't have a Tableau Server or a Tableau Online access, we can also publish our work on Tableau Public, which is a free cloud service provided by Tableau. However, please note that, as the name suggests, any work that we publish on Tableau Public will be publicly accessible and hence it is advised not to publish any confidential views on Tableau Public.

Read more about Tableau Public from the following link: `https://onlinehelp.tableau.com/current/pro/desktop/en-us/publish_workbooks_tableaupublic.html`.

10
Formatting in Tableau for Desserts

In this chapter, our focus will be on formatting and we will look at the following topics:

- ▶ Formatting across our entire workbook
- ▶ Formatting within a worksheet
- ▶ Using and formatting labels and annotations
- ▶ Using and formatting titles and captions

Introduction

At this point, we have a very good understanding of the various concepts and functionalities in Tableau. We started by creating individual worksheets, then moved on to creating dashboards as well as storyboards. While doing so, we briefly looked at some quick and very basic formatting techniques. Even though it seems to be the most neglected functionality in Tableau, I believe formatting has a tremendous potential to make your views stand out and get the necessary attention. I see a lot of potential in formatting and many a times I feel that formatting is like the icing on the cake; we can eat our cake and enjoy its taste without the icing, but it is the icing and the way the cake is decorated that tempts us to want to eat it in the first place.

The same goes for formatting. We can create all those views and charts and build all the wonderful interactivity, but it is the formatting that will actually make our work stand out and make the user want to use it.

Formatting across our entire workbook

So far we have been working on our `My first Tableau Workbook` and we have created multiple sheets, dashboards, and storyboards. Now, let us say that we need to follow a consistent font type across our entire workbook. If we decide to go to every single individual sheet and change the font type, it is going to be very difficult and time consuming. In earlier versions of Tableau, this was often the most challenging part. However, since version 10.0, Tableau has made provisions for us to change certain aspects of formatting and make them consistent across the entire workbook.

Let us look at the following recipe to see how it is done.

Getting ready

For this recipe, we will continue using our `My first Tableau Workbook` file. We will work on the already created dashboard called `My first Tableau Dashboard`. Let us get started with the recipe.

How to do it...

1. Using the forward and backward arrows in the status bar, which is at the bottom right-hand side section of our workbook, we will go to our previously created dashboard called **My first Tableau Dashboard**. Refer to the following screenshot:

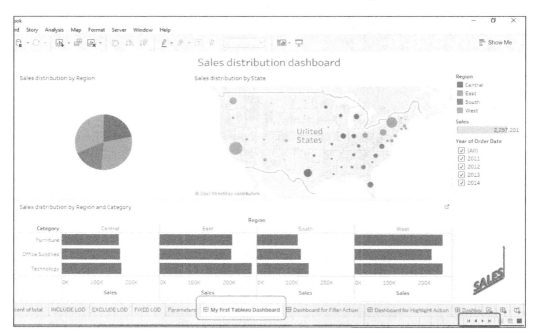

2. Once we do that, let's choose the **Format | Workbook...** option from the toolbar. Refer to the following screenshot:

3. Once we do that, we will get the following view:

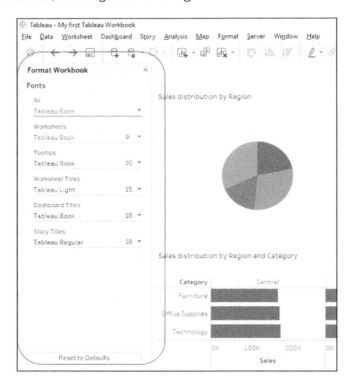

4. The left-hand side section now reads as **Format Workbook** and we get the option of changing the fonts across the entire workbook in terms of the fonts that are used within **Worksheets**, **Tooltips**, **Worksheet Titles**, **Dashboard Titles**, and also the **Story Titles**. We will click on the down arrow of the **All** option and change the font type from **Tableau Book** to **Tableau Regular**. Refer to the following screenshot:

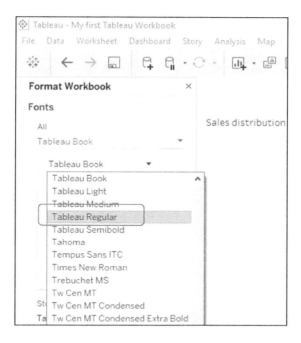

5. This action will update our view and we will notice the change in the dashboard title, worksheet titles, and so on. Refer to the following screenshot:

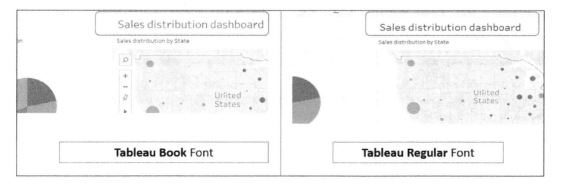

How it works...

In the preceding recipe, when we changed the font type in **All**, Tableau applied that font type within all the worksheets that are part of the workbook despite having different data sources. The change is also applied on the tooltips. The worksheet titles, dashboard titles, as well as the story titles will also be affected by this change.

At any point, if we feel like reverting back to the way things were, we can always click on the **Reset to Defaults** button. Refer to the following screenshot:

Formatting within a worksheet

In the preceding recipe, we saw a quick option for formatting across the entire workbook, which was great. However, there can be situations where we need some specific formatting within a particular worksheet. Let us see the following recipe to see how we can do formatting within a particular worksheet.

Getting ready

We will continue working in our existing `My first Tableau Workbook` workbook and use the already connected **CoffeeChain Query (Sample - Coffee Chain)** data source. Let us see how this is done.

How to do it...

1. Let us create a new sheet and rename it as **Formatting within a Worksheet**.

2. Next, let us make sure that we select the **CoffeeChain Query (Sample - Coffee Chain)** data source from the **Data** pane. Following this, we will create a text table by dragging the **Product Type** field from the **Dimensions** pane and dropping it into the **Columns** shelf, followed by dragging the **Market Size** field from the **Dimensions** pane and dropping it into the **Rows** shelf. Next, we will drag the **Market** field from the **Dimensions** pane and drop it into the **Rows** shelf, just next to the **Market Size** field. Lastly, let's drag the **Sales** field from the **Measures** pane and drop it into the **Text** shelf. This will create a view as shown in the following screenshot:

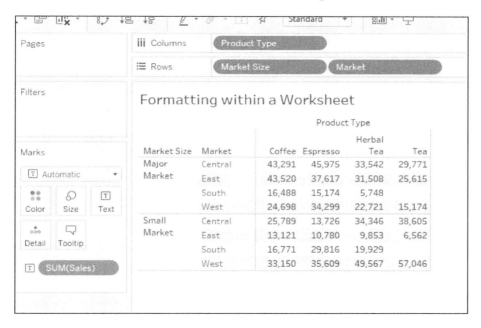

3. Once we are done creating our basic view, let us then add our **Totals** and **Subtotals** by dragging the **Totals** option from the **Analytics** pane and selecting the **Subtotals**, the **Column Grand Totals**, and also the **Row Grans Totals**. Refer to the following screenshot:

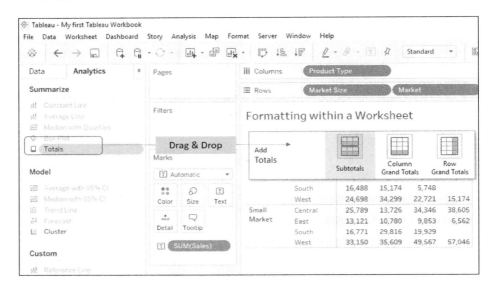

4. Once we enable our totals, our view will update, as shown in the following screenshot:

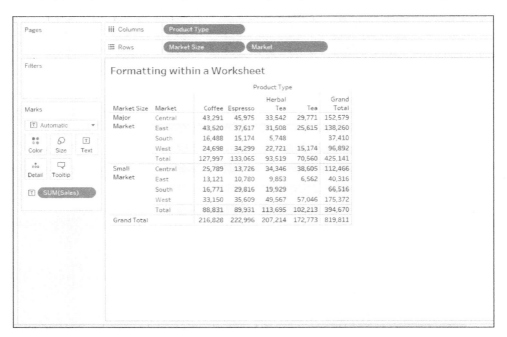

5. As we can see, our worksheet currently has a lot of white space around a text table. To change this, let's click on the dropdown in the toolbar that currently reads as **Standard** and let's change it to **Entire View**. Refer to the following screenshot:

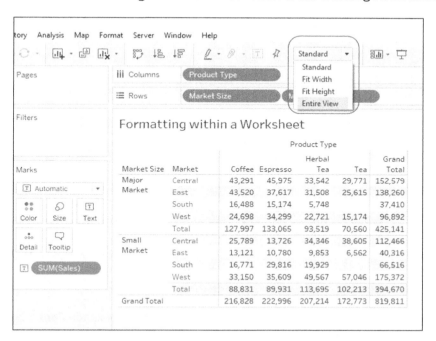

6. This action will update our view to what is shown in the following screenshot:

7. Next, let's click on the **Format** option in the toolbar and select the **Font...** option. This will show a new section on the left-hand side that reads as **Format Font**. Refer to the following screenshot:

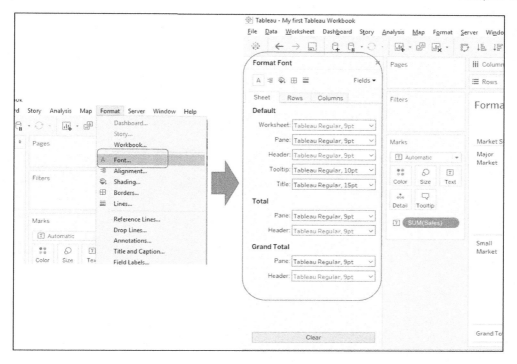

8. The current workbook font type is **Tableau Regular** with a font size of 9pt. Even the **Total** and **Grand Total** have the same font type and font size. Let's quickly change the font size of **Grand Total** from 9pt to 10pt in the **Pane:** section as well as the **Header:** section. Refer to the following screenshot:

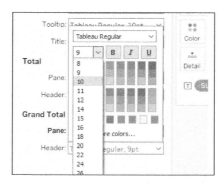

9. This will change the font size for both the **Grand Total** text and the **Grand Total** numbers. Refer to the following screenshot:

iii Columns	Product Type				
≣ Rows	Market Size	Market			

Formatting within a Worksheet

		Product Type				
Market Size	Market	Coffee	Espresso	Herbal Tea	Tea	Grand Total
Major Market	Central	43,291	45,975	33,542	29,771	152,579
	East	43,520	37,617	31,508	25,615	138,260
	South	16,488	15,174	5,748		37,410
	West	24,698	34,299	22,721	15,174	96,892
	Total	127,997	133,065	93,519	70,560	425,141
Small Market	Central	25,789	13,726	34,346	38,605	112,466
	East	13,121	10,780	9,853	6,562	40,316
	South	16,771	29,816	19,929		66,516
	West	33,150	35,609	49,567	57,046	175,372
	Total	88,831	89,931	113,695	102,213	394,670
Grand Total		216,828	222,996	207,214	172,773	819,811

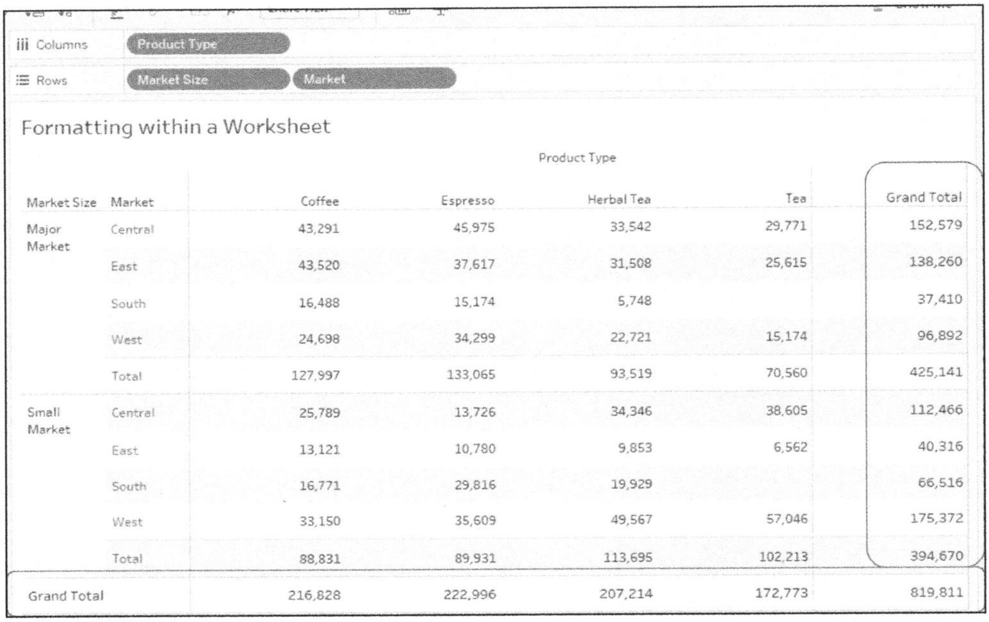

10. As a next step, let us change the alignment for the **Sales** number from right aligned to center aligned. To do so, let us click on the **Alignment** icon, which is next to the **Font** icon. Refer to the following screenshot:

11. Under the **Default | Pane** section, let us change the alignment from **Automatic** to **Center**. Refer to the following screenshot:

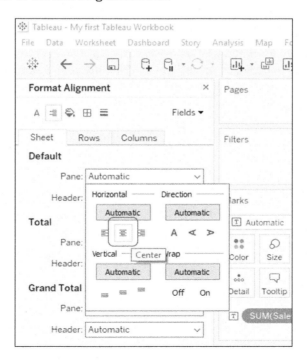

12. This will update our view, as shown in the following screenshot:

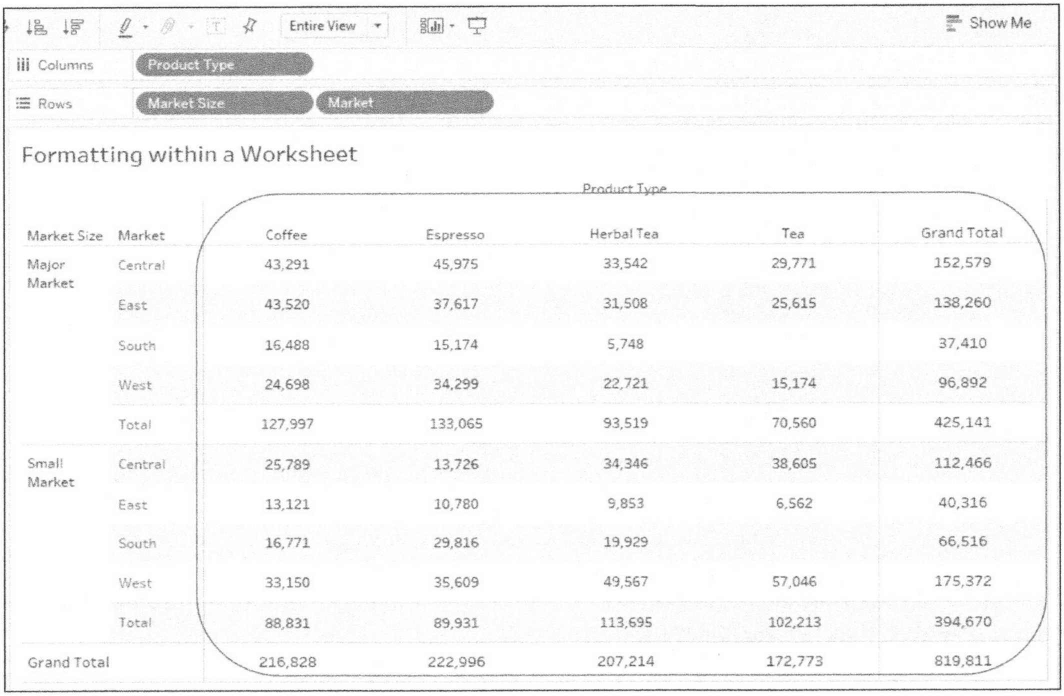

13. As a next step to formatting, let us remove the gray bands and color only the **Grand Total** sections. To do so, let us click on the **Shading** icon on top, which is next to the **Alignment** icon. Refer to the following screenshot:

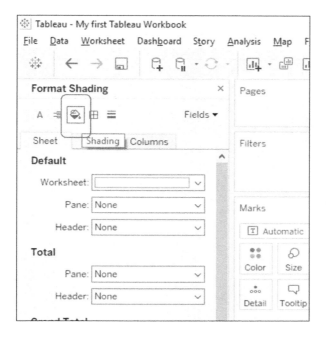

14. Once we are in the **Format Shading** section, we will go to the **Grand Total** section and click on the dropdown for **Pane**; to select a gray color. Refer to the following screenshot:

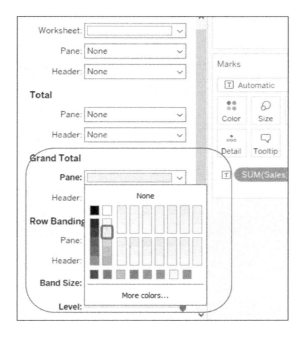

15. After we are done with that, we will go to the **Row Banding** section and move the **Band Size:** slider to the left most side or lower side. Refer to the following screenshot:

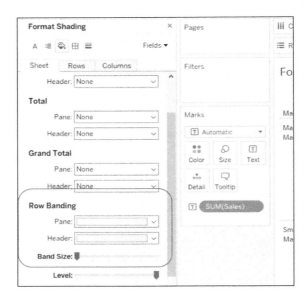

16. Both these actions will update our view, as shown in the following screenshot:

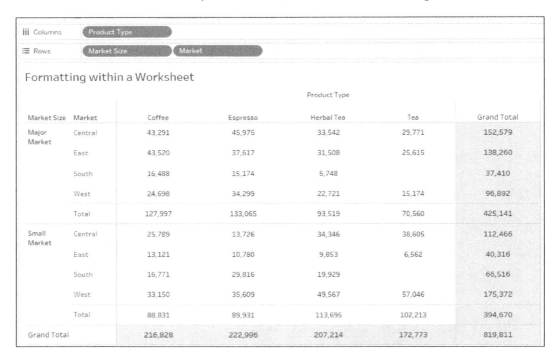

Formatting within a Worksheet

Market Size	Market	Coffee	Espresso	Herbal Tea	Tea	Grand Total
Major Market	Central	43,291	45,975	33,542	29,771	152,579
	East	43,520	37,617	31,508	25,615	138,260
	South	16,488	15,174	5,748		37,410
	West	24,698	34,299	22,721	15,174	96,892
	Total	127,997	133,065	93,519	70,560	425,141
Small Market	Central	25,789	13,726	34,346	38,605	112,466
	East	13,121	10,780	9,853	6,562	40,316
	South	16,771	29,816	19,929		66,516
	West	33,150	35,609	49,567	57,046	175,372
	Total	88,831	89,931	113,695	102,213	394,670
Grand Total		216,828	222,996	207,214	172,773	819,811

17. Now let's also add some of the column dividers between different product types. To do so, let us click on the **Borders** icon, which is next to the **Shading** icon. Refer to the following screenshot:

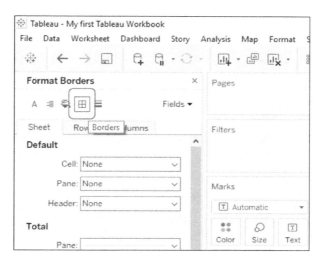

18. Let's scroll down to the **Column Divider** section and move the **Level:** slider to the right most side or higher side. Refer to the following screenshot:

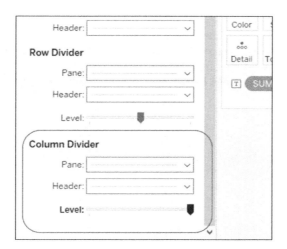

19. This action will update our view, as shown in the following screenshot:

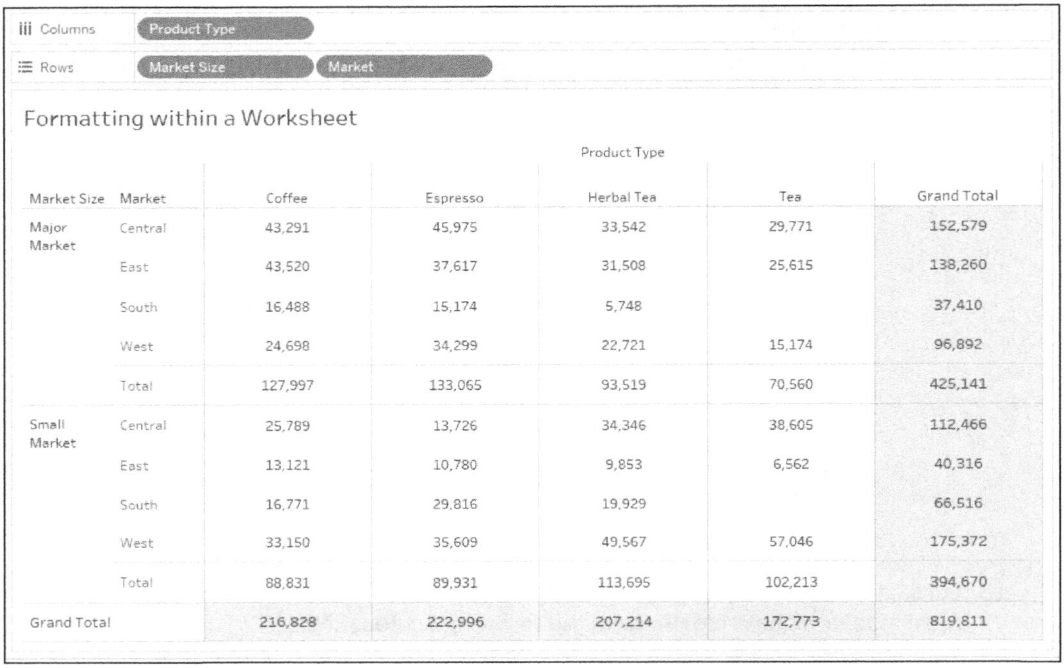

iii Columns   (Product Type)

≡ Rows   (Market Size)   (Market)

Formatting within a Worksheet

			Product Type			
Market Size	Market	Coffee	Espresso	Herbal Tea	Tea	Grand Total
Major Market	Central	43,291	45,975	33,542	29,771	152,579
	East	43,520	37,617	31,508	25,615	138,260
	South	16,488	15,174	5,748		37,410
	West	24,698	34,299	22,721	15,174	96,892
	Total	127,997	133,065	93,519	70,560	425,141
Small Market	Central	25,789	13,726	34,346	38,605	112,466
	East	13,121	10,780	9,853	6,562	40,316
	South	16,771	29,816	19,929		66,516
	West	33,150	35,609	49,567	57,046	175,372
	Total	88,831	89,931	113,695	102,213	394,670
Grand Total		216,828	222,996	207,214	172,773	819,811

20. Notice the sales values, currently there is no way for our end users to find out what currency they are looking at. We know that these are US dollar values, so let us go ahead and change the number format of our sales values. To do so, let us click on the dropdown that says **Fields** and select the **SUM(Sales)** option. Refer to the following screenshot:

21. This will update our **Format** section, as shown in the following screenshot:

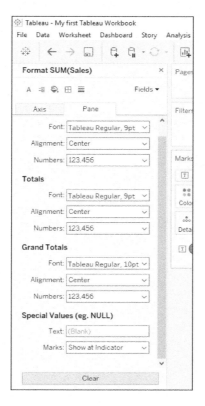

22. Let us select the **Currency (Standard)** option from the first **Numbers**: section and then select the **English (United States)** option. Refer to the following screenshot:

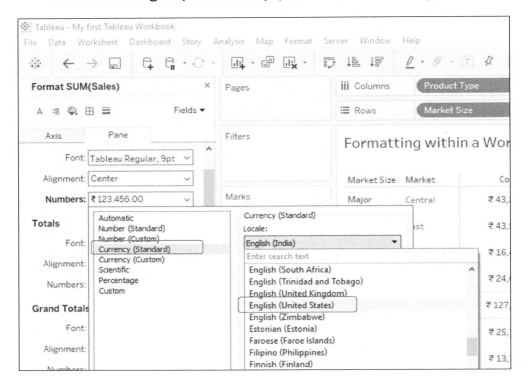

23. This will update our view, as shown in the following screenshot:

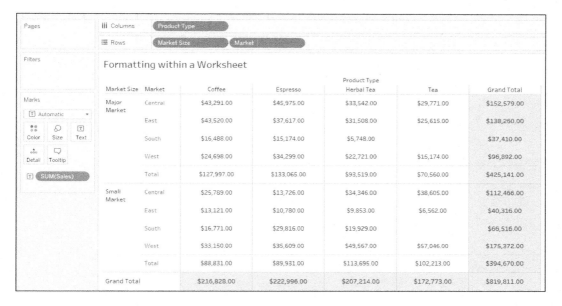

| Pages | iii Columns | Product Type | | | | |
| | ≣ Rows | Market Size | Market | | | |

Formatting within a Worksheet

				Product Type		
Market Size	Market	Coffee	Espresso	Herbal Tea	Tea	Grand Total
Major Market	Central	$43,291.00	$45,975.00	$33,542.00	$29,771.00	$152,579.00
	East	$43,520.00	$37,617.00	$31,508.00	$25,615.00	$138,260.00
	South	$16,488.00	$15,174.00	$5,748.00		$37,410.00
	West	$24,698.00	$34,299.00	$22,721.00	$15,174.00	$96,892.00
	Total	$127,997.00	$133,065.00	$93,519.00	$70,560.00	$425,141.00
Small Market	Central	$25,789.00	$13,726.00	$34,346.00	$38,605.00	$112,466.00
	East	$13,121.00	$10,780.00	$9,853.00	$6,562.00	$40,316.00
	South	$16,771.00	$29,816.00	$19,929.00		$66,516.00
	West	$33,150.00	$35,609.00	$49,567.00	$57,046.00	$175,372.00
	Total	$88,831.00	$89,931.00	$113,695.00	$102,213.00	$394,670.00
Grand Total		$216,828.00	$222,996.00	$207,214.00	$172,773.00	$819,811.00

Marks: T Automatic; Color, Size, Text, Detail, Tooltip; T SUM(Sales)

24. Lastly, let us remove the word **Product Type** from the top of our view and to do so, we will right-click on the **Product Type** text and select **Hide Field Labels for Columns**. Refer to the following screenshot:

Formatting within a Worksheet

Market Size	Market	Coffee	Espresso	H...		Grand Total
Major Market	Central	$43,291.00	$45,975.00	$3...		$152,579.00
	East	$43,520.00	$37,617.00	$3...		$138,260.00
	South	$16,488.00	$15,174.00	$5,748.00		$37,410.00
	West	$24,698.00	$34,299.00	$22,721.00	$15,174.00	$96,892.00
	Total	$127,997.00	$133,065.00	$93,519.00	$70,560.00	$425,141.00
Small Market	Central	$25,789.00	$13,726.00	$34,346.00	$38,605.00	$112,466.00
	East	$13,121.00	$10,780.00	$9,853.00	$6,562.00	$40,316.00
	South	$16,771.00	$29,816.00	$19,929.00		$66,516.00
	West	$33,150.00	$35,609.00	$49,567.00	$57,046.00	$175,372.00
	Total	$88,831.00	$89,931.00	$113,695.00	$102,213.00	$394,670.00
Grand Total		$216,828.00	$222,996.00	$207,214.00	$172,773.00	$819,811.00

Context menu:
Sort ascending
Sort descending
Format...
Hide Field Labels for Columns

25. This will update our view, as shown in the following screenshot:

		Coffee	Espresso	Herbal Tea	Tea	Grand Total
Pages						
Columns	Product Type					
Rows	Market Size	Market				
Filters						

Formatting within a Worksheet

Market Size	Market	Coffee	Espresso	Herbal Tea	Tea	Grand Total
Major Market	Central	$43,291.00	$45,975.00	$33,542.00	$29,771.00	$152,579.00
	East	$43,520.00	$37,617.00	$31,508.00	$25,615.00	$138,260.00
	South	$16,488.00	$15,174.00	$5,748.00		$37,410.00
	West	$24,698.00	$34,299.00	$22,721.00	$15,174.00	$96,892.00
	Total	$127,997.00	$133,065.00	$93,519.00	$70,560.00	$425,141.00
Small Market	Central	$25,789.00	$13,726.00	$34,346.00	$38,605.00	$112,466.00
	East	$13,121.00	$10,780.00	$9,853.00	$6,562.00	$40,316.00
	South	$16,771.00	$29,816.00	$19,929.00		$66,516.00
	West	$33,150.00	$35,609.00	$49,567.00	$57,046.00	$175,372.00
	Total	$88,831.00	$89,931.00	$113,695.00	$102,213.00	$394,670.00
Grand Total		$216,828.00	$222,996.00	$207,214.00	$172,773.00	$819,811.00

Marks panel: Automatic; Color, Size, Text; Detail, Tooltip; SUM(Sales)

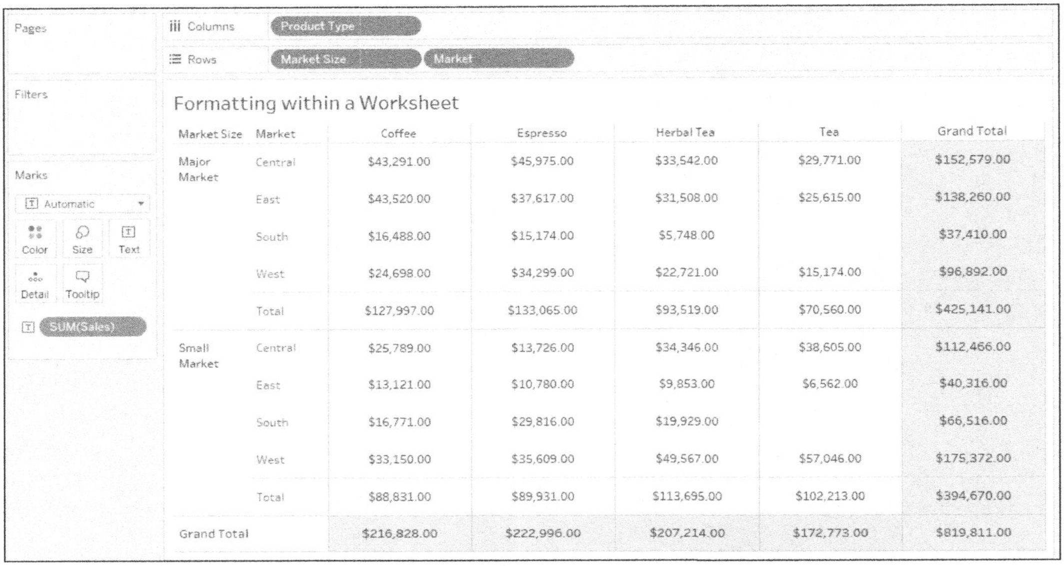

How it works...

The preceding recipe explains how we can format the objects within our worksheet. In case we need the similar formatting across multiple worksheets, then instead of formatting the relevant sheets individually, we can simply format one sheet and copy and paste the formatting to the other sheets.

To do so, all we need to do is right click on the sheet tab and select the **Copy Formatting** option and then go to the relevant sheet and select the **Paste Formatting** option. Refer to the following screenshot:

Using and formatting labels and annotations

Labels and annotations are another important aspect of our visualizations. Even though the science of data visualization suggests that we declutter our views by removing or not adding unnecessary information, there are times when we simply can't get away without showing the labels or annotations.

In the following recipe, we will see how to add labels and annotations and how to format them.

Getting ready

We will continue using our existing `My first Tableau Workbook` workbook and create a quick bar chart by using the **Deadliest Earthquakes (Deadliest earthquakes)** data source. Let us get started.

How to do it...

1. Let us create a new sheet and rename it as **Formatting Labels & Annotations**.

2. Next, let us select the **Deadliest Earthquakes (Deadliest earthquakes)** data source from the **Data** pane and create a line chart by selecting the **Date** field in the **Dimensions** pane followed by doing a *Ctrl* + select on the **Number of Records** field in the **Measures** pane. We will then select the continuous line chart option from **Show Me!**. Refer to the following screenshot:

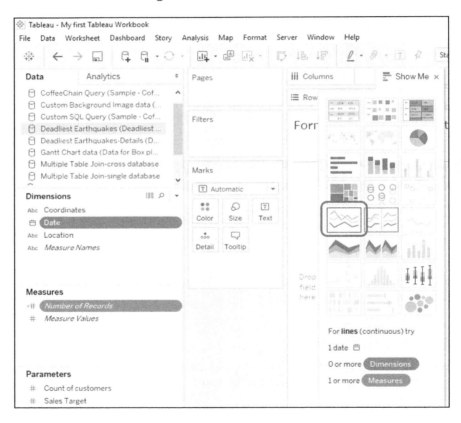

3. This will create a view, as shown in the following screenshot:

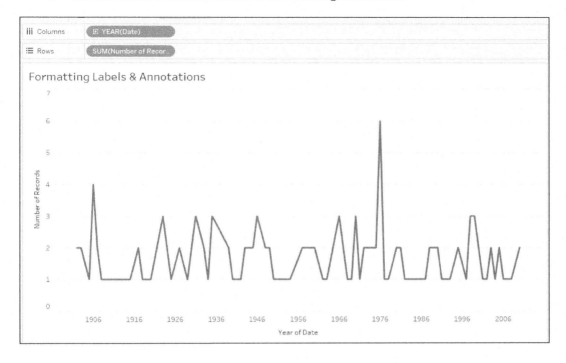

4. Let us now label the point that has the highest number of earthquakes. To do so, let us click on the **Label** shelf in the **Marks** card and enable the **Show mark labels** option. Refer to the following screenshot:

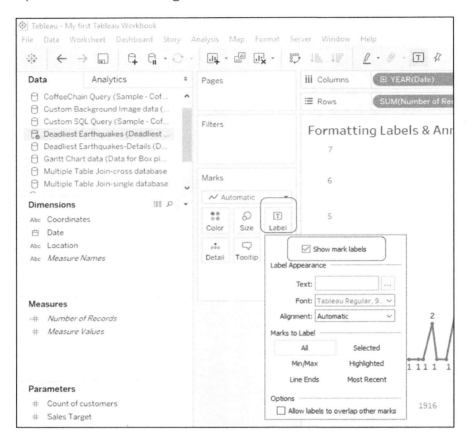

5. Once we do this our view will update, as shown in the following screenshot:

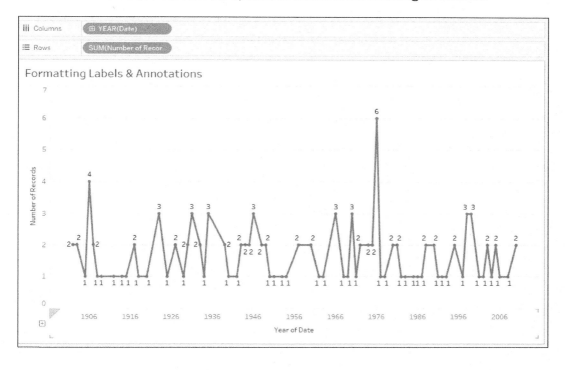

6. As mentioned earlier, we wanted to label only the data point that had the highest number of earthquakes, whereas our last actions seem to have labeled every single data point. To rectify this, we will select the **Min/Max** option under the **Marks to Label** section and then uncheck the **Label minimum value** option. Refer to the following screenshot:

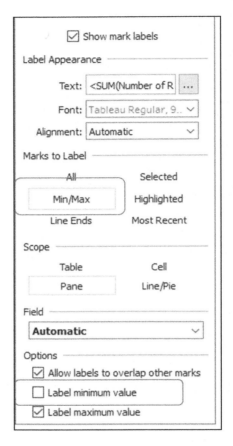

7. Once we do that, our view will update, as shown in the following screenshot:

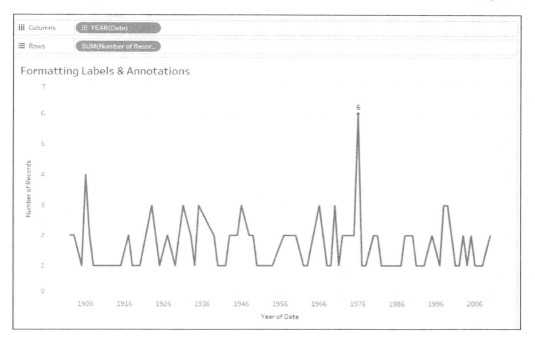

8. Next, let us right-click on the labeled point and select the **Annotate | Point...** option, as shown in the following screenshot:

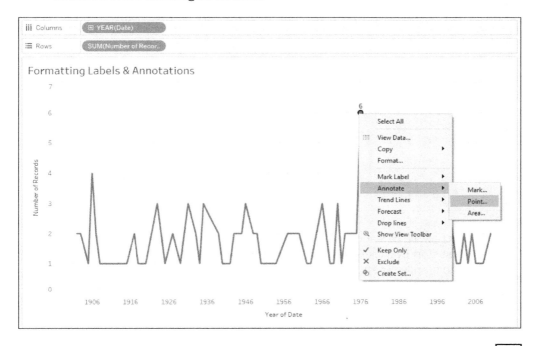

9. This will open a textbox where we will clear the default text and type `Highest number of Earthquakes`. Refer to the following screenshot:

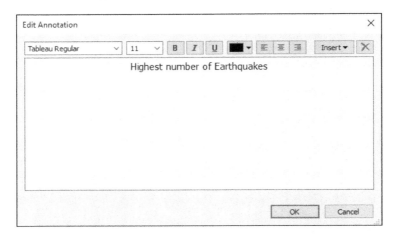

10. Once we click **OK**, our view will update, as shown in the following screenshot:

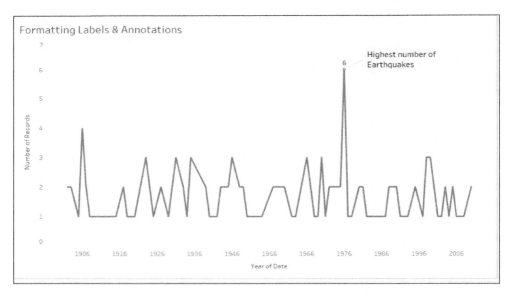

11. This is how we can add labels and annotations to our views. Now to format them, we will first start by clicking on the **Color** shelf in the **Marks** card and changing the line color to orange, as shown in the following screenshot:

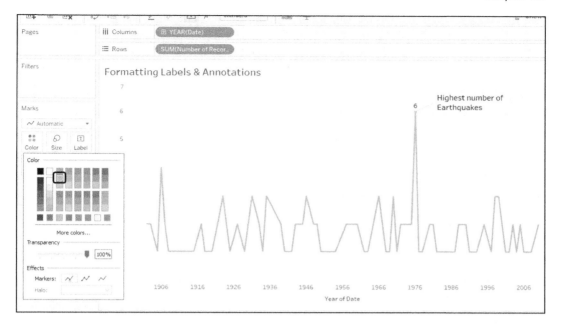

12. Next, we will click on the **Label** shelf in the **Marks** card, change the font size from 9 to 11 in the **Font:** dropdown, and then select the option of **Match Mark Color**. Refer to the following screenshot:

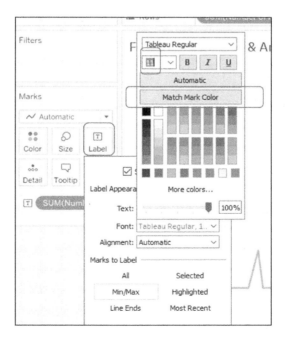

13. Once we do that, our view will notice that the label has increased in size and now has the same font color as the line. Refer to the following screenshot:

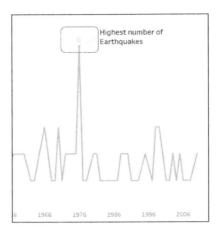

14. Next, let us right-click on our annotation and select the **Format...** option, and then change the **Shading:** from the gray color, which is currently at 90% transparency to **None**. Refer to the following screenshot:

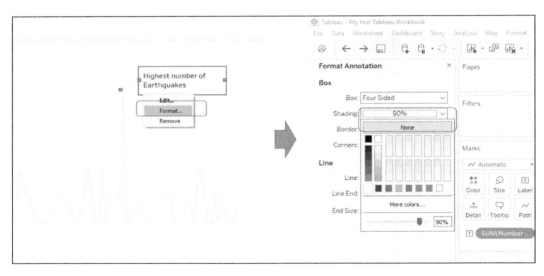

15. This action will update our view, as shown in the following screenshot:

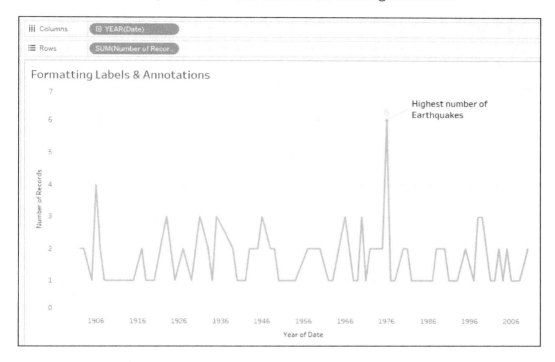

How it works...

In the preceding recipe, we saw to enable labels and annotations as well as how to format them.

For enabling labels, we simply checked the **Show mark labels** option in the **Labels** shelf. As an alternate approach, we could also have dragged our **Number of Records** field from the **Measures** pane and dropped it into the **Label** shelf. Refer to the following screenshot:

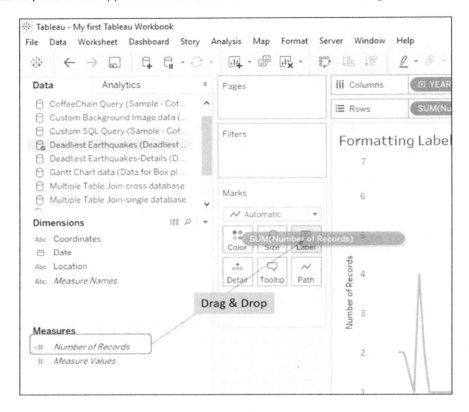

Once we do that, we will see that the **Number of Records** field is placed in the **Label** shelf, which was earlier missing when we simply selected the **Show mark labels** option. Refer to the following screenshot:

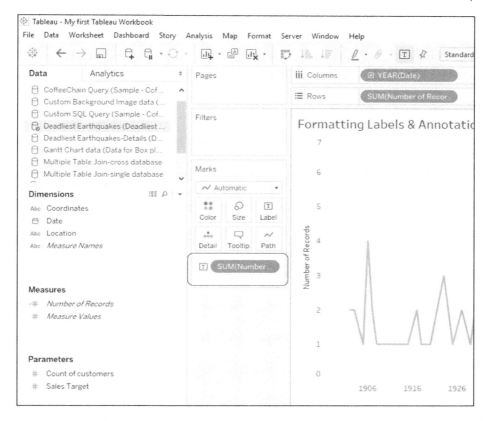

Using and formatting titles and captions

Naming our sheets and giving them titles not only helps us find the relevant sheets while working on our dashboards or storyboards, but it also helps our end users understand what we are trying show in our views. Tableau will, by default, take our sheet name as our title for that sheet, which we can change if we want to.

While working with dashboards, we briefly saw how to add titles to our worksheets and dashboards and how to do some basic formatting on them. In this recipe, let's relook at how we can add titles to our worksheet, format them, and even make them dynamic based on what the user selects.

Getting ready

We will continue using our existing `My first Tableau Workbook` workbook and create a quick bar chart by using the **Orders (Sample - Superstore)** data source. Let us get started.

How to do it...

1. Let us create a new sheet and rename it as **Formatting Titles & Captions**.

2. Next, let us select the **Orders (Sample - Superstore)** data source from the **Data** pane and create a bar chart by selecting the **Sub-Category** field in the **Dimensions** pane followed by doing a *Ctrl* + select on the **Profit** field in the **Measures** pane. We will then select the bar chart option from **Show Me!**. Refer to the following screenshot:

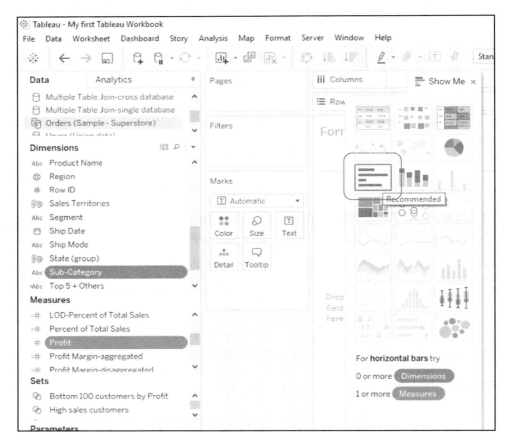

3. This will create a horizontal bar chart for us, which we will sort in descending order by **Profit**. Refer to the following screenshot:

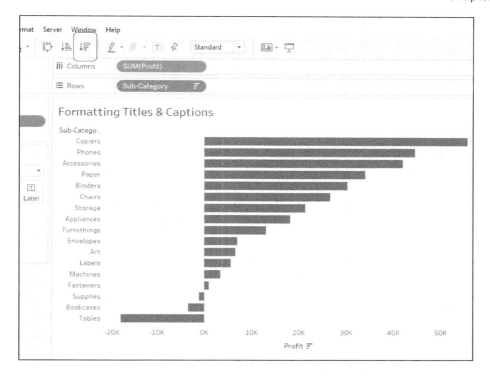

4. Now, let us right-click on the **Region** field in the **Dimensions** pane and select the **Show Filter** option. Refer to the following screenshot:

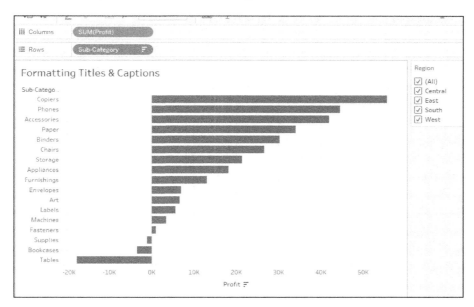

5. Next, let us make this filter a single select radio button instead of the multiple value select by clicking on the dropdown of the filter control and selecting the **Single Value (list)** option. Refer to the following screenshot:

6. Now, if we notice, the `Sheet Name` as well as the `Worksheet Title` are exactly the same. Let us change the title of this worksheet to something more meaningful that will help our users understand what we are trying to show using the bar chart that we have created. To do so, let us double-click on the title and it will open a textbox for us. Refer to the following screenshot:

7. As we can see in the preceding screenshot, the text box contains the **SheetName**. We will remove this and type **Subcategory wise Profit**. This will change our title. Refer to the following screenshot:

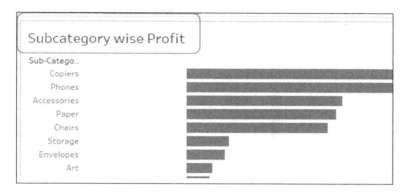

8. Now, this is how we can add titles to our sheet. The earlier textbox gave us a couple of options to format. However, if we wish to add background color and borders to our titles, to make them stand out, then we can do so by right clicking on the title and selecting the **Format Title...** option. Refer to the following screenshot:

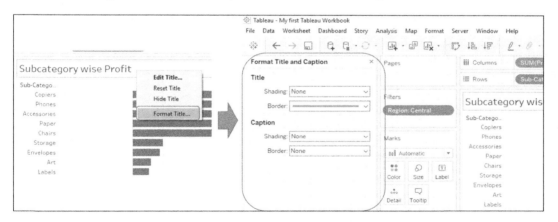

9. Under the **Title** section, we will begin by keeping the **Border:** section as is. We will add a gray background color to our title by using the **Shading:** dropdown. Refer to the following screenshot:

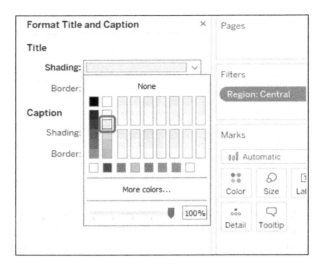

10. We will then go to the **Caption** section and keep the **Shading:** dropdown as is. We will instead add a border from the **Border:** drop-down menu. Refer to the following screenshot:

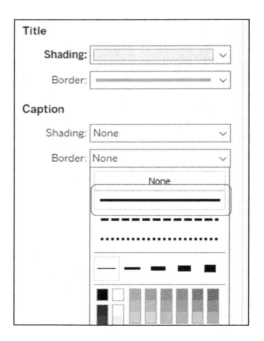

11. This will update our view, as shown in the following screenshot:

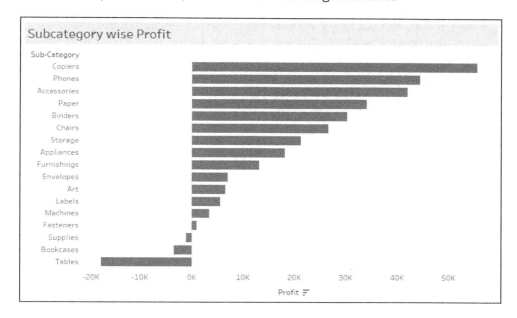

12. In previous steps, we formatted our caption; however, our worksheet currently doesn't have a caption, and to enable it we will select the **Worksheet | Caption** option from the toolbar. Refer to the following screenshot:

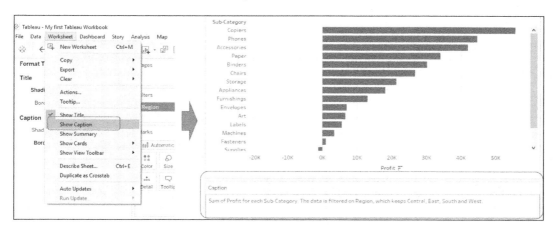

13. Lastly, we have a **Region** filter and it would be great if we can customize our title to show which **Region** is selected in the filter. To do so, double-click on the title and this will open the text box for us. We will go to the end of the current text, insert a space, and then type the word *for*. After we do this, we will then select the **Insert | Region** option and then click **OK**. Refer to the following screenshot:

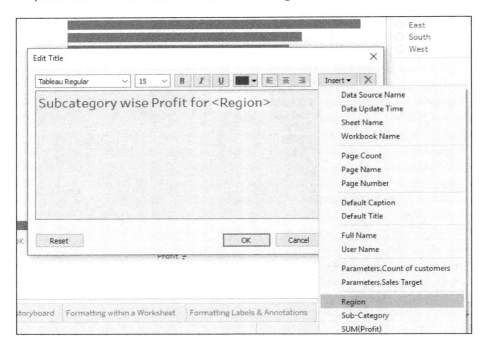

14. Now if we change the filter selection from **All** to **Central**, our title will read as **Subcategory wise Profit for Central**. Refer to the following screenshot:

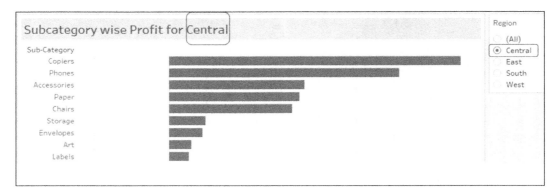

How it works...

The preceding recipe explains how we can add **Titles** and **Captions** to our worksheets and format them. We also saw how we can make our titles dynamic to give more context to our visualizations by using the **Insert** option.

We can also format our **Tooltips, Reference lines, Legends, Filter controls, Highlighter controls,** and **Parameter controls**.

To format our **Tooltips**, we will have to click on the **Tooltip shelf** in the **Marks** card, which will enable a textbox where we can do the desired formatting. Refer to the following screenshot:

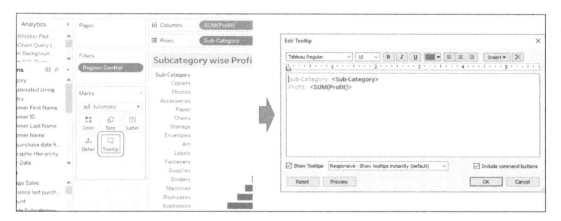

Next, to format our **Reference Lines**, we can select the **Reference Lines...** option from the **Format** menu in the toolbar. Refer to the following screenshot:

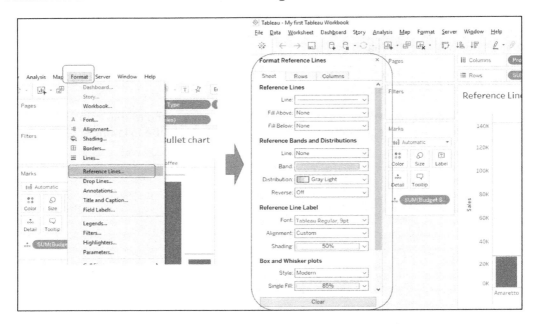

To format our **Legends**, **Filter controls**, **Highlighter controls**, and **Parameter controls**, we can select the relevant options from the **Format** menu in the toolbar. Refer to the following screenshot:

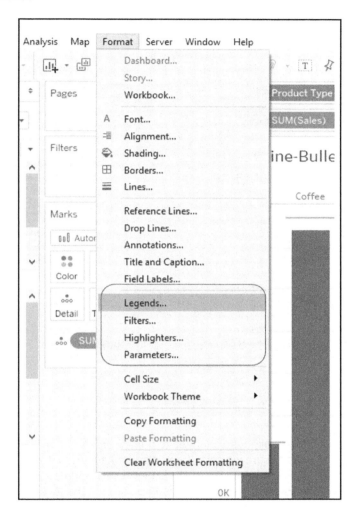

Another quick point to explore is the **Workbook Theme**. We can change the default workbook theme by selecting the **Format | Workbook Theme** option. Refer to the following screenshot:

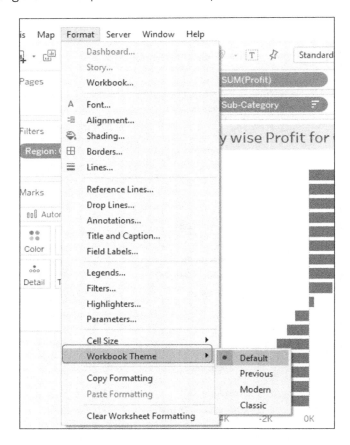

Lastly, now that we have made all these changes to our `My first Tableau Workbook`, which is a `.twb` file, let's make sure we save it and also make sure that we keep our `My first Tableau Packaged Workbook`, which is the `.twbx` updated as well. We will select the **Export Packaged Workbook...** option from the **File** menu in the toolbar and replace the existing `My first Tableau Packaged Workbook.twbx`.

Formatting is a vast topic and is very subjective as well. Even though we saw a whole lot of options, there is always more to explore. To read more about formatting in Tableau, refer to the following link: `http://onlinehelp.tableau.com/current/pro/desktop/en-us/formatting.html`.

Index